THE

Family Firm

Also by Emily Oster

Expecting Better: Why the Conventional Pregnancy Wisdom Is Wrong—and What You Really Need to Know

Cribsheet: A Data-Driven Guide to Better, More Relaxed Parenting, from Birth to Preschool

THE
Family Firm

A Data-Driven Guide to
Better Decision Making
in the Early School Years

EMILY OSTER

PENGUIN PRESS
New York
2021

PENGUIN PRESS
An imprint of Penguin Random House LLC
penguinrandomhouse.com

LIBRARY OF CONGRESS CATALOGING-IN-PUBLICATION DATA

Names: Oster, Emily, author.
Title: The family firm : a data-driven guide to better decision
making in the early school years / Emily Oster.
Description: New York : Penguin Press, 2021. | Includes index.
Identifiers: LCCN 2020057449 | ISBN 9781984881755 (hardcover) |
ISBN 9781984881762 (ebook)
Subjects: LCSH: Parenting. | Technology and children. | Children—Education,
Elementary. | Education, Elementary. | Decision making.
Classification: LCC HQ755.8 .O78 2021 | DDC 306.874—dc23
LC record available at https://lccn.loc.gov/2020057449

ISBN 9780593299746 (international edition)

Printed in the United States of America
1st Printing

Book designed by Cassandra Garruzzo

To Jesse

Contents

PART I

The Family Toolbox

PART II

Big Data

PART III

The Data Studies

THE
Family Firm

Introduction

If you are parenting in the modern age, there will come a time when you will face the great question: "When can I get a phone?" The question might come when your child is ten, but more likely five, or eight.

"All my friends have one!" "If I don't get one, I'll never be invited to X or Y or Z." "Don't you want me to be able to call you if there is something wrong?" "Lauren at tennis camp already has one and she's younger than me." At some point, a friend of your child may get a phone, and then they may start texting your phone. "How r u" "i miss you" *emoji-emoji-emoji*. Perhaps it is worth it just to avoid these texts.

However, when you investigate, the internet is a source of cautionary tales: "Phones Linked to Anxiety in Teen Girls" or "Phones Shown to Lower Student Achievement." An article about Silicon Valley parents says they are eschewing phones, along with all plastic toys. The latter seems unrealistic, but maybe the phones are a possibility. And yet everyone else's kid does seem to have a phone. Are you going to be the only one? What do they know that you do not?

This is a new kind of parenting dilemma. When you're parenting a baby, and wondering about questions like "Is it a good idea to swaddle? Should I feed them solid foods at four or six months? What about sleep training?" the decisions feel overwhelming in their frequency and their newness. Also, you are making them in an exhausted, dreamlike state.

But from the vantage point of having an older child, these choices can seem incredibly tractable. There is, for example, an actual answer to the question of whether swaddling is a good idea (yes). It's based on data, research, evidence. It's reasonably consistent across healthy babies. And it is also simply not that important in the grand scheme of things. If you swaddle your baby, they will sleep better early on. But if you do not, nothing terrible will happen.

On the other hand, when to get your child a phone feels nothing like this. There isn't much data on it, certainly nothing that would rise to the level of what we know about swaddling. It almost certainly has wildly different effects depending on the child. The best answer to this question could well be different for two children in the same family, let alone two different families.

Adding to the problem, for many older-kid decisions, the question itself may not be immediately clear! Is the question whether the kid should have a "dummy phone" that only calls their parents and the police? Or whether they should have the latest, slickest Google phone? Your partner may be thinking about the second question while you are contemplating the first. Forget about *solving* the same problem—sometimes we aren't even talking through the same choices.

This book is focused on the post-toddler but pre-teenager stage—let's say, the ages of five to twelve. We'll begin with seeing your kid off to elementary school and walk through the very beginnings of puberty. We'll leave teens for another day.

Parenting decisions in this age range do not come with the frequency that they do with a baby, but they are almost always more complicated. What's the right kind of school and at what age should they enter? How do you get them to eat a healthy diet? Should they play a sport, and if so, how seriously? Are you a helicopter parent, a free-range parent, a tiger parent, an ostrich parent? Is that last one even a thing?

These issues are all a bit like the phone: they feel big and important, and it's not always clear even how to start. It's easy to see how they can overwhelm harried families.

That brings us to the other hallmark of this period of parenting: logistics. For many of us, parenting in the twenty-first century is an exercise in extreme logistical complexity. Nowhere is this more vivid, for me, than in the case of summer camp.

My younger brother has four kids. Many kids means lots of logistics, so I wasn't too surprised when he signed off an email exchange with me by saying he had to get back to the spreadsheet he was working on to plan the kids' camps.

This was in *November.*

It turns out his kids go to a tremendous number of different camps—various sports, sleepaway, sailing, something called "Muskrat Camp" (or maybe I'm remembering the rodent wrong?), which is apparently so popular you have to plan before Thanksgiving to get the "right week." Because most American school systems take almost three months off in the summer, summer camp is a large—and very complex—piece of the school-age family puzzle.

Where we live, one of the most popular camps is Zoo Camp. Sign-ups open for one day in February, and if you miss it, you're out of luck. Or, worse, stuck with an inferior week, *not* the one your kid's friends are in (*their* parents remembered the sign-up day).

Even if, by some miracle, you remember to sign up, you've got to contend with the logistics of camp once summer arrives. Inexplicably, in the period before camp starts, the famous Zoo Camp requires you to sign up for what sandwich your child wants. If you forget (yes, I forgot), you get a significant "tut tut" at drop-off, plus your kid is stuck with the last available sandwich type (sunflower-seed butter and jelly on wheat—clearly no one's first choice).

And the timing! Zoo Camp, for example, is from 9 a.m. to 3 p.m., with no before- or after-care. Who's going to arrive late and leave early from work to make this doable? Can the grandparents come in that week? Do you need a babysitter on top of camp? Camp is expensive, and so is the babysitter. Logistics relate to time, but also to money.

In my mind, these two scenarios—the phone and camp—illustrate the two key problems of this era of parenting. The day-to-day is a series of logistical challenges. This is then punctuated by big, complicated, weighty, consequential decisions that you often have no idea how to even think about. And by the way, the choices you make about those complicated decisions will feed back into the logistics.

This is, again, fundamentally different from many of the challenges of early parenting. There, you had more relevant data (as with swaddling), but your problems were also simply more immediate. They required, and were satisfied by, a more in-the-moment approach to the solution.

Consider this baby situation: the baby has pooped in their crib during a nap, and it's gotten everywhere, including the rug—and, also, the poop is green. What to do? It's clear: Quickly clean it up, wash the sheets, change the baby, shampoo the rug. Then immediately call the doctor to ask about green poop (it's fine, by the way).

This is physically draining, and a bit gross, but it's over fast. A small fire arises, and you put it out, and you move on.

You may have found this green-poop stage wasn't really your thing (to be honest, it wasn't mine). Maybe you expect later parenting to play to your strengths more. Which is good! But even if you are more comfortable making a decision about whether your third grader should participate in travel soccer, that decision requires a contemplation of whether this is the right activity for them and what the benefits and costs of this type of team sport are. Is there a reason to start now? And how would it actually *work*? Is this going to get in the way of something else your family cares about? How do you know whether this is more or less important than other priorities?

There isn't just one piece of data here—it's not just "Is green poop okay?" There's now a lot of data to bring in, both information on soccer itself but also (probably more) information on your family structure, your central values, the day-to-day structure of your lives. And if you make these choices wrong, you may end up in a situation that makes you unhappy.

Imagine you have two kids. Simon is nine (third grade); Ellie is six (first grade). They go to public school a couple of miles away. Morning bus pickup is at 7:30; school ends at 2:45. Let's imagine your household has two parents—Mom and Dad—with the acknowledgment that your adult configuration may well look different.

Here's one way your day might go: Kids wake up at 6:30, get themselves dressed, and come downstairs. Family eats a quick breakfast together, then the kids are hustled out of the house to the bus stop (check: Do they have their lunch cards?). Mom and Dad clean up and head off to work. At 3:15 the bus drops the kids off at home, to be met by the babysitter and taken inside. Two days a week, Simon goes to soccer after school and another parent drops him back home at 5:30. Mom and Dad arrive home around 5:45, say goodbye to the babysitter, and dinner is on the table at 6:30 (okay, it's not a gourmet meal, but everyone likes pasta again, right? RIGHT?). Dinner, bath, some homework for the older kid, and both kids are in bed by 8:30.

Or here's another way: Kids wake up at 6:30, get dressed, and eat breakfast. Mom is out the door shortly after they get up; Dad is in charge. Kids are off to the bus, Dad returns to his home office. At 3:15 the bus drops the kids off, to be met by Dad. One day a week, he shuttles both kids to music lessons; two days a week, the older child has soccer and the younger has gymnastics at the same time (soccer drop-off, drive to gymnastics, wait, drive back, soccer pickup). Most days they are home by 6:30. Kids eat something while doing their homework or watching some TV. Mom returns around 7. Kids are in bed by 8:30 most nights, and Mom and Dad eat a late dinner together.

Or here's a third: Kids get themselves up at 7:10 and grab a granola bar on the way out the door to the bus. Dad has already left for work by 6; Mom is at home, organizing the chaos. Mom does school pickup at 2:30 and they're off to a neighboring suburb. Both kids do their homework in Starbucks with a snack and then head to the ice rink. Figure skating is 5 to 8 most nights. Mom picks up some dinner around the corner for the kids, or, if the day was calm enough, she brings sandwiches. Meanwhile, Dad arrives at the rink around 7 to take over and get some time with the kids. Everyone is home by 9 and (on a good day) in bed by 10.

There isn't anything inherently wrong with any of these family setups. There are lots and lots of different (good!) ways to organize your family life. The trouble arises, though, when expectations do not match reality.

If you envisioned yourself in version 1 of this story, and you find yourself in version 3, you may not be happy. If you have always felt that family dinner together is a top priority, and in fact 6 out of 7 nights a week you're eating on the road between events, it's a recipe for frustration.

The choices you make about logistics may seem like just that—logistics. But at this age, logistics are a lot of the puzzle. What your kids (and you!) do with each hour of each day will affect your budget, your time, how you feel about your connection with your kid.

For me, adapting to this new era of parenting required a pretty fundamental change. I have two children: a daughter, Penelope, and a son, Finn. I'm an economist by training and I've been a professor for many years. My work is data focused. I do research on health—Why do people make the health choices they do?—and also on methods for learning from data. I try to understand questions like "What makes this evidence more reliable than other evidence? Are there ways to learn from imperfect evidence?"

When I was pregnant with Penelope, and then over the course of both kids' early childhoods, I brought these data skills to my parenting life. Virtually any pregnancy- or kid-related problem that came up—what kind of prenatal testing, should I get an epidural, do I really need to breastfeed until a year, circumcision, potty training, toddler screen time—my first instinct was to refer back to academic research on these topics, to systematic data and evidence. I did this even in places where the problem was, quite frankly, unimportant (I am thinking, specifically, of the time I tried to find academic papers on whether infant Penelope should wear baby mittens).

The data wasn't always perfect—indeed, sometimes pieces of it were downright bad—but for most of the decisions that felt big, weighty, and important, there was at least some data I could hang my hat on. The evidence on the benefits (or not) of breastfeeding has some holes, but there is a lot to learn from it. I wrote two books using this approach—*Expecting Better*, on pregnancy, and *Cribsheet*, on early childhood.

I figured I'd rely on data in this way forever. But as my kids got older, the problems changed, and I found that the data-oriented solution wasn't always available. It wasn't that the problems felt less important, but they felt more specific, more unique. The data alone couldn't help me.

For example, at some point, we were looking to choose a school. There are data and research on schools. But it is very general. The academic literature doesn't ask the question "From my personal option set, what's the best one to pick?" We wondered about sleepaway camp, but there was no place to search for "Is *my* kid ready to spend time away from home?" And it's hard to even get started on framing questions about social issues—bullying, behavior challenges, anxiety, self-esteem.

It was tempting to throw up my hands and decide that data wasn't relevant, that I should just give up on being systematic with all this and go with my gut or whatever random thing had occurred to me most recently. But that wasn't right. There was still relevant data. I still needed to find the best evidence, to sort out the good data from the less good. But that data wasn't useful alone anymore. I needed more scaffolding surrounding it, on both sides.

On the one hand, we needed to think much more about the *question* we were asking, and about framing. "Is green poop normal?" is a pretty basic yes-or-no question. But take a question like "What kind of school is right?" That question is too vague. There is no way to bring data to it because you haven't asked it correctly. A better one is "Should I choose school A or school B for this particular kid at this time?" Of course, this requires you to think about what the options are even before you get started with evidence. You need to stop and first think about how to frame the question. Is there even a school B option?

It's not that this kind of thing never happened in early parenting, but in this phase, I found myself wondering: *What is the question?* Much more frequently, I found that moving forward required my husband, Jesse, and I to step back and frame things before we could even start to think about which evidence was appropriate to gather.

There were other adjustments. It had always been clear to us that family preferences were important. Indeed, a central point of *Cribsheet* is that different families will make different choices about things like breastfeeding and sleep training, and that family preferences should play an important role in those decisions. But now the choices we made were all linked. It was necessary to step back, to think more carefully about the bigger picture, about the basic structure of our family. We could no longer separate individual decisions from these larger issues.

Think back to the three family scenarios. The choice to be serious about ice skating isn't made in isolation. This shapes the whole day, the whole week, the year. It's a primary choice. Family dinner and ice skating are one choice, not two.

The more I thought about it, the more I realized we had started running our house like . . . well, like a firm. I hadn't left my job behind in my home. I'd just switched out my statistical-methods-researcher hat for my former-business-school-professor hat. Before I came to Brown University, I worked for five years at the University of Chicago Booth School of Business, teaching microeconomics to MBA students. I spent an awful lot of time explaining to my students there how to use tools from economics to organize their future business dealings, as well as mentoring students with big, entrepreneurial ideas.

It dawned on me that the lessons I tried to impart to them about running their businesses had value in how I ran my house. This idea crystallized for me when Jesse and I scheduled a meeting (using Google Calendar) with eight-year-old Penelope to discuss the school-year schedule. We presented an agenda and draft schedule in advance. (Good meeting! Penelope and Jesse noted some errors in the documents I drafted, but I felt it was largely successful.)

I would argue that, in fact, many of the tools and processes you most need to manage this period of life are exactly the ones that many businesses use to function well. Yet I think even people who *use* these tools every day at work do not always see their parallel uses at home.

Let's imagine your day job is managing the shampoo line at a haircare company. An opportunity comes up to purchase a smaller firm that makes a particular type of scented shampoo. There is a process to think about this. You'd likely start by asking whether this purchase fits with the mission of your firm (for example, maybe your firm's motto is "All Natural, No Scents," in which case this is probably not a good acquisition). You'd look at the data on their sales to see if it's a successful brand. You'd have meetings, and you'd frame the decision in a specific way ("How many dollars should we bid for the company?"). You'd use scheduling tools, probably some kind of task-management software, and you'd think about the benefits and costs of buying the smaller company. In the end, you'd decide, and then you'd move on to the next thing. There is an ease of process here, at least in theory, that we don't often have at home.

Now think about a (possibly) familiar family scenario: travel soccer. Nine-year-old Sofia is invited to join the travel soccer team. She really, really wants to do it. Her best soccer friend is doing it. If you do not let her do it, *you will literally ruin her life.*

It may be tempting to approach this decision based on what is happening right in that moment—how much whining there is, what other parents are doing—or to go with your first basic gut instinct. But this decision deserves more attention than that. It's four evening practices a week for the fall, plus one weekend day (at least!) spent at tournaments. If you say yes, this will be a huge part of your life. If you say no, though, see above—*you will ruin Sofia's life forever.* Quite a trade-off there.

This decision deserves the same attention you'd give to buying that scented shampoo company. Does this fit in your family's "mission"? Is it consistent with your basic values, or the central pieces of family life that you find important (for example, family dinners might be key for you)? You need to look at the data. Are there risks (Concussions?) or benefits (Healthy lifestyle? Benefits of team sports?) to soccer you should be thinking about? You need to think about a specific question: Should Sofia sign up for travel soccer or . . . what's the alternative? No soccer? Local soccer? Volleyball?

Just like in your shampoo firm, this decision will be helped by having some processes around it. Some meetings, perhaps some shared documents. You may not need to go as far as having a dedicated Slack channel, but this is a big enough choice that it likely makes sense to keep track of your discussions. At the end of all this, you get to a decision, hopefully one that is better thought out than one you'd make on the fly.

It probably does not escape you that this seems like a lot of work. And up front, there is no question that it is. Relative to going with your immediate gut instinct, deliberate decision making is going to take more time. But I'd argue that spending this time up front will save you time—and pain—later. If you decide to do this on a whim and then spend hours every week fighting about who is going to spend their weekend at the soccer tournament, that's a lot of wasted time and lost family harmony.

In addition, sometimes making big decisions up front will allow you to make smaller decisions faster. This book will advocate taking serious time to think about the question of family meals: Which ones do you eat together, how do you prepare them, how do you coordinate? But once you've made decisions like those, other decision making may be very fast.

For example: My daughter Penelope's main athletic activity is running, after a brief and unsuccessful foray into youth soccer. At some point around second grade, a fellow parent in the class told me about a youth running club that met twice a week at the local high school. It seemed on the face of it like it might be great for Penelope—an opportunity to run with someone who wasn't me, a chance to have a teamlike atmosphere, exercise.

But when I looked into it, I found that it met at 6 p.m. One of the central organizing principles of our household is that we eat family dinner at 6 p.m. every night. So that made the decision for us—I didn't even have to raise this with anyone else.

Your choice perhaps would be entirely different, but I'd argue that all families of school-age kids would benefit from more ease of process.

This book is, at its core, a business book. The business of parenting. I'm going to outline a framework and some systems. A way to run your family a bit more like a firm. And I'm going to argue that this approach is suited to this new age of parenting.

Concretely: we begin by outlining the "Big Picture" for your family.

This first step will require *thinking deliberately* about your household and parenting style. What do you want your family life to look like? It may seem mundane, but a lot of this really does come down to the basic structure of your day-to-day. Do you want to eat meals together? Which ones? What does the end of the day look like—is bedtime early or late? What are the weekends like? When it's midweek and you look forward to Saturday and Sunday, are you going to be excited to see a bunch of extracurricular activities and social events on the calendar, or do you want those days to be more family- or religion-oriented?

This Big Picture extends to slightly larger questions as well. Do both parents work outside the home, or do you want to adopt a more traditional approach where Mom stays at home (if there is at least one mom)? Or a less traditional one where, say, Dad is at home (if you've got at least one dad)? Even more broadly, it's worth thinking a little bit about your "parenting philosophy"—how much do you want to lean into encouraging independence in your kids, and how much scaffolding do you want to provide them?

Working through the Big Picture goes beyond just thinking about it in passing. I'm going to suggest you actually sit down—alone, or with your partner if you have one, or with any other family stakeholders—and work out what you want your life to look like. You can do this at any time (and there is probably some benefit to having some of these conversations even before you have children), but around the age of school entry is a natural time to at least revisit them because with the advent of more full-time school, a lot of logistics change for many families.

This is a lot of up-front work, but some of the payoff is immediate. Having this Big Picture in place has the side benefit of making task delegation smoother. I'd argue that once you know some basic principles, many decisions can be "triaged"—made immediately by one person, without consulting the other decision maker(s) in the family—which makes delegation simpler. And the ability to delegate, in turn, can reduce family conflict.

There are a lot of reasons you may have conflict with a partner, but in this phase of parenting, I would venture that at least some of them revolve around the tendency to deal with the aforementioned complexity by micromanaging. And I'd also venture that at least some of us do this micromanaging at home in a way we'd never do it at work.

Let's imagine your workplace provides a weekly lunch, and one of your tasks is to order the food. Usually, you get a selection of sandwiches, cookies, and drinks. Everyone likes it.

One week, you ask a colleague if they can take care of the ordering since you're swamped with a project. Sure, they say, that's fine.

Your coworker gets on the computer to order, and all of a sudden you are compelled to stand over them and comment. "Don't get that many turkey options, no one likes turkey. No, that's the wrong kind of veggie sandwich. Not too many peanut butter cookies! Wait, we do not usually order fruit. What are you doing!?"

You would never do this.

Why not? First, it's a waste of your time. You presumably asked your colleague to do it so you could get something else done. Second, it's disrespectful. This isn't how you talk to other adults, to people you trust, respect, and work with. Finally, it doesn't matter! Maybe people actually do like turkey sandwiches. And even if they don't, the worst that will happen is some people eat a lunch they like slightly less for this one week.

Now imagine you're the person who typically gets your five-year-old ready for camp: you get their shoes and socks on, pack up their requested snack, apply their sunscreen. One morning, you're busy reading to the two-year-old, so you ask your partner to get the kid ready.

When the book is done, you go down to see what is going on. "Those aren't the right shoes! He likes a less ripe banana than that! He'll never eat one with a brown spot! We don't use the blue spray sunscreen in the mornings, we use the green spray one!"

Maybe you'd never do *this*, either. But I bet it sounds a lot more plausible than the work scenario.

Yet the reasons *not* to do it are all the same. You're wasting your time. You're disrespecting your partner. And it doesn't matter! Any shoes are fine. You might be wrong about the bananas, but even if you are not, your child missing a snack one day is not a crisis. And why do you have two different spray sunscreens, anyway?

It's not that there isn't anything in this decision that would ever require discussion—for example, you may at some point discuss the issue of what is an appropriate snack. That's part of your family's Big Picture. But the reason you did that was so every morning you wouldn't have to discuss whether they can have a chocolate chip granola bar; now anyone can decide. Including your partner, who has made a perfectly reasonable choice, even if it is not precisely the snack you would have picked.

For many of your day-to-day experiences, having made choices about your family Big Picture will determine what you do. But not all decisions will be made here.

From time to time (or more often), bigger questions will come up: what school to choose, how to think about homework, which summer camp to choose, what to do if your child is being bullied (or doing the bullying). The second big piece of the Family Firm approach is designing a framework for making these big decisions.

The goal in this framework is to ask "How can we make this choice *well*?" Note that it is not "How can we make this choice *correctly*?" You cannot guarantee that you'll make the correct choice. Parenting involves mistakes. It's inevitable that sometimes you'll make a choice that turns out to be the wrong one. But what you *can* do is approach the choice correctly, and make the choice *well*.

When your family faces a big choice, I give you **The Four Fs**:

- *Frame the Question:* Think about the question you are asking. This is often the hardest step. It may seem easy, but in many cases, our starting-point question is too vague to really be answerable. "What kind of school is right?" isn't a question you can answer well. Much better is "Should we send our child to school A or school B?"
- *Fact-Find:* Gather the evidence, data, and details you need. This may involve learning more about the logistics and thinking through how you could make this work (or not). Or it may involve data on benefits and risks of each option. This step (the longest one) is a chance to get all the factors together, clearly, in one place.
- *Final Decision:* Once you have the evidence, have a meeting, and use that meeting to make a decision. This may seem obvious, but I think people often fail to have this single decision meeting and instead revisit the question again and again with different information. Let the decision take a lot of headspace in a single moment, decide, and move on.
- *Follow-Up:* Most decisions deserve follow-up. Once you've made a choice and implemented it, the last step is to make a concrete plan about when you'll revisit your choice. Hopefully you made the right choice, but if you didn't, better to rethink it sooner than later.

The combination of these structures—the big-picture approach and its accompanying schedules and principles, and the Four Fs for more infrequent decisions—provides an overall structure for your household firm. You may be wondering, though, *Where is the data?* Despite the emphasis

I've placed on decision structures so far, most of the content of this book is, presumably, data. Where, precisely, will that come in here?

The short answer: everywhere! More specifically, it will come in both your Big Picture development and in your individual decisions. To take a concrete example, one of the areas of the Big Picture you'll need to think about is family meals: Do you plan to eat dinner together every night? There are a lot of considerations inherent in that. But one of them is likely to be whether this is important for your children's development.

(My friend Ben told me that their family eats together because "People told me otherwise our children will be serial killers." Clearly, if true, this would be a factor to weigh in your choice.)

But without evidence, you cannot know whether the link between family meals and outcomes is real or just something people say. You need data, and just like with many decisions in pregnancy and early parenting, you need to sort out the good evidence from the not-so-good evidence. There may be a *correlation* between eating family meals and better outcomes, but this is different from saying the family meals *cause* these better outcomes. It could be that families who have meals together are different in other ways as well. Thinking clearly about correlation and causation is a big piece of this work—and, indeed, of my previous books.

When we turn to individual decisions—about school or sports or social development or media consumption—we will also find data is important. This data will not always be specific to one particular decision. Indeed, when we look at evidence on something like the efficacy of homework, it is likely to be key to a bunch of different family decisions, though maybe not the same ones for each family. But having all these pieces of data at your fingertips will help with the second of the Four Fs—Fact-Find—regardless of your specific question framing.

It's hard to see how all this will work without an example. So the next chapter starts with one. Specifically, a common one in early school age: the problem of kindergarten entry age, or "redshirting." My hope is that this example will give you an understanding of how to work through a problem like this, even if you never have to face this particular question.

Then I'll step back and give a little more detail on the approach. This begins with the idea of developing a family Big Picture, and the fact that doing so can help you make daily decisions faster. And then I'll provide more details on the Four Fs. The toolbox rounds out with a review of my love of Google Docs, task management apps, and other computerized solutions to your coordination issues.

The third section of the book turns to the pieces of data I think are useful in developing your Big Picture: sleep, nutrition, evidence on parental work, and a bit of discussion of whether the data tells you anything about what "kind" of parent you should be.

And finally, the last section dives even more deeply into the data, in the form of, effectively, case studies. For example, I'll talk about the data we have on schools. And then I'll develop just one example of a question that might come up around school, and talk you through how you could use the data and the Family Firm approach to solve it. Just like the case studies you'd work through in "real" business school, it's not likely you'll face this *specific* question. But we can learn from what comes before us, and we should. Reading through a worked-out example may be the best way to visualize how to work through your own.

This age of parenting is a little scary. I mean, all parenting is scary, but this age feels daunting in a way that younger kids do not. Messing up—saying the wrong thing, making the wrong choice—and the consequences of messing up can feel more extreme. But there are also greater possibilities! We have a little breathing space to take more time with choices, to craft a lifestyle that works for our families.

In a way, you can think of this as a promotion. We're all in management now. And as with all promotions, while it's good to be the boss, sometimes we wish we could go back to being told what to do. But I would suggest we embrace our promotion rather than fear it. We can do it, and creating the Family Firm can help.

People will often tell you parenting is a job (albeit an underpaid one, where the employees frequently tell you they hate you and you've ruined their life). So maybe it's time to start treating it like one.

A Sample Case Application

Red Shirt, Green Shirt, School-Entry Age

Time was, you entered school when they told you to, usually in the September you were five years old, maybe just before you turned five in some school districts.

Of course, there have always been small exceptions. Even when I was a kid, children with a birthday at the very end of August were sometimes held back to start school the following year, on the premise that it could be hard for a just-five-year-old to adjust. But on the whole, school entry happened at a prescribed time, without much parental choice or consideration.

No more. We have entered the era of the "redshirt."

Historically, "redshirting" has referred to the practice of recruited college athletes (usually football players) delaying the start of their college sports participation for a year so that they are larger and stronger than their peers for their four years of collegiate sports. It was not coined as a term for kindergarteners. And yet it has trickled down. It is now common to consider "redshirting" kids, delaying kindergarten entry for a year so that they enter at an older age, presumably more able to handle the structure of school. And this isn't just for kids with summer birthdays, either. Based on news reports, it seems that parents are now sometimes considering it even for kids born smack in the middle of the school year.

Why would one do this?

The main reason seems to be the feeling that if children are older for their grade, they'll do better; conversely, they may be at a disadvantage if they are very young. A just-five-year-old can be quite different from an almost-six-year-old. The worry is that if your child is the youngest in their school peer group, they'll struggle to keep up academically early on, or be unable to connect socially with their much-older classmates, and that this will have both short- and long-term consequences.

There is actually quite a lot of evidence that relative age matters in the arena of kids' sports. Elite athletes, in both youth and adult sports, are more likely to have birthdays that fall on one side of the youth sports age cutoff.[1] For example, many more professional baseball players are born in August than in July due to the August 1 cutoff for Little League. That cutoff means that if you were born on August 1, you are the oldest kid on your age-defined Little League team; if you were born on July 31, you're the youngest. If you're older, you're bigger and stronger and more likely (but still very, very, very unlikely) to end up playing baseball in college and professionally.

But kindergarten is not a sporting league, and being *bigger* isn't necessarily the key to success. It is certainly true that on average, kids who are older than their peers when they enter school will have had more prior exposure to letters, numbers, colors, and shapes. To the extent that kindergarten is increasingly focused on academic learning, this added preparation could help; as kids age through early childhood, they are also better able to sit still and focus, which will help in at least some kindergarten environments.

Reading the internet, one might be forgiven for thinking all other parents are waiting until their kids are eight or nine before enrolling them in kindergarten. Is that the case?

The answer lies in the data. One simple way to see it is to look at how the age of kids in *first grade* in the US has changed over time. You can see that in the following graph, which shows the share of six-year-olds enrolled in school at all (the dotted line) and those enrolled in first grade or above (the solid line). In 1968, the two lines are virtually the same, meaning all six-year-olds were enrolled in first grade or above. By 2005, only about 84 percent of six-year-olds were in first grade or above, meaning 16 percent of them were in kindergarten.[2] There is no reason to think this trend hasn't continued to the present.

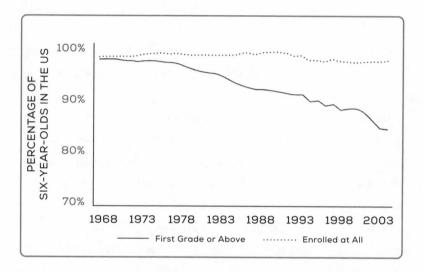

Put differently, in 1968 virtually all kids entered kindergarten at five, and then first grade at six. By 2005, 16 percent were entering *kindergarten* at six.

This overall trend tells us that on average, kids are entering kindergarten later. But it doesn't fully answer the question about redshirting. Some of this later entry is due to the school districts changing their age cutoffs over time, meaning even if parents did exactly what was expected, kids were older entering school in 2005 than they were in 1970.

But by using more granular data, it is possible to actually observe how much redshirting goes on. Writing in the journal *Educational Evaluation and Policy Analysis* in 2013, researchers looked into two nationally representative datasets that had detailed information on children's birthdates.[3] They matched these kids with the states they lived in so they could compare their school-entry dates to what would be expected in their school district.

These authors found that on average, across all kids, about 4 percent were redshirted. The vast majority of these—nearly all—were born in the three months before the school-entry cutoff date. In other words, it looks like parents tended not to do this unless their child would be among the youngest students. Boys were about twice as likely as girls to be redshirted, consistent with the general rhetoric that boys at this age develop a bit more slowly.

(Interestingly, the authors found that about 2 percent of students are "greenshirted," meaning they enter kindergarten early. These tend to be kids with birthdays right after the cutoff. The decision about whether to do this with your kid follows the same contours but is likely to be less common if only because many districts will not allow it.)

The figure 4 percent may seem small, but since nearly all these kids were born in the three months prior to the cutoff date, these figures actually mean that about 16 percent of children with summer birthdays were held back. For boys, where 5.2 percent of the overall sample were redshirted, over 20 percent with summer birthdays were held back.

In addition, these figures vary by demographics, both of the kids and of their schools. Children from higher-income families were more likely to be redshirted, and higher-income school districts do much more of it (this may be due to the fact that it is easier for these families to afford childcare). The researchers estimated that in some school districts, up to 60 percent of children with summer birthdays entered the year they were six years old, rather than five.

This prevalence data may be helpful in starting to frame this decision. It says, among other things, that this is most likely to be an important decision if your child is born right around the age cutoff. You may read anecdotes about people holding back their winter-birthday children, but these aren't representative. You may still choose to do that, but if your child enters kindergarten when they are almost seven, they'll be outside the norm.

But if you do have a child with a birthday just before—or just after—the age cutoff, this data says that you'd be in good company thinking carefully about this decision. And it matters! Even if it didn't matter to your child's long-term outcomes, it would affect the logistics of your family life.

HOW TO DECIDE: THE FOUR Fs APPROACH

The redshirting decision is emblematic of many of the hard choices in this period of parenting. It's hard precisely because there are so many moving parts, so many considerations. There's a data piece: What do we know about the impacts of school entry on our child's outcomes? And then there's a family piece: How does this fit in with other goals for our family? There are logistics, but maybe also budget considerations. It means evaluating, perhaps, how you trade off other core family values with this consideration.

The Four Fs approach is built for exactly this kind of decision. I'll say much more about the details of this approach in part 2 (and I'll have more examples in part 4). But let's start by seeing how this would look in regard to the question of school-entry age.

Frame the Question

Perhaps the hardest part of this process is this initial step: framing the question. Before you get into any details, you need to figure out what the question is *in your situation*. In the case of this choice, the first question may simply be "Is this relevant for my family?"

There are other situations—like "Should my kid get a phone?"—where you've got to actually decide, because there is no obvious default. Here there's a clear baseline option: go with whatever is the standard school-entry age in your district. The first conversation about this is likely to focus on whether there is a reason to consider deviating from this default.

One key question is just how young your child is, really—are we talking about a late August birthday, or late May? In the latter case, it's more likely you'll be able to decide that, really, the default works fine.

Also central is the question of logistics. What will your child do if you hold them back for a year? Do you have another childcare solution? Will there be implications for spacing with respect to your other kids in school—for example, if holding this kid back means they'll be in the same grade as a younger sibling, that could be a good reason not to do it. If it avoids the younger sibling being in the same grade as an older sibling, on the other hand, that may be an argument in its favor.

Finally, you'll probably want to do some due diligence at this phase to determine what is acceptable in the school or school district your kid will attend. On the parent side, it can be really helpful to have friends with slightly older children, so you can see what the school is like and bounce your thinking off the parents. On the school side, you'll find that some schools will virtually default children with birthdays close to the cutoff to being held back, while others really frown upon it. Still others have some creative solutions—"transition kindergarten," for example—which you surely want to know about before discussing your options.

This first F is likely to involve a family meeting; maybe multiple meetings. You probably want to do this far enough in advance that you have time to gather the evidence you need, but not so far in advance that you can't gather all of the relevant facts. Occasionally a woman pregnant with a baby due in the summer will ask me about redshirting, sometimes motivated by a fight with her partner (or her mom) over this question. You cannot make a decision about this while pregnant. It's too dependent on the circumstances at the time, on your child, on where you live.

It's possible that you'll realize that, in fact, the default is fine. But the resolution of this first step isn't (typically) a decision. What is the evidence you need to gather? This framing will tell you where to look. And then you get to it.

Fact-Find

In the world of early parenting choices, most of the evidence required was data based. Breastfeeding: What does the data really say about the short- and long-term benefits? Potty training: Is there any data-based guidance on when to start?

That's not as true here. In many cases, the evidence you'll need to gather lies outside the data. For example: If the key issue in school-entry timing is logistics, the evidence you need to put together may be some summary of the non-school childcare options. If the issue is budget, you need financial planning tools. The Family Firm toolbox is very helpful here, and I'll talk some in part 3 about using elements of the toolbox to handle questions like this.

But often there is also a data-based piece, and school-entry age is no exception.

What the Data Says

Is an older school-entry age good (or bad) for kids?

Before getting to the conclusions, let's try to be clear on how we might (or might not) answer this question. One simple, intuitive approach may to compare some outcome (say, test scores) for children who enter school at five years old with those who enter at six. Or, to get more granular, you could compare within five-year-olds, looking at those who enter at (say) five years three months to five years six months.

This approach has a basic problem. Parents are choosing—at least in some cases—the time of entry based on other things they know about their child. This means that when you look at the actual school-entry ages and kids' outcomes, you can get a misleading answer.

To be more concrete, imagine the school cutoff date is September 1, so if a child is born in August and they enter on time, they'll be the youngest child in school.

As discussed, the data show that some parents will choose to hold their child back. Which children will be held back? The data tells us it is more likely to be children from families with more resources, but it's also probably the case that parents are more likely to hold back children who are less prepared. If your August-birthday child is reading fluently at four, you'll probably send them to school.

But both of these facts—and others you can probably come up with on your own—mean the actual age at which a child enters school is related to other characteristics of both the child and their family. In econ-speak we'd call it "endogenous," as in, "Age of school entry is endogenous to demographic and personal characteristics." That's a great conversation starter for your next cocktail party.

This, in turn, means that if we look at just the actual age at which a child enters school and try to relate that to how well they do, we will struggle to learn whether it's the age of school entry that matters or the other differences.

Fortunately, this problem has a solution. Rather than use the age kids *actually* enter school, you can use the age they *should* have entered. It goes like this. Let's keep with our example of a September 1 school-entry cutoff. If a child is born on August 1, their default, non-redshirted school-entry age is five years one month, and if they are born January 1, it's five years eight months. Since (in practice) most kids enter at the normal, non-redshirt time, on average the kids who are born in August enter school at a younger age than those born in January.

By comparing the children with August birthdays to the children with January birthdays, we can learn about the effects of entry age. It's true, of course, that some of the August birthday children are held back, but as long as the average age of entry for August birthdays is younger than the average age for January birthdays, this will be informative. In fact, sometimes you can get the timing even closer and compare, say, kids with August birthdays to those with July birthdays, to draw conclusions about even smaller age differences.

Most of the literature will take this approach and use it to look at a variety of different outcomes.

First things first: There are some outcomes that are necessarily linked to *school-entry age* because they are a result of *school-completion age*. If your child enters school a year later, they'll finish each grade a year older. This has two direct implications. First, it affects the amount of school they are legally required to complete. Children can drop out of school at sixteen in the US; depending on the age of school entry, this could occur when they are in tenth grade or eleventh grade. By having your child enter school later, you leave open the possibility that they might complete less school.

One of the most famous papers in economics—"Does Compulsory School Attendance Affect Schooling and Earnings?"—looks at this relationship in the data.[4] (This paper is most famous for the methods it developed, although I'll focus on the conclusions here.)[5] The authors found that children who enter school at an older age due to their birth timing complete less school on average—and as a result, their earnings are lower as adults.

A second direct implication is that, holding constant how much school they complete, children who enter school later will enter the workforce later. As a result, their earnings will be lower early in life; certainly, if you look at their total earnings at age twenty-four, someone who completes college and starts work at twenty-two will have more than the same person completing college and starting work at twenty-three. This difference seems to fade out over time, however, perhaps as early as thirty.[6]

My guess is that most parents are not thinking about either of these considerations when deciding on school entry. That may be appropriate, given that high school completion rates in the US are high and the effects of school-entry age on earnings are short-lived.

On the other hand, it may be worth including some of these mechanical considerations in your calculus: later entry means, for example, a kid may be able to get their driver's license earlier in high school. Could be good or bad, but it's probably something to put on the radar even if it's not the first thing that comes to mind when looking at your four-year-old attempting to ride their balance bike.

Beyond these long-term mechanical impacts, however, there is also evidence of short-term effects of age of school entry. These effects extend to both test scores and learning differences.

To set the stage, we can start with a study from Norway that used the timing-of-birth approach to look at the impact of school-entry age on test scores (this is the same study that shows some long-term earnings effects).[7] In terms of data, these authors have an interesting advantage:

they have scores both from tests administered at school and a test required for the armed forces, administered out of school, which every Norwegian takes at eighteen. This means they can look at the impacts of age at school entry on test scores *in a particular grade* (when the students who entered school younger will be younger at the time of the test) and *at a particular age* (when the students who entered younger will have completed more school).

The authors found, first, that kids who enter school younger did slightly better on the military test when they were eighteen, likely due to having completed more school years on average. If your goal is to have the highest test scores at the age of eighteen, this suggests earlier entry is (a little) better. However, on the flip side, they found that when you look at test scores in a fixed grade, the kids who entered school earlier did a lot worse. Being young for your grade seems to predict worse school performance.

This conclusion is consistent with what other researchers have found in various datasets covering a wide range of locations. On average, kids who enter school at younger ages have worse test scores than their peers in the same grade.[8] They are also more likely to repeat an early grade (kindergarten, first, or second).[9] (I'll come back to this fact later and argue that it isn't obviously bad, since it could simply reflect parents changing their minds in the face of new information.)

Test scores and school performance are one thing. The other very significant effect is on the diagnosis of learning disabilities, most notably ADHD. We can see detailed evidence on this in a paper published in 2009 in the *Journal of Human Resources*.[10] The authors of this paper collected data on school-entry cutoffs from many states in the US. As I described above, they were able to look at the impact of age at school entry by looking at outcomes for kids born in different months.[11]

The bottom line, the paper reported, is that being a year younger at school entry increased the chance of being diagnosed with ADHD by 2.9 percentage points. The baseline rate of diagnosis is around 4.1 percentage points, so this is a 70 percent increase. This is really very large. Out of 100 kids who enter school, about 4 of them will be diagnosed with ADHD, but among those who enter at very young ages, it's 7 out of 100.

Let's be clear on how to read this. The authors' approach allowed them to isolate the effect of school-entry age, so this is *not* saying that kids who enter school earlier are predisposed to have more ADHD diagnoses, but rather that *the fact that they entered younger* means they are more likely to be *diagnosed* with ADHD. Those extra 3 diagnoses per 100 kids are a result of the age of school entry; we would not have expected these children to be diagnosed if they entered at an older age.

Why might this be? Mechanisms are always hard to identify, but one possibility is that younger kids are less able to sit still (this is certainly true) and teachers (or parents, or other school personnel) naturally compare kids to the other students in their class. If a child is the youngest kid in the class, their age-appropriate inability to sit still as compared to their older peers may be interpreted as hyperactivity.

Other evidence in this paper points to this as the likely explanation for the discrepancy in ADHD diagnoses. The authors were able to show that when a child's class cohort is (randomly) older, the child is more likely to be diagnosed with ADHD. In other words, even conditional on a child's own age of entry to school, if they are in a class with older kids, they are more likely to be identified as having a learning disability. These effects are not unique to this study; they are echoed in other papers, with different data.[12] And these learning-difference diagnoses seem to persist over childhood.[13]

It is important to say, of course, that there should be no shame or stigma in learning disabilities. Early recognition can lead to better, faster, more effective treatment. Kids who might otherwise have struggled all through elementary school and beyond are now able to excel and achieve with the help of therapy and medication. That's all great!

These results on school-entry age are worrisome, however, because they suggest that age-of-entry-driven diagnoses are the result of circumstance and not fundamentals. These kids would not have been diagnosed if they had entered school later, and this overdiagnosis *is* a cause for concern.

So that's where the data is on this. Kids who enter school earlier have (in the short term, at least) lower test scores and are persistently more likely to be diagnosed with learning disabilities. Based on what we know about age and sports, it seems likely that we can also conclude that younger entry means less school-sports success.

On the flip side, kids who enter school at younger ages learn more in the early years: at age eight, you'll know more if you entered school at five years old than if you entered at six. They'll also graduate high school or college at younger ages and get into the workforce faster.

As a parent, you may find this data informative but incomplete. You probably have a lot of other questions: How will they fare socially? Being older seems like it could be good or bad. Is there a chance your child will be really bored at school if they enter when they are older?

These studies rely on evidence we can get from schools, which inherently limits what the data can tell us. This doesn't mean you shouldn't think about them in your decision, just that you will not have hard data to rely on.

In fact, there are a lot of additional considerations that may factor into this decision—finances, logistics, what your child is like. It is also likely to interact with the choices in the first chapter ahead. Which school you choose may dictate what the right entry age is. We'll come back to the question of school choice in part 4.

The (Data) Bottom Line

- Benefits to entering school early: Fewer childcare expenses at young ages; graduate high school or college and enter the workforce sooner.
- Benefits to redshirting: Lower ADHD diagnoses, better test scores.
- Benefits are larger in locations where more people are redshirting; it seems problematic (on average) to be the youngest in a class.

Final Decision

The title says it all. Having framed the questions you need answered and gathered evidence, you have to make a choice. Visualize logistics, or the budget, if that's the issue. Think about how this intersects with your family priorities. Think about the data I've detailed and how it applies to your kid.

It almost certainly makes sense to have a family meeting about this. The goal of this meeting should be to make a decision. Sometimes it's impossible; considerations you didn't think about may surface, ones that need more research. (Hopefully, if you do the evidence gathering right, that will not happen.)

So you meet, you talk, you decide. Even after all this careful thought, evidence gathering, and discussion, the answer still may not be obvious. This is a complicated choice with a lot of uncertainty. You will never know for sure how your child will react to school until they get into it, nor will you know for sure what the school is really like until they start.

What this process can give you is not certainty that you made the right choice but the confidence that you made it thoughtfully.

This last point—that at the time you make the decision, you cannot be sure it is the right one—is, I think, what holds people back most from facing these choices head-on. By really leaning into the process of making the decision, you also lean into the possibility that you'll do it wrong. But *not* thinking carefully about choices like this won't help your decision be right, either.

Follow-Up

Your kid is finally starting school—either on time or early or late, whatever you decided. But wait! You're not quite done. At some point, likely within the first year of school, it will make sense to go back and review your decision. This is especially crucial if you decided to enroll your child on time, so they're young for their class. If that's the case, you have the opportunity to effectively change your mind and have them repeat a grade.

A big part of this review should be talking to your child's teacher about how your child is doing. They'll know, probably better than you do, whether your child is keeping up in the classroom and if they are ready to move on.

There are good reasons to do this review in your child's first year or two of school rather than waiting until something prompts it. It's likely to be much harder socially to hold back a kid in the fourth or fifth grade than in kindergarten. If you skip the review step, you may find yourself forced into it later, when the options aren't as good.

As with other aspects of this approach, I make a push to build the infrastructure now and reap the benefits later. More up-front investments let you make better decisions in a calmer way, to use your time more effectively. It isn't necessarily parenting less, but it's parenting smarter.

School-entry age is just one example—maybe not even one you'll have to face—but the intention of this approach is to be flexible. And to see that, we'll work through many examples. But first, I'll take a step back. What is the Family Firm system, anyway?

Part I

The Family Toolbox

When my daughter, Penelope, was in third grade, her school decided to put on the musical version of the Disney film *Frozen*. All the second through fifth graders were invited to participate. Rehearsals would be three days a week after school for two months, followed by a few more intense days and a weekend with performances. Many of her friends were going to do it.

On the one hand, whether Penelope chose to do this was not, in the scheme of things, very important. On the other hand, the decision *was* going to influence the shape of the next months of our lives. For example, it would mean some changes to the school pickup schedule, and more after-dinner homework.

No book could tell us what to do in this situation. Even the most specific set of parenting guidance does not contain an index entry for "Lower School Musical Participation, *Frozen*." For this, and for a million other decisions, we needed to establish not *what to do*, but *how to decide*.

Making decisions—big and small—is something firms do all the time. When you enter business school, one of the primary things you are trying to learn is how to make good decisions. A key component of this is setting up good decision-making structures and approaches. Although it doesn't always work this way, business decision making is ideally organized and deliberate.

If your family is going to work like a firm, you need a family decision-making process, too. When a choice comes up—rules at dinner, screen time, school choice, whether to do the *Frozen* musical—do you have the processes in place to make it thoughtfully? This is where the Family Toolbox comes in.

In the process I'll outline on the following pages, you start by making some *really* big decisions, establishing some of the key structures for how your Family Firm will operate. This will take some time, but once you have these key structures in place, a lot of small decisions will be obvious. The principles will dictate the choices, and you'll never need to discuss them.

And then you'll put a structure in place to make the medium-size decisions that come up from time to time—kindergarten entry age, summer camp, and, yes, the musical. This is where the Four Fs come in: Frame the Question, Fact-Find, Final Decision, Follow-Up. (We used this for *Frozen*. We skipped it that year. If you never see my kid play Elsa on Broadway, now you'll know why.)

You may find yourself thinking it would be a lot easier if you had a way to coordinate that went beyond, say, a discussion in the hallway or writing something on a sticky note or (Jesse's personal least-favorite) bringing up a logistical discussion right after the lights go off for the night. The last chapter in this section nods toward some basic workplace tools—I mean *really* basic, like Google Docs—that can help.

Creating the "Big Picture"

In his book on families, Stephen Covey, of *The 7 Habits of Highly Effective People* fame, argues that your family needs a "mission statement." This is a grounding document to highlight your central family values. It's not dissimilar to the mission statement a firm might have. Your central family values may be religious or articulate a family-first focus. They might say something like "Prioritize family time and raise thoughtful kids." Maybe your mission articulates a particular approach to child independence (i.e., are you a free-range parent, or more of a helicopter type?).

You should have such a mission statement! But I'm going to suggest going beyond that and directly addressing the interaction between these broad priorities and concrete decisions. When I talk about creating the family Big Picture, I'm talking about these overall principles, but I'm also talking about confronting "What does Thursday night look like?"

There's a parallel to firms. The statement "Create a great search engine and don't be evil" is perhaps a good mission statement for Google, but it's not a recipe for how to run the firm. Just as "Prioritize family time and raise thoughtful kids" may be a good broad mission, but it doesn't tell you the right bedtime.

These logistical details matter, because if you fail to think about the logistics holistically, you could find yourself almost accidentally in a very different place than you imagined. Each individual choice may seem inconsequential in the moment, but they add up.

Think, for example, about birthdays. Imagine you have three kids, all in school, in classes of twenty kids each. And imagine that each kid in each class has a birthday party. That is *sixty* birthday parties a year. When each Evite rolls in, you think, "Oh, okay, it's just one birthday party." But by the end of the year, you've spent literally every weekend at Sky Zone, Jump For Fun, Kidz Kastle, or, my personal favorite, Dave & Buster's.

At some point you may think, "Enough is enough," and put the kibosh on attending any more parties that year. But then it's your middle daughter's best friend's birthday and she *absolutely has to go*. So that's another weekend down.

In economics parlance, your sequential birthday approach means you're making each invite decision "on the margin." But while adding each marginal birthday has a small effect, the aggregate may be, quite simply, not acceptable.

In the grand scheme of things, birthday parties are a minor issue. But this kind of slippery-slope experience can pervade our parenting decisions. You let in one late-night extracurricular, then another, and pretty soon your image of dinner as a family at six every night has vanished. And if this dinner is a priority for you, that's a problem.

It shouldn't escape our notice that failing to articulate these priorities is a recipe for conflict in cases where there are multiple decision makers (say, two parents) in the household. Let's say bedtime by 8:30 is a key priority for me, and I've worked out the family schedule so it happens every night that I'm around. Now imagine that I'm out of town for work and I call my partner at 10 p.m. to learn that the older child is still up, watching *The Great British Baking Show*.

"WHAT IS THE MATTER WITH YOU?!" I yell through the phone.

"This is your rule, not mine," comes the retort. "You want it done your way? Don't leave town."

What is the problem here? Perhaps many things, but at least one is failing to get on the same page about bedtime as a priority. If you have two (or more!) parents involved in raising a child, they'll inevitably parent at least slightly differently. My husband, for example, adheres much less stringently to the every-other-day bath system than I do. When he's in charge, baths tend to be a little less frequent. And this is okay, because although I have a particular bath system, it's not actually that important to me. In contrast, maintaining a fixed bedtime is *extremely important* to me. But unless we had talked it through, how would Jesse know that my feelings on bath frequency and bedtime are fundamentally different?

It is also useful to recognize that every small thing cannot be a hill to die on. If you start this process and it turns out one of you has rigid preferences about *everything*, that doesn't leave much space for joint problemsolving. Articulating priorities together may help you recognize which are really important to you and realize that they cannot all be equally crucial.

The first step in creating your Family Firm is to outline your mission, and then think carefully about what your family will prioritize, what your day looks like, and the basic logistics of your family. To be clear, you could think about this at any time in life—before kids, with an infant, with a toddler—but around school-entry time is a good point to revisit your mission statement carefully. For one thing, once your kid is in school, you'll adopt a schedule that you will keep—more or less—for the next thirteen years (or longer, if you have other kids). For another, this is often around the time things calm down at least a bit and you get more mental space to think about your choices.

THE PROCESS

Creating the family Big Picture is not the activity of a single afternoon, and you'll probably need to revisit pieces of it more than once as your children age. And you may choose to do this a bit differently. That's okay! Think of this as a guide or a starting point.

To help you out, I've made a workbook. In the pages that follow, I'll talk about structuring some of these conversations, about writing things down. You don't need a workbook to do this, but I think it will help.

(Also, I love workbooks. True story: My mother still remembers that at my third-grade parent-teacher conference, Mrs. Totman said, not entirely positively, "I just cannot understand why she likes workbooks so much.")

There are two basic steps. First, at the broadest level, expressing and aligning values and priorities. Second, getting to the more granular: creating the day-to-day schedule, establishing some family principles, and assigning responsibilities.

But before you get into actually *doing* any of this, please read the next section of the book, which has some big data pieces you might want to consider. As you think about the family schedule, knowing more about sleep—Is it important? How much do kids need?—is important. As you think about your level of parental involvement with your kid, you may want to consider what the evidence says on the relationship between parental involvement and children's independence or performance in school. The data chapters won't tell you how to make these choices for your family, but they may provide some important input.

Step 1: Values and Priorities

In a business-school class in negotiations, a common topic is the "Theory of Anchoring." Basically, the opening bid in a negotiation "anchors" the price. By the same token, collective decisions can be thrown off by having one person publicly state their views first. If we are trying to decide, as a firm, how much to bid for a company, and the first person to speak suggests $20 million, I may be embarrassed to say I thought it was worth only $2 million. But knowing that we disagree is valuable! One approach to learning that is to ask people to write down their valuations privately and then share them simultaneously.

We'll take a similar approach here. Start with all the parenting stakeholders, whoever that is in your family. This exercise is likely to be useful even if you are parenting alone, just not for quite the same reasons. Everyone gets a piece of paper (or a copy of the first workbook page) and writes down:

- Your overarching family mission statement. Whatever you want! One sentence: What is your main goal for the family?
- Three main goals for your children (big life goals; not something like "Use a fork better," even if you desperately, desperately want that).
- Three priorities for you, things you care about (could be working, exercising, seeing friends); what do you want to make sure *you* get time for?
- Three activities you see as *must do* on (most) weekdays. (For example, mine would be: [1] eat at least one meal with the kids; [2] get some work done; [3] be there for bedtime. If I get all three things in a day, I'm likely to be happy.)

- Three activities you see as *must do* on (most) weekends (for example, religious services, extra tutoring, competitive sports, hiking, seeing grandparents).

And then you switch papers and discuss.

What comes out of this? Well, it depends. Maybe you're completely aligned and what comes out are some touchpoints you both agree on for developing your family schedule and principles. Or maybe you're not aligned. Maybe my ideal weekend is competitive sports and math tutoring, and yours is hiking the Appalachian Trail and camping. Would be good to know now.

This may also reveal things we care about and agree on but that differ from what we are doing now. For example, this may reveal that I would like to be a stay-at-home parent. And my partner might think that's a great idea and even have some thoughts on how to make it work financially. If we haven't discussed it before, I may not know that my partner would support that. Or the inverse: Maybe I've been staying at home, but I'm dying to go back to work and was afraid to bring it up. For these reasons, it is important to be *honest* in these discussions, even if you think what you want isn't achievable.

(A note: If you are parenting alone, I still think this is a valuable approach, since in the chaos of parenting, you may not stop often enough to reflect on what you really *want* to be doing in each moment.)

There is no obvious end to this conversation. It's one you've probably started before you got to this point, and one you'll continue. But have the conversion until you feel like you're in enough alignment to put your mission statement into concrete practice.

Writing down your goals for your family will not give you control. Control in family life is illusory—things happen that you do not expect, the world throws you curveballs. No amount of note-taking and planning can avoid this. But not everything is unexpected, and we can avoid much daily stress by at least being clear about our real hopes for our family.

Step 2: The Details

SCHEDULE

The approach in this book—perhaps fitting for an economist—focuses on the practical. So while I'd urge you to start with the values and principles, the next steps dial into the details. Starting with the schedule. Literally, this step involves looking at calendars (in the workbook!) for the weekdays and weekends, and filling them in.

Give everyone a calendar. All the adult decision makers. If they are old enough, some of the children as well. Have everyone outline their suggested schedule for the week; adults, you need to do the kids' schedules, too. Note that this shouldn't be your "dream schedule" (for my kids: breakfast, TV, lunch, app time, snack, movie, dinner, bed). It should be a realistic expression of what you think the day should look like. It needn't be hyperdetailed, but it should go beyond "eat, work, eat, sleep." Try to think through some details—for example, if you agreed in step 1 to eat dinner together most nights, you need to figure out how said dinner will be produced (and by whom).

I've given an example on the next page—this is a Tuesday, and I've put in a proposal for me and each of the kids. I left Jesse on his own, but I'll note that having been married so long and having the same job, we basically have the same schedule. Although he wakes up an hour later and runs less frequently.

Once you've got these schedules written down, compare them. You're not likely to agree on everything. Maybe your ten-year-old thinks that

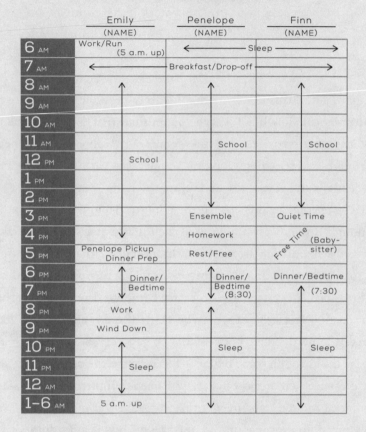

Creating
YOUR SCHEDULE

	Emily (NAME)	Penelope (NAME)	Finn (NAME)
6 AM	Work/Run (5 a.m. up)	← Sleep →	
7 AM	← Breakfast/Drop-off →		
8 AM	↑	↑	↑
9 AM			
10 AM			
11 AM		School	School
12 PM	School		
1 PM			
2 PM		↓	↓
3 PM		Ensemble	Quiet Time
4 PM	↓	Homework	Free Time
5 PM	Penelope Pickup Dinner Prep	Rest/Free	Free Time (Baby-sitter)
6 PM	↑ Dinner/	↑ Dinner/	Dinner/Bedtime
7 PM	Bedtime ↓	Bedtime ↓ (8:30)	↑ (7:30)
8 PM	Work	↑	
9 PM	Wind Down		
10 PM	↑	Sleep	Sleep
11 PM	Sleep		
12 AM	↓		
1–6 AM	5 a.m. up	↓	↓

homework should be an after-dinner activity, whereas you are adamant that it should happen right after school. Maybe your partner thinks four nights a week of take-out is a good idea, whereas you are more of a once-a-week kind of person.

But you'll come together. It's easier to coordinate schedules than values, in most cases, and you've done the work to get to the shared values.

Once you do agree on everyone's schedules, get them in writing. At a minimum, print out the family schedules and keep them somewhere (do not necessarily trust your children to keep them—one of mine just came in while I was writing this to tell me she "lost" her schedule several weeks ago). You may also consider entering these into a Google Calendar, if you choose to go all in on that (more on computing tools in the last chapter of this section).

These schedules will not keep forever. New school years or terms will bring new activities. You may need a big revisit at least once a year, and perhaps smaller revisits more often than that. But these later revisions should be easier. Like many aspects of this approach, there is a big up-front investment and a payoff later.

PRINCIPLES

The second practical component of the Big Picture is a set of principles. That is, a set of family rules that are more specific than "here is our mission" but general enough to speak to decisions that come up frequently. Some of your family principles may be closely related to schedule—for example, one family principle may be "Bedtime is at 8 p.m."—but they will go beyond this.

The goal of principles, really, is to translate the set of shared values into a set of shared "rules" that anyone can implement. Consider this example: Can twelve-year-old Alexandra have a sleepover tonight? It's a Wednesday. She wants to go to her friend's house after dinner to work on their social studies project and then sleep over. Mommy arrives home from work; Alexandra asks her. Mommy knows the friend, knows that her parents will enforce a reasonable bedtime, but still, it's a weeknight sleepover.

Mommy says she has to talk about it with Mama. Mama arrives home at 6:10, dinnertime is 6:20. She is immediately accosted by the question, Alexandra standing impatiently while her parents attempt to discuss.

Mama really has to pee. Regardless of the outcome, everyone ends up frustrated and annoyed.

Or Mommy just says yes. Then Mama comes home and cannot believe she wasn't consulted about this, since she is categorically opposed to school-night sleepovers. Whether Alexandra goes or not, the day ends with everyone mad.

Neither of these is a good outcome. There isn't time for this to involve a long discussion in the moment, but it's also not a completely trivial decision. Put differently, you need a way to make the decision quickly, but not arbitrarily.

Or consider this scenario, drawn from my own family: It's the start of the school year, and one morning four-year-old Finn decides he does not want to come down to breakfast, he wants to color. HE IS NOT HUNGRY. I think we should make him come down to eat; I entice him with frozen muffins. Jesse thinks we should leave him. We equivocate.

Finn finally does come down on his own, but he only has 8 minutes to eat, and he wants a bagel. It takes 4 minutes to produce this. I want to tell him he can't have the bagel, he has to pick something fast; Jesse wants to let him work it out himself and ultimately realize it was a mistake to wait so long. We end up giving him somewhat conflicting advice; he ends up upset. Breakfast ends with us telling him he has to stop eating and him running away from the table with a mouth full of bagel. We are late for school.

In both cases, the problem is the lack of an articulated principle. It's not your fault! This hasn't come up before. But you do need a principle. Are weeknight sleepovers allowed? What is the rule about sitting at meals? If you had a principle, both of these situations would be simple to resolve.

Writing out your family principles should address some of these questions. You are likely able to write down some of them immediately— rules for bedtime, for what is an acceptable snack, maybe some rules around whether kids are allowed to go outside on their own and, if so, how far.

But these principles will evolve over time. In the case of Finn and breakfast, Jesse and I had a quick discussion later that day and established a new family principle, specifically: You must be downstairs by 7:05, or else someone will come get you. We cannot force you to eat, but we'll make you come downstairs and at least briefly sit at the table. Breakfast has a hard stop at 7:25. This was entered into the family meal policy (right under "No carbs for snacks").

It may be helpful to think of these principles as a system of triage, the parenting equivalent to what happens in the emergency room.

When someone comes into an ER, the first thing they do is find the triage coordinator and explain their complaint. The ER has set up some systems, they've agreed ex ante on what to do in each type of case. Someone with shortness of breath? Immediate full workup. Someone with a cut on their foot? Waiting room. Once these systems are in place, all the staff know what to expect from the triage coordinator, and it makes their jobs much faster.

Of course, the key to this system is that the hospital spent some time up front deciding on some general principles for the ER; this is what allows them to do the sorting. The principles may have taken time to set up, but they pay dividends.

The same is true here. You'll spend some initial time setting up your guidelines, but then many of your family's day-to-day decisions can be made by anyone in the household.

RESPONSIBILITIES

The final piece of the Big Picture is responsibilities. That is, thinking deliberately about who in the family is going to be responsible for what.

I'm talking here about significant, repeated family tasks. This isn't

"Who is responsible for getting the hats that were left outside this morning?" but rather, "Who is responsible for planning meals and shopping for groceries? Making lunches? Packing backpacks?" and on and on.

Check out the worksheet on page 273 for this, which suggests writing down the main family activities, thinking about their time commitment, and allocating them. I'll note that I'm far from the first to suggest this approach—among many others, Eve Rodsky's book *Fair Play* has a more detailed version of this system for dividing spousal responsibility.

This responsibility allocation should, by the way, involve your children. There's much more on parenting approaches in chapter 7, so I'd suggest you read that first to prepare. And you may decide that your parenting approach does not involve having your children take ownership of many family tasks. But if you do decide they are a piece of this, this responsibility allocation is a time to involve them.

Exactly how will depend on their age. A nine-year-old may be old enough to have lunch-packing responsibilities. A five-year-old probably isn't. But maybe the five-year-old is old enough to have the responsibility of putting lunch *in* their backpack. Given that children mature, responsibilities change, and parents' out-of-home activities may vary, this responsibility allocation should be revisited with some frequency, probably similar to how often you revise the family schedule.

Developing guiding principles and allocating responsibilities is a way to divide work. In its best form, this should give everyone the ability to do these activities *on their own*. This means that everyone else needs to stay out of their way as they're doing their tasks. If you are the person who does most things, allocating work to another member of the family may seem great. But it is easier said than done.

Think back to the example in the introduction about micromanaging your spouse as they get your child ready for camp. Now extend this to your child packing their own lunch. You told them it's their job to pack their lunch (allocating responsibility), and you have some basic guide-lines for what to pack (veggie, fruit, main dish, small dessert).

It may drive you crazy to watch your ten-year-old eat the exact same thing every day. You may think those tomatoes would be a lot nicer with a little salt on them. Maybe you wouldn't have put that soft nut bar in a plastic bag where it would melt. But—and I cannot emphasize this enough—*keep your mouth shut.*

The Four Fs

S etting up the Big Picture and establishing principles is a lot of work, but once you've done it, you can cruise along. Your food policy is in place, the bedtime plan is organized, and, in principle, everyone can make many decisions on their own.

Until, all of a sudden, you face a big choice. What school to pick. When to start it. How much to invest in an extracurricular. Sleepaway camp. The dreaded phone.

On the plus side, decisions of this importance do not come up all the time. You'll make maybe one, two of these a year. You can recognize these decisions in part by their impact on your life. Will a choice you make have repercussions for how your day looks for a few months, or for years (competitive volleyball at a school that's a 45-minute drive away)? Will it be something you experience every day (like the phone)? These are hallmarks of decisions that deserve the Four Fs treatment. When you face one of these, they require more effort. You cannot make a decision in a quick email exchange. You need more time, more reflection.

What makes this hard? One issue is that there are many considerations to these decisions. Think about a decision that, in a way, seems simple—like "Should my kid do travel soccer?" Making the right choice here requires thinking through your family logistics, the impact on your other children (their schedules, their time with parents), the impact on things like sleep and mealtimes, the benefits (Possible future Major League Soccer player? College scholarship? Exercise? Value of team sports?), and the costs (Giving up the opportunity to do other things? Concussions?). You will almost certainly think of other factors specific to your family that would never even occur to me.

A second problem is that the arrival of these decisions is inherently unpredictable. Yes, there are a few you know you'll have to make—school choice, school-entry age, probably something about extracurriculars. But a large share of these decisions will spring up unannounced. I had understood that at some point, Penelope might want to go to sleepaway camp. But in the moment, in the winter of her third-grade year, when she seriously raised the issue of wanting to go to camp the following summer, I was totally unprepared.

And with an older kid, even a decision that many others have made before you (like sleepaway camp) is unique to your family because kids are so different. There will be times when you can rely at least in part on data from people who have made these choices before you (indeed, data like that is a focus of the third part of this book). But such data is rarely, if ever, going to provide the *answer*. It may reinforce or refute your concerns, but it won't tell you what to do.

Making these big decisions is much less about finding the answer in someone else's choices or the data, and much more about taking the right *approach* to the decision. A hallmark of poor decision making is to seesaw between choices based on your last conversation. For this reason, when a decision is important to a (well-run) firm, there is a framework in place for making it. Your Family Firm needs a framework, too. And so we have the Four Fs.

THE FOUR Fs

Frame the Question

The Four Fs start with framing the question. What is the actual decision you need to make—what is the question you need to answer? In the context of the example at the start of the book, it was "Should I wait a year to enroll my young-for-his-year preschooler in kindergarten?" Some questions are easier to identify than others. Sometimes your family's version of the question—what your choices really are—will be kind of unique.

Frame a question, then plan an initial meeting where all the involved adults, plus (maybe, in some cases) the relevant child, can talk about the decision. The goal should be to air all the possible issues—logistics, costs, benefits, risks, what people are worried or excited about.

You probably won't make a decision at this meeting, since you'll likely need more information about the question. The goal is to leave the meeting with a plan for what information you need to gather. Figure out how you'll get that information (more on the tools for this in the next chapter). Assign responsibilities. And plan a date for a follow-up meeting.

Fact-Find

Gather the evidence you need. What does that involve? For decisions with complicated logistics, one thing that has worked well for my family is actually populating a (fake) calendar and looking at it. Can you be really specific about what this decision will mean for the family schedule?

If there is relevant data, try to collect it. This could involve evidence from published literature (for example, is there a serious concussion risk associated with the sport your child wants to play?). Here's where a lot of data will come in. The last part of this book tries to work through some of these general data pieces; not all of them will be helpful to you, but I've tried to cover many of the big questions that come up.

The fact-finding may also involve information more specific to your particular circumstances. For example, if you're deciding whether to hold a child back for later kindergarten entry, it may be useful to know how common this is in your particular school or school district. That's something you can find out directly.

You may need to talk to other people. I always find this part the hardest—I really, really hate the telephone—but when we've thought about extracurriculars, camps, or school choice, it's been valuable to talk to parents whose kids already do the activities or go to the school. You can get a good sense of, among other things, whether the families involved share your values and whether you think your kid would fit in. Here's another place where having friends with slightly older kids can be pretty helpful.

This process should ideally be interactive. You get some evidence, share it with others, if necessary, and think about what else you might need. By the time you get to the follow-up meeting, you should have the necessary information.

Final Decision

You actually have to decide. This probably requires another meeting, possibly more than one (although hopefully not). It may be harder than you think, since there probably isn't an obvious choice (otherwise, this elaborate procedure wouldn't be required). But at this point, you have what you need, and the question is simply what you want to do. Plan to leave this meeting with a decision *and* a plan for follow-up.

You cannot be sure you've made the right choice, but none of this is about making sure your choice is right—that is impossible! What you can do is make sure you made the choice thoughtfully. Whether it is right will be revealed over time—that's what the fourth F is for.

Follow-Up

This is the least obvious but may be the most important step in the process. You need to have a concrete plan for reviewing the decision. Let's say you decide to do the travel soccer team. Schedule a time at the end of the season to discuss how it went. Do not decide to do it next year just because you did it this year! Really think through all the angles: How did it go? Was it worth it? Is there anything you would change if you do it again?

In any decision-making process, there is hysteresis—you just want to keep going on the path you are going on. But new information can and does crop up over time. Let that information help you. Don't wake up in six years and realize you wasted thousands of hours driving around to distant towns for soccer games and no one enjoyed it.

PRACTICAL CONSIDERATIONS

Implementing the Four Fs approach to decision making will not happen overnight, and your system may not look exactly like what I've described. Maybe you want to have a few meetings during the fact-finding. You may be more or less inclined to involve your children. You may want to talk through most decisions over the phone with your child's grandparents or some other trusted advisors.

The core idea to build on here, though, is that these decisions should be made *deliberately*. There should be some process for doing so. You should give these decisions the space they deserve to make them thoughtfully. But conversely, you shouldn't give them all your attention. When large choices like this come up, it is easy to let them take over your thinking. You're thinking about them in the shower, on the way to work, talking them through in all your conversations with your partner.

This constant consideration isn't obviously helpful. A structured approach to these decisions lets you devote the needed time to the choices without letting them take over.

When you do implement this approach, some tools will be useful. Specifically, things like task management systems or shared documents. A Google Sheet is no substitute for good decision making, but it can help you follow through. So, we turn to this now.

The Efficiency Frontier

A confession: I am a sucker for a Google Form. I use them all the time. As I was writing this, I agreed to run a large university committee, and I lay awake for 2 hours that night planning the set of Google Forms I was going to send out.

It is not just forms. I have a generally high level of confidence in business process organization. (As a reader of this book, you should hope I would.) I use two different task management programs at work. I have a slew of shared Google Sheets and Docs, and routinely try to insist that the basic tracking of things (any things!) happens in a formalized way.

A hard-won lesson for me has been that business processes are not a substitute for good decision making. All the Google Forms in the world cannot rescue you if you disagree about fundamental principles. But there is no question that, in at least some work situations, introducing better tracking and organizational technology can help.

The same is true at home. There is no reason you cannot adopt some basic workplace tools to make your house function more smoothly. These will be helpful in facilitating the decision making I talked about in chapter 2, but they can also be useful to your family in their own right.

Think about the example of the summer camp decision. One of the problems many of us grapple with in organizing our summers is remembering to register *right when camp sign-ups open*. This is typically some-time in February, when you are more worried about the chaos of the next snow day than what to do the week of July 4. And yet each year, you must remember the sign-up date.

For many of us, this information resides in a corner of our brain, waiting to wake us up at 2 a.m. on February 17 and cause us to rush out of bed in a wave of panic: *What if I missed it?!*

Even if you didn't miss it, you might be close to doing so. And now you've got to frantically spend the next four days coordinating camp with your partner, maybe the grandparents, two sets of other parents (your kids can't do art camp without their friends!), and on and on. On top of this, maybe this isn't the *best* four days to do this. No one wants to juggle a series of important conference calls with frantically reviewing the weekly offerings at Adventure Fun Ropes Camp.

You'd be much better off if you had remembered to do this in January, when you had more calendar time to make these choices. Calendar time, in this case, buys you peace of mind, but also the ability to fit the planning into your schedule in a way that isn't so frantic.

But why does your brain have to hold this information on its own? It's busy. Your computer, however, is more than happy to remember the date for you. It's not busy. Imagine that instead of your brain waking you up in a panic on February 17, your inbox pops up a camp sign-up reminder on January 15.

Ideally, this reminder comes up in your task management software as a task. Perhaps it's labeled "Book kids' camps" and is already linked to the same task from last year. You click into it to see what you did last year, immediately providing some context. There's also a note in the task description about a school trip planned for your older daughter, and the fact that your younger daughter asked to do a two-week tennis camp with her friend.

The extra calendar time helps, as does the task management software. Rather than sending a series of frantic, uncoordinated emails and texts, you can interact with your partner through the software in a series of quieter moments. By the time the camp sign-up day arrives, you've got a coordinated schedule planned and it's simple to execute. You book the camps, and maybe you assign your partner the task of populating the kids' Google Calendars with their plans. And by early March, you're all set. Never mind that in April, your older daughter informs you that eleven is *much too old* to go to camp and she will be staying home by herself in the summer, thank you very much. You put in your (well-worn) parental earplugs for this discussion.

In some sense, having such an elaborate process might seem like overkill. Seriously, is this really saving time relative to the frantic two-day emergency camp push? And this instinct might be right; you might not save hours doing this. But it does give you the ability to use your time efficiently and to make better decisions. By giving yourself more calendar time, you can do the actual work in a moment that works for you. You probably recognize this logic in tasks at work, but you don't necessarily recognize it at home.

If you're working with a partner, this approach may also mean less conflict between the two of you. Setting up the task like this lets you share the work—at least a bit—and if you don't end up scrambling around to work this out in a really inconvenient moment, it may breed less resentment.

Having these tools in place will also help you manage the Four F process. Business-based toolboxes provide a natural way to track decisions, have discussions, and keep tabs on any family policies you've developed.

What, exactly, are the tools in this toolbox? There are many—but here's a few you might explore.

TASK MANAGEMENT SOFTWARE

Broadly, this refers to a suite of software products (mostly online, and mostly free in at least some version) that allow you to manage tasks with a team. Inside the program, you can create a project, assign tasks within it, and track and comment on them. Tasks can have due dates and sub-tasks, and you can reassign them as needed.

This kind of system combines efficient tracking, reminders, and transparency about what has to be done and who is doing it. For my family, a big plus is that it puts all the relevant comments about the task in one thread. If you try to do the same thing over email, it can be tempting to create a new email each time something happens (I do this a lot and it drives Jesse crazy). But then you're not reminded of what came before, and you end up searching through past emails to see what you previously decided.

Task management software is most useful for managing concrete but slightly lengthy tasks. Camp booking is a good example, or figuring out after-school schedules. We've also used it for regular reminders for things like reviewing the kids' clothes to make sure they are not too small and other household stuff (most notably when we did a house renovation).

A number of task management software platforms are available, and many programs used by businesses may work for your family. We have used Asana at home, and I use Jira at work. Other families swear by Trello. There's also a whole world of family-specific task management apps. Personally, my feeling is you might as well go all in and be a firm, but a family-oriented app could be a place to start.

Shared Calendars

If you look at my Google Calendar display, it appears to be a mess. I'm in blue. Penelope's in red. Finn is purple. Jesse is kind of a dark pink, and our babysitter's schedule is orange. Here and there are a few other work calendars—seminars or lunches—in various other shades. But you quickly learn to read it, and (for me) the value of having all this information in one place is enormous.

Having a shared kid-and-childcare calendar means that all of us (me, Jesse, the babysitter) can quickly see when the kids are in school and when they're not. It means that when our schedule for the babysitter changes (due to the fifteen thousand school holidays), I know she can see it on her calendar. When I'm looking at weekend activities, I don't have to remember when soccer starts up again—it's in there.

Spousal calendar sharing is also worth a lot to us, although the logistics of this may be more complicated for some people, especially if one or the other's work calendar is private. The value here lies in the ability to coordinate without checking in.

An example: The babysitter emails to ask if she can have a day off around her birthday. I look at my calendar for that day and see that I can cover the time, other than an hour near the end of the day when I have a meeting. Because I can also see Jesse's calendar, I can see that he's free for that hour. I tell her yes, and send Jesse a calendar invite for the time he'll be covering. It saves a conversation, or rather, saves time for more interesting topics in later conversations.

Google Docs

It is useful to have the ability to share documents among your family. A family packing list could go here, for example. Or an agenda for a parent-teacher conference, pediatrician visit, or session with a family therapist. When Penelope entered third grade, I used a Google Doc to create her first-ever meeting agenda (to discuss the after-school schedule).

When I was writing this chapter, I reviewed the old contents of our "Oster-Shapiro Household" Google Drive folder and found a document Jesse shared with the grandparents when Penelope was three, outlining some principles for how to best deal with her. I am sure it was much appreciated—everyone knows how much grandparents like to be told how to do stuff!

Google Docs is simple and flexible. It's easy to use and share. It's the obvious choice here.

Other Apps

Calendars, documents, and tasks are likely to come up in many families. But when you review what you need, you may find there are some specific pressure points that are amenable to a more targeted approach. For us, one of these was menu planning. For a bunch of reasons, I have found it's useful for me to spend 20 minutes on Thursdays planning dinners for the week ahead. I tried Google Docs for this, but in the end I found that a menu planner with built-in recipes was more useful (I use one called Paprika).

There are apps for all kinds of stuff like this—planning travel sports or even dealing with custody arrangements. The question is just what you need.

IT'S NOT ALL PARENTING

This book is focused on parenting. And many of the tools here are well suited for this particularly logistics-heavy phase of parenting. But I would be remiss not to mention that many other forms of household operations may be assisted by the same tools.

For example: When Jesse and I bought a house, we used Asana to track the details of our house-buying process and then, later, to track house renovations. We use Google Docs to keep track of movies we want to watch. (It is a list of Marvel superhero movies; I actually do not like these, so the list keeps getting longer and longer and we never watch any of them. Still, it's the thought that counts.) The menu-planning app I use would be helpful even if we did not have kids.

These tools can also be helpful for cross-family coordination. I joked earlier about Jesse's instruction document for the grandparents, and it is true that they ignored it. But we have successfully used shared calendars to coordinate grandparent visits and Google Docs to share information with them. In the broadest sense, these processes share the burden. It can feel to some of us that we are constantly holding all the household and family information in our heads. This is inefficient at best, and can breed anger and resentment at worst. Let the computer do it for you. It does not get tired, it has plenty of memory, and it won't get passive-aggressive if you do forget something.

Part II

Big Data

T he core of the Family Firm approach is an overall household structure and set of decision-making processes. Into any of your important family decisions, there will be many inputs. Your core values. Constraints put on you by financial or other circumstances. What you *like* to do. Your family preferences. All these will matter.

Most of these are likely to be specific to your family. Part of the reason you need a family decision-making process is precisely because all families are different, and you cannot expect someone else's decision to necessarily work for you. *But.* Underlying many of these decisions, there is at least some data.

Understanding the data on these topics is one crucial input to good decision making. When you think about bedtime, you want a familiarity with the data on sleep. As you consider your family eating patterns, you might actually want to know what the evidence says on whether "family meals" are really all that and a bag of chips. The evidence on these topics can provide a common touchpoint when there are disagreements, and they may lead you to prioritize differently. To be clear, the data will not always (indeed, will rarely) *make* decisions for you, but it can make them easier.

For this book, I'm going to separate the data into two groups. First, there is some general data that will help you craft the Big Picture for your family. This includes evidence on sleep, food, parental work, and some (limited) evidence on parenting philosophy. These topics will be covered in this section, and I recommend you read the information before you try to put together your family Big Picture. There is some interesting stuff here! Not all of it will be relevant, but it may help you structure your broadest conversations.

And then there's some more specific data, targeting a particular set of big decisions, which are common to many families. That includes data on (for example) schools and homework, sports and socioemotional development. I'll leave that for the third part of the book.

Sleep

The summer between second and third grade, Penelope expressed some interest in learning more about the brain. In typical academic parent fashion, I decided this meant we should get a high school–level brain book and work through it. Let's just say the experience had some ups and downs, although we did make an awesome pipe-cleaner neuron.

In terms of the book's actual content, by far the most interesting topic for me was sleep. All animals sleep, or have a sleeplike resting state. Some ocean dwellers (dolphins, for example) keep one side of their brain awake while the other sleeps so they can keep swimming, follow the group, and watch for predators while they rest. But as you think about it, this is surprising: sleep seems incredibly maladaptive. In a world where other creatures want to eat you (which, let's face it, is the world that most animals currently live in, and that your ancestors survived if you're here reading this book), it is crazy to spend a good chunk of the time comatose.

The fact that sleep persists in the face of evolutionary pressures not to sleep suggests it must be really, really important. And it is! Rats will die after two to three weeks if kept awake, even if they are otherwise well fed and cared for (thanks, brain textbook).

But the thing is, we don't really know *why* sleep is so important. It seems to matter for memory consolidation, and recent work has specu-lated that the brain needs a resting period to "clear out" some debris (the academic phrasing is more technical). Some theories suggest that while you sleep each night, the information your brain collected during the day is organized so it can be better utilized later, but this is largely an intu-ition, and why we need *sleep* to do this is not completely clear.

What *is* clear is that without sleep, people do not function well, or at all. We know from sleep-lab studies that adults who are sleep deprived do poorly on a variety of mental tasks, including on tests of attention, memory, and cognition.[1] And it is not just the amount of sleep you get but also the *quality* of sleep that matters. Researchers often measure sleep efficiency alongside time in bed, and various sleep disorders (e.g., sleep apnea) or low-quality sleep environments (sleeping on the floor, sleeping with the lights on) can make sleep less effective.

Kids need sleep just like adults, and in general, we tend to think they need more hours.[2] I'll get more into what we know about amounts of sleep in a bit, but the official recommendations are that kids between the ages of four and thirteen need 9 to 11 hours of sleep a night. If your kid has to get up at 6 a.m. for school, this means they should be asleep between 7 and 9 p.m. Frankly, it can be hard to meet that bedtime amid homework, sports practice, dinner, and maybe a little family time.

A decision to prioritize sleep time will dictate—or at least play into—a huge number of decisions about your child, and about your family schedule, so it is worth at least dipping into the science. How important is sleep for kids, really? How much do they need, and what happens if they don't get it? This information alone may not tell you how to orga-nize things, but it's one of the crucial pieces of data for making a lot of schedule choices.

DOES SLEEP MATTER FOR KIDS?

Yes.

As a first piece of evidence for this, we can look at studies that show correlations between the amount of sleep, daytime sleepiness, and various outcome measures for kids. One notable example comes from a survey of about three thousand high school students in four school districts in Rhode Island.[3] The participants were surveyed about their sleep habits—bedtime, waking time, how much they sleep during the week relative to the weekend, and so on.

The authors found that sleep time correlated with academic grades. Kids with worse grades slept less, went to bed later, and had more of what the researchers called "weekend oversleep" (meaning they slept a lot more on the weekend than during the week, a signal of being tired). They also found that kids who sleep less say they are more tired during the day and have a great incidence of depression.

This is just one study (although it's among the larger ones), but the findings are consistent with a lot of other papers. A meta-analysis from 2010 summarized the results of seventeen studies with almost twenty thousand children and found that a lower amount of sleep, worse sleep quality, and "sleepiness" were all associated with poor school performance.[4]

In this meta-analysis, the largest correlation was seen between measures of daytime sleepiness and school outcomes. This relationship is more important than, for example, the actual amount of sleep time. This distinction appears in other papers as well. Data on a sample of Korean teenagers shows that sleep duration per se doesn't predict academic performance, but whether the kids are sleepy does.[5] Another paper—this one about kids in Israel—shows that the quality of sleep kids get matters more than time in bed.[6]

The necessary amount of sleep may vary from kid to kid. What is important may not be the absolute amount of sleep, but whether the amount of sleep your kid gets is sufficient for your kid in particular.

This evidence (laid on top of our general evidence on the importance of sleep) is suggestive. But if you are a savvy consumer of research studies, you may start to wonder if this relationship is really *causal*. Does lack of sleep or sleepiness actually cause worse school performance, or are they just correlated? Maybe there are other factors (poverty, for example) that generate worse sleep quality and also cause worse school performance for other reasons.

To try to get to the bottom of this, we can look for experimental data—evidence where the amount of sleep is manipulated by researchers—or what we call "quasi-experimental" data, where there is some random variation not necessarily generated by a research experiment. In this case, we have both true experimental data, where researchers do the manipulation, and some quasi-experimental data, where the world manipulates for us.

Many studies of adult or college-student sleep rely on extreme manipulations—keeping people up all night to see how they perform on tests (they do worse, but they think they do better).[7] For kids, it wouldn't really be ethical to do this, so experimental manipulations rely on small changes in sleep duration. We can consider one nice example from Canada.

Researchers in this study took thirty-two children ages eight through twelve and followed them over three weeks.[8] In the first week, the children were told to sleep normally. In the second week, they were told to either add an hour of sleep ("long sleep") or subtract one ("short sleep") each for four days. In the third week, they switched: the kids who slept less in week 2 slept more, and vice versa.[9] At the end of each week, the researchers brought the kids and their parents into the lab. They did a bunch of cognitive testing on the kids, and asked their parents all about their behavior, sleepiness, etc.

It is worth saying that this manipulation seems pretty minor—just an hour on either side. I'd wager that for most of our kids, their sleep schedules vary a bit; even the most rigid bedtime-setters may find a little wiggle room. So you might have the instinct that an hour of sleep wouldn't matter. And yet, in the data, it does. The researchers found that during the kids' "short sleep" week, they did worse on tests of working memory and math fluency, and their parents reported lower attention and worse emotional regulation.

An earlier study with the same basic structure—short-lived changes in sleep duration—found similar negative effects for fourth- to sixth-grade students in Israel.[10] A different kind of experiment, using younger children, was oriented around a program designed to improve sleep habits.[11] This study found that sleep education—telling families that sleep is important and giving them some tools to improve their child's sleep—increased sleep duration and improved grades in school.

All this suggests that sleep matters, even within the range of what is typical. These studies tend to be small, though, and they are expensive to run. As a result, researchers looking to analyze this question have tried to be creative about strategies with data. And when they do this, it turns out that there is a very helpful source of variation: school start times.

This approach works because, in practice, when school starts earlier, kids tend to get less sleep. This doesn't have to be true; an earlier start time coupled with an earlier bedtime could preserve sleep amounts. But in practice, it seems like kids and their families do not alter bedtime that much in response to earlier school start times. This means that kids who live in school districts with an early school start time get less sleep. Studies exploit this by using the variation in school start time as a source of sleep amount variation.

Start times, at least historically, have been determined not by students' need for sleep but by other factors (school bus schedules, mostly). Researchers doing these sleep studies about children argue that start time variation is partially random, making them more confident about drawing causal conclusions.

A representative example is a paper from 2017 that studied eighth graders in a large school district.[12] Some kids started school as early as 7:20 a.m., others as late as 8:10. The authors collected data on almost 27,000 children, asking them questions about the amount of sleep they got and their grades. They found that kids in schools with an earlier start time got less sleep and reported worse grades than those in districts with later start times.

This basic pattern—that kids whose school day starts earlier get less sleep and are sleepier in school—is echoed in other studies.[13] One especially good one is from a boarding school (with high school students) that changed its class start time from 8 to 8:30 a.m.[14] The change in start time increased sleep—in fact, it increased it *more* than the start time change, since kids started going to bed earlier (the authors included some quotes from kids saying that when they realized how much sleep mattered, they wanted even more). There were huge reductions in various self-reports of daytime sleepiness, falling asleep in class, and need for naps. The school health services reported a reduction in kids needing to nap there during the day (yes, if you go to boarding school, you can nap at health services), and teachers reported that fewer students were late for class.

This school had intended the change in start time as a short-term experiment, and in fact, teachers were very resistant because it meant some loss in class time (they couldn't extend the day due to sports schedules). In the end, though, it was a huge success, and the school kept the later start. One teacher is quoted in the study as saying it was the best change in his many years at the school.[15]

And it's not just grades and school performance. Studies of school start time differences in Virginia have shown lower car accident rates for districts with later high school start times.[16]

These studies tend to focus on high school students, although there is a bit of work on middle school.[17] In my view, this shouldn't be taken to mean sleep matters less for younger children; indeed, it probably matters more. The difference is that younger kids may have an easier time adjusting to an earlier bedtime when wake-up is earlier, and the impacts on their sleep are less.

This is a lot of evidence to support that sleep matters. If your kid isn't sleeping enough, they will be tired in school, they'll need a nap, they'll be less able to focus. Also, they will be a jerk some of the time. This will be familiar to you from their younger years, especially as they transition out of taking a regular nap. It will probably manifest differently with an older child (less throwing trucks, more telling you they hate you), but it's the same basic principle.

There is an obvious follow-up question: How much sleep is enough?

THE RIGHT AMOUNT OF SLEEP

In 2015, the National Sleep Foundation convened a panel of eighteen experts to review the evidence on sleep, and to address the question "How much sleep do people need, and how much does it vary by age?" Their conclusions about kids suggested that preschoolers need 10 to 13 hours a night, school-age kids 9 to 11 hours, and teenagers 8 to 10 hours.[18]

This is more than most kids get. Although it can be hard to know exactly how many hours children are sleeping, studies that monitor sleep carefully (through a device similar to a Fitbit) suggest that school-age kids sleep about 8 hours a night.[19] And this seems to have declined a bit over time, decreasing an hour or so between 1905 and the present.[20]

But unlike the evidence on the importance of sleep in general—which I find quite compelling—the data on how much sleep is the right amount is less conclusive. For one thing, the range of recommended sleep—9 to 11 hours for a school-age kid, for example—is very wide. And the National Sleep Foundation caveats this average recommendation by saying that as little as 7 or as many as 12 hours may be appropriate. That range is huge!

This seems to reflect that sleep needs vary from person to person. Some people—kids and adults alike—simply need more sleep than others to function. When I was in college, my best friend seemed to have no trouble functioning normally on 5 hours of sleep (this proved helpful later at Goldman Sachs). But another roommate clearly needed at least 10 hours to have any hope of getting out of the room. Left to our own devices, I would sleep much less than my husband. Kids' sleep needs can vary, too, which makes the question of the "right amount" of sleep a tricky one.

Fortunately, you can experiment here. Your goal (presumably) is to figure out the amount of sleep your child needs to function well. And this is a process where there is a lot of immediate feedback. Put differently, you should be able to tell if your child needs more sleep.

How?

There are a few ways. A child who is well rested should not feel sleepy during the day or be falling asleep in class. When they go to bed, they should take a little time to fall asleep—perhaps 15 to 20 minutes—but not hours. Falling asleep as soon as your head hits the pillow may sound good, but it's not a good sign of sleep quality. And if you give your kids a chance to sleep in—say, on the weekend—they shouldn't actually sleep in that much. If your kid is sleeping 2 extra hours when you let them (the dreaded "weekend oversleep"), they need more sleep on a regular basis.

With a younger child, you control bedtime (I mean, hopefully? Okay, maybe it doesn't always seem that way). If you're worried they are not sleeping enough, try moving bedtime an hour or a half hour earlier. On the other side, if they're taking an hour to fall asleep, try moving bedtime a bit later.

You have less control over an older child—the idea of "lights out" may be harder to enforce with a twelve- or thirteen-year-old. On the other hand, a kid this age is old enough to understand the evidence behind sleep and to reflect more on their own experiences. In the boarding school experiment I talked about, the authors argued that the reason sleep increased by even *more* than the start time change is that students realized that more sleep was beneficial, and they changed their bedtimes on their own in order to get even more. This is an age when a family discussion and reflection may work better than rules (which may be true for many things with a preteen).

The (Data) Bottom Line

- Sleep matters!
- Kids need more sleep than you might think, even as they age through middle school, and not getting enough can affect their school performance, among other things.
- Different kids need different amounts of sleep, but if your kid is sleepy during the day or sleeping in a lot on the weekend, this is a clue that they are not getting enough. Try an earlier bedtime!

ADDING TO THE BIG PICTURE

The evidence suggests that kids really need to rest. When you make up the family calendar, it makes sense to protect those hours. Adding extra math classes isn't useful if your child doesn't sleep enough to pay attention in them.

Sleep needs will dictate various aspects of your calendar. The family wake-up time will be determined, probably, by the start times of school and work (or by a child who is always up at 5:30!). But you will choose bedtime, or at least the time scheduled activities end. If you decide your child needs 10 hours of sleep and they need to wake up at 6:30 a.m. for school, then bedtime needs to be 8 or 8:30 p.m. Working backward, this will dictate when you eat and what type of evening activities you can actually do.

It can be easy to undervalue sleep—honestly, most of us adults (especially parents) do not get enough of it and probably do not think of it as something to prioritize. In my case, when I get stressed or anxious about not getting enough done, sleep is the first thing I think to give up. As I frequently tell my kids, I'm old enough to make my own mistakes; I don't want to make the same ones for them, though.

Childcare and Parental Work

Yrou may think, if you are the parent of a school-age kid, *I already decided whether to work or not.* You probably did carefully deliberate this choice when your child was a baby. But just because you have thought about it before doesn't mean you are done thinking about it. When your children are in school, the decision morphs. An infant or toddler is a full-time job for someone—a parent, grandparent, nanny, day care, some combination. For a school-age kid, a huge chunk of their day is taken up by . . . school. This underscores the importance of choosing schools (more on that later in the book), but it also means that your childcare needs will change a lot and, by extension, decisions about parental work may as well.

Around school entry is a key time to think deliberately again about this choice. Even if you have no interest in revisiting the choice about parental work, if all the adults in the household work full time, you'll need to think about logistics.

To give an example, here's our family's basic problem. Both of my kids are in school, which starts at 7:45 a.m. and ends at 3 p.m. If Jesse and I both choose to work in our current jobs, we need to be in the office around 8 or 9 and stay until around 5, or sometimes a bit later. Assuming this basic structure, we face a few key questions.

- Who takes the kids to school? (For us, the early start of school makes it possible for us to both walk them in on the way to work.)
- Who picks them up, and at what time? More specifically, what happens between 3 and 5:30 p.m.? We have a few options. They could stay at school for after-school care. Or we could decide one of us will work a more part-time schedule and be the one to pick them up. Or we could have a nanny or babysitter do it.
- What if they have after-school activities outside of school? Who takes them to those?
- And even more complicated, what happens when they are sick? What about school holidays, winter break, spring break? The dreaded long summer break? Who covers those?

These issues evolve over time. When my son was in pre-K, we picked him up at 12:45, making our childcare needs a bit more complicated. When my daughter hit third grade, suddenly she was spending at least two afternoons at school doing various extracurriculars, meaning even if we had wanted to, we couldn't pick her up before 5:30 p.m.

Of course, our logistics are specific to us. Your school day may be longer or shorter, the after-school options may differ. When I was a kid, my grandmother lived around the corner, substantially simplifying the problem of who would cover holidays and sick days.

All this means the decisions you make about both parental work and childcare may be very different than they were with a younger child. And it's worth saying: this could be in any direction. I certainly know women (mostly women) who stayed home until their children were in school and then returned to work. But I also know people who did it the other way—they worked while their children were little, and then decided that they'd like to be home when the kids got older. Or decided to pull back on work time to be able to do the afternoons, the school holidays.

The data here is not going to make decisions for you. It echoes something I've said in many other places in this book: families are too heterogeneous for a one-size-fits-all solution. The best we can hope for is to use it as *input* in a larger family discussion. And here, I do think there is some good input data. It really comes in two forms: data on whether outcomes for kids differ if their parents work, and data on how work choices affect parents directly.

PARENTAL WORK AND CHILD OUTCOMES

When you come to think about this for your family, there are likely to be a million considerations even when you focus just on your children. What will be best for your relationship with them? Is there a particular out-of-school activity they are really committed to, and does parental work interfere with this? Really, what will make them happy?

I am sorry to say that researchers cannot measure most of these things. Research on this topic is heavily reliant on outcomes we can measure in the data. It's very hard to figure out whether people are happy or to evaluate the quality of their relationships. This issue will come up again and again in the book—most notably in the context of studying schools. What we can measure, both here and in the school context, is academic achievement (as measured by test scores). This will be a lot of the focus. In addition, a number of studies look at links between parental work and child health outcomes, specifically obesity.

Test Scores

It's easy to find data to help you understand the link between parental work and test scores. Much harder to find is data with a compelling causal interpretation. A representative paper looks like the following: Get some data on kids that includes information on whether their mothers worked during their childhood, and also information on test scores or school performance. The data will typically also use information on other characteristics of the family, like race and maternal education. Note that nearly all these papers focus on maternal employment; they assume fathers are employed if they are present in the household.[1]

(Many, many research studies about maternal employment use data from a survey called the National Longitudinal Survey of Youth, which recruited several thousand women in 1979 and has followed them and their children over time.)

With this data in hand, researchers will look at the links between child test scores and whether Mom is employed. They will usually try to hold constant some basic factors about families (income, race). And sometimes they'll divide the kids into groups—for example, they'll look at kids whose families have higher income separately and see if the effect is different for them.

There are challenges with interpreting the results from this kind of analysis. The choice of whether both parents work is not made randomly. Right now, you are reading a whole chapter of a book about how to make this decision in the "best" way. This is only one of many books about this! People really think about this decision, so it's difficult to imagine that there aren't other differences across families who have both parents working and those who do not.

It's actually not even obvious the direction of the bias in these results. Families where both parents work may be better off than others in some ways, perhaps worse off in others.

Basically, it will be hard with data like this to know if the links we see between parental work and child outcomes are causal or just correlational. The ideal, of course, would be a randomized experiment—we randomly force some families to have both parents working and others to have one parent stay home. Ethics prevent this (never mind the difficulty of recruiting subjects!), so we should take the results here with a grain (or a pinch) of salt.

Having said this, I think the volume of evidence points to two conclusions.

First, to the extent that there are either good or bad effects, they are small. To see this, we can turn to meta-analyses. Studies like this are a good way to see many, many results on the same scale and leverage the power of a bigger sample size. (This doesn't magically fix our correlation-versus-causation problem, but it does give us a more comprehensive view of the correlations.)

In the case of maternal work and test scores, in 2008 researchers in California published a meta-analysis combining data from 68 studies that reported a total of 770 different effects.[2] Where they tried to combine as many results as possible, the authors found a very, very slight positive correlation between maternal work and test scores. They reported in terms of a coefficient called "r."[3] This is a general measure of effect size; in research on education, we typically think that a value of $r = 0.1$ is small, $r = 0.3$ is medium, and above $r = 0.5$ is large. This study found values of r in the range of 0.001 to 0.05—so, typically less than half of what we'd consider a "small" effect. And in many of their analyses, the values were extremely close to zero.

The second finding is that there do seem to be some differences in these effects across groups. The effects of maternal work seem to be slightly more negative in studies that include a greater number of wealthier families, and slightly more positive in those that include a greater number of poorer families. Similarly, the effects seem to be more positive in samples that include more families of color and more single-parent families. The effects are also more positive for girls.

If we take this at face value, it could imply some negative effects of parental work for certain groups (say, more educated moms). But even in the extreme, these effects are very small. And when we dig into individual papers—say, a 2008 paper by an economist named Christopher Rhum that tries to isolate different effects by groups—we tend to find that the more we can do to adjust for differences in the home environment, the smaller the effects are.[4] This suggests that even the small effects that we'd be tempted to attribute to maternal work may, in fact, reflect other family differences.

Obesity

In contrast to the effects of maternal employment on test scores, the effects of parental work on obesity are more consistent: when both parents work, children seem to be at a higher risk for obesity.[5]

As in the case of test scores, though, these effects are fairly small. And like test scores, the increase in obesity seems larger among the children of more highly educated moms (although this may be due to their lower starting weights).[6]

When researchers have tried to dig into *why* we might see these obesity effects, they tend to focus on what kids are doing in their out-of-school hours. After all, obesity isn't that much of a mystery: if you eat more and exercise less, that will generally lead to more weight gain. This means that looking for mechanisms here boils down to figuring out whether kids with working moms are eating more calories or burning fewer calories (or both).

This is simple in concept, although in practice it asks a lot of the data. You'd need to see not only information on moms' work and children's weight, but also information on how kids use their time (specifically, do they exercise?) and what they eat. Fortunately, at least some data sources are up for the challenge.

We can consider one example, a 2014 paper published in the journal *Social Science & Medicine*.[7] The authors showed first that children whose moms worked were more likely to be obese. The effects were moderate—going from 0 to 40 hours of work increased the risk of obesity by about 4 percentage points (in this study, on average about 20 percent of children were obese).

The paper then goes on to look at details of behavior. Kids with working mothers ate fewer vegetables and fruits and more fast food, drank more soda, and watched more TV. They actually also seemed to exercise more through organized sports, although the added TV time may have meant an overall more sedentary lifestyle.

These results may be intriguing, but it's important to note that they still don't prove a *causal link* with maternal work. We don't know if those kids would be doing the same things if their moms were home. Papers on this topic often speculate that the links result from moms having less time to drive their children to sports or lovingly prepare home-cooked meals.[8] That could be, but when you actually look at how parents spend their time, it isn't clear that working parents spend less time on these activities than those who don't work.[9] So it still may be the case that it's simply other differences across households that matter, not work per se.

And So This Means . . . What?

Given all the flaws in the data, we should be clear that there isn't any smoking-gun causality in this evidence. We have suggestive correlations and, with only two outcomes, not nearly the full range of things you care about.

We can clearly see from these results that it may matter at least a bit what your child does out of school. One interpretation of the fact that maternal work seems to matter more in higher-income families is that the kids would be more likely to be doing "enriching" activities if they were with their parent. This is different from saying that both parents shouldn't work; it does argue for giving thought to out-of-school hours and to things like food options. Basically, be deliberate. (Good news! This whole book is about that.)

But even if we were willing to assume that all these effects were causal, they are still *really small*. The school performance effects are mostly insignificant, and even when they are statistically precise, they are tiny. The obesity effects are perhaps a bit larger but still swamped by other factors that drive children's weight.

The (Data) Bottom Line

- There are many interesting outcomes for kids that we cannot measure; the two we focus on in parental work are test scores and obesity.
- The impact of working parents (in the data, specifically moms) on kids' test scores does not go in a consistent direction, and in any case, is small.
- There are stronger correlations between having two working parents and childhood obesity, but causal evidence is limited. To the extent that there are links, they probably reflect the activities kids do, not the parental work per se.

BEYOND THE DATA: CONSIDER THE PARENTS!

Let's take a step back from the two-parent, heteronormative, mom-working world that our data seems to reside in, and return to the world in which your family gets to allocate parental work in whatever way works best for you.

There are really two reasons to work. One is to get money. The other is that you like it. Making the right choice is going to require thinking through both of these, ideally with some numbers.

Let's start with the money. How much does it matter to the family budget if all the adults in the household work? Obviously, this depends on what they would be doing (i.e., what job they would have). If you are currently working, you know your income. If one adult has been out of the labor force for some time, it may be harder to know *exactly* what their income might be if they returned. But it's not unknowable! And you can probably make a good rough guess.

As a side note: The idea of reentering the labor force after a break is daunting to a lot of people. And it's right that if you've been out for five years, you're not likely to pick up exactly where you left off. But that is different from saying it should not be something you consider. And employers may be more understanding of this than you expect. Some evidence from résumé audit studies (basically, studies where people send out fake résumés and see who gets a call back) suggests that explained gaps in the résumé are not as damaging to a job search as unexplained ones.[10] Kids are a good explanation!

Any added income from having all adults working is likely to be partially offset by additional childcare costs. What will the kids do after school and how much will that cost? One parent working part-time may be one answer to this problem, but there are many other childcare solutions.

There is a long-term piece to this budgetary discussion as well. In many jobs, your income goes up over time, and childcare costs are likely to go down (at least until your kids hit college). So the financial benefits of working are likely to evolve.

Finally, when you sit down to think about budget numbers, it's worth considering not just the *number* of dollars but the *marginal utility* of those dollars. How much extra happiness will more money buy you? One way to think about this is to ask what else you'd do with the funds. This may help frame how valuable they really are (or, perhaps, aren't).

Money isn't the only thing. The truth is that it probably does come first, since for many families, having all adults working is necessary to have basic necessities. But if you are lucky enough to have a choice, the question of what you want to do should factor in. You might like working. Or you might prefer full-time parenting. Or you might prefer some of both.

I think many of us do not consider this question of what we want out of the combination of our professional and personal lives often enough. Maybe we think carefully about it when our kids are born, but we don't necessarily do it again. And sometimes the answers change in surprising ways.

My desire to spend time with my kids has gone up, not down, as they've gotten older. I did not expect this. Before they arrived, I had an idea that the first couple of years—with all the breastfeeding and so on—would be the really time-intensive period, and once they were in school, I wouldn't feel as much of a pull for extra time with them.

Instead, I enjoy being home more during the after-school hours than I did when they were smaller. I value that time, in part to get to hang out with them and, honestly, in part because I do not think anyone else is tough enough on supervising violin practice.

Look, we all have our things, okay? Don't judge me.

I am very, very lucky to have a job that can accommodate some of this (albeit at the cost of working before they get up and after they are in bed). But my desire to be around more has caused me to rethink some professional choices, to hold back from taking on more responsibilities at work, to put on hold some possible next steps, careerwise.

One of my former colleagues at the University of Chicago, Marianne Bertrand, has done some interesting work on happiness, focused in particular on women.[11] She found that life satisfaction is enhanced by having a career, and it's also enhanced by having a family. But they don't add up together—you don't get both the family and career satisfaction boosts. And among more highly educated women, those who work and have a family are more often unhappy, stressed, and tired than those who stay home.

I would like to think things do not have to be this way, and if we all thought a bit more about what we wanted, we might find better solutions. More institutional flexibility, both from the government and from private enterprise, would also be hugely helpful.

And let's say it again: Those solutions do not have to be all about Mom. As I've said before, in the context of younger children, the question shouldn't be "Stay-at-home mom or stay-at-work mom?" but "What is the optimal configuration of adult work hours?"

Adding to the Big Picture

There is a fairly stark contrast here between your choice set if you choose to have a parent at home and your choice set if you do not. If you decide that one parent is going to stay out of the labor force, there are still likely to be some logistical challenges—e.g., what do you do when one kid needs to be at piano lessons and the other at soccer practice?—but the basic structure of who covers the after-school hours is decided.

If all the adults in the household work outside the home, the logistics are simply more complex, and you want to make sure to think through all the pieces.

What do kids do after school in the business-as-usual scenario? Depending on where you live, your family situation, and their school, there are likely to be a few options. The school may offer after-school care, or there may be another location (a YMCA or JCC, for example) that offers after-school care. You could get a babysitter to pick them up or meet them at home, or maybe a grandparent or family friend can do this.

The after-school routine is slightly complicated if you're trying to fit in "enrichment" activities. This may necessitate a childcare provider who can drive. Or perhaps another parent can fill in. (Oddly enough, some of the most complicated issues with other parents filling in involve car seats, which kids now need until they are really quite old. Once your child is old enough for a booster seat, I highly recommend the Bubble-Bum, which is inflatable. Genius.)

It's also worth thinking through planned and unexpected school absences. How do you deal with school breaks and sick days? Who takes time off, or who do you get to fill in? Unexpected absences—mostly sick days—are probably the most complex. There's no good solution when all the adults need to go to work and one kid has a fever, and you cannot fully plan.

It may help to outline some basic orders of priority for work obligations. In our house, teaching usually takes priority. Meetings get canceled before classes. This occasionally means we are frantically switching off who is home with a sick kid (for example, if my class ends at noon and Jesse's starts at one), but at least we do not argue about it.

Indeed, when Penelope was a baby, one of the best pieces of advice I got (from my friend Nancy) was to decide up front who would be backup if the nanny was sick. The principle applies to the older kids, too. It's stressful enough to figure out logistics without resentment. And it may help to accept that sometimes, despite your best-laid plans, you will find yourself with a marginally ill child sitting in your office/the break room/your classroom watching TV on their iPad while you have meetings. It could be worse; maybe they'll learn something.

Nutrition

Eating, preparing to eat, and planning what to eat is a big part of your day. For many of us, this is probably more true after kids than before. When it's just you, or just you and a partner, food can be much more flexible. For the year that I lived alone between college and graduate school, I literally ate the same salad (mixed greens, goat cheese, walnuts, dried cranberries, balsamic) every day for dinner. Even when Jesse and I lived together before kids, food was more flexible; we went out a lot, got takeout, made decisions at the last minute.

With kids, this type of spontaneity is harder, in part because they *must eat* right when it's their scheduled dinner time. While it is true that Jesse can get cranky when he is hungry, it's nothing compared to the "hangry" state that Finn can get into between 5:30 and 6 p.m. The idea that the timing of dinner could move around flexibly to suit the day is . . . laughable.

On top of that, feeding kids is more complicated than feeding adults. They have more preferences, and you're probably a lot more worried about developing and getting them to eat a healthy diet. You might be concerned that your partner doesn't eat any vegetables, but you might also recognize the futility of trying to change a thirty-seven-year-old.

But your kids! They are still young enough to be malleable. At the same time, they resist such malleability by requesting pasta *every single day*.

It's easy to get overwhelmed by the process of feeding kids, and organizing the feeding of kids, but from the Big Picture standpoint, I'd say there are really two key decisions: What are your general rules going to be about food (if any), and how are you going to structure meals?

Will you allow sugar? How much? Are you going to have rules about snacking? Are you going to do anything to encourage fruit and vegetables?

And then, for meals outside of school hours, will you eat together? In what configuration? Is there a family dinner? A family breakfast? Both? Neither?

Not surprisingly, much of this is going to come down to your family logistics and preferences. But first, the data.

WHAT'S IN A HEALTHY DIET?

Nutrition science is notoriously bad. You can perhaps infer this from the fact that every week there is another news story about what foods to eat, or not. One week, coffee is good for you; the next, it kills you. One week, red meat causes cancer in everyone; the next, it's totally fine. This whiplash has real impacts on what people consume.

I recall that for breakfast most days when I was a small child, my father would make us eggs (actually, cheese omelets, which I have to say I find impressive even now, as I serve my children bagels and mini pizzas). And then one day, in the early 1980s, nutrition science decided that eggs were out—too much cholesterol and fat—and a high-carb, low-fat diet was in. Gone were the eggs, replaced by breakfast cereal.

Of course, fast-forward to my young adulthood, when we learned that, in fact, the low-fat diet wasn't any better for you; we've also seen a backlash against carbs, in favor of foods like eggs. Dad was about twenty-five years ahead of the curve.

There are all kinds of examples of this. Remember margarine? It was the healthy alternative to butter, until it turned out that it contained a lot of trans fats and, right, they kill you. Oops.

Why is it so hard to learn about what is in a healthy diet? There may be many reasons, but I think a central one (indeed, this is the subject of at least some of my academic work)[1] is that choices about diet are intimately related to many other things about you. People who eat "healthy" foods—or whatever is in vogue at the moment—tend to also undertake other healthy behaviors, like exercising and not smoking; they also tend to be better educated and wealthier. It's extremely hard to separate those factors.

As a simple way to show this, I once took a widely used, nationally representative dataset that collected information on food consumption and weight (specifically, body mass index, or BMI, a rough measure of body fat based on a person's weight and height). I compared BMI across people who ate different foods, focusing on cases where it was *very unlikely* that the food itself contributed to differences in weight. In the graph on the following page, you can see the relationship between eating each food and BMI for four kinds of lettuce and two types of sugar substitutes.

What you see is that the "fancier" the food, the more it is associated with a lower weight. Iceberg and romaine lettuce? They appear to be associated with increased weight. Arugula and dandelion greens? Make you skinny. Similarly, chemical-based sugar substitutes are associated with a higher BMI, and plant-based ones are associated with a lower BMI.

But of course, it isn't really that one kind of lettuce is better than

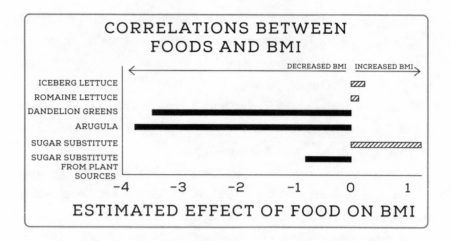

another. No lettuce has a lot of calories! It's just that other features of people who eat these kinds of lettuce differ. (A broader issue is that, of course, measures like BMI are very poor proxies for actual health. Even if you were confident of the relationship between some food and weight, it wouldn't be the same as linking that to the elements of health we care about.)

This type of analysis makes clear that it is simply very hard to learn about what makes a "good" diet by comparing people, and nearly all the evidence we have is of this type. We do not have a lot of large, randomized-trial evidence that we can really trust. One big randomized trial showed health benefits from the Mediterranean diet (fish, vegetables, olive oil, red wine), but among older and mostly unhealthy adults. How applicable is this to healthier, younger adults and, especially, their kids? It's hard to know.

At best we know it's probably a good idea to eat at least some fruits and vegetables. And that foods like soda and candy deliver a lot of calories without making you feel very full, which is not good if weight is a concern. This doesn't mean there isn't some secret magical diet (although given that humans have evolved eating a wide range of foods, I doubt there is), but at this point the data we have doesn't especially suggest one.

This may relax you a bit, but before you relax too much, there is good evidence that tastes are stable and are formed in childhood. This means what your kid eats now may impact what they like for the rest of their lives. No pressure!

How do we know this? You might think that it would be simple: look at diet in children, and then look at their diet as adults and see if they are related. And we do have studies like this—for example, a 2015 study that surveyed college students about the foods they liked currently and what they ate as a child.[2] The authors found that students seemed to like the foods they ate as a child, and their current diet and (recollected) childhood diet overlapped a lot. This result is echoed in data on younger children where you see (for example) that children who eat more vegetables at the age of one also eat more at the age of six,[3] or children with a poor diet in sixth grade are much more likely to retain this poor diet as they age.[4]

Among my favorite of the studies in this range is one that tracked girls' taste for snack foods from age five to eleven.[5] The researchers found moderate stability even across snack foods—girls who ranked Skittles highly at age five were likely to rank them highly at age eleven, although they did find that some snacks (pretzels, ice cream) became more liked over time. Notable research-based fact: Fig Newtons are widely disliked.

These results are suggestive, but we worry that they may be driven by something other than tastes. Observing that college students who ate more vegetables as a child eat more vegetables now could be due to their having developed a taste for vegetables, or could reflect that their circumstances (i.e., access to vegetables) have been consistent over time. This is even more true for results with younger kids: the fact that vegetable consumption is related at ages one and six probably largely reflects consistency in what parents cook and offer over time.

On the flip side, though, there *is* evidence suggesting that early exposure to flavors can affect how much people like them. One piece of this is about very early life exposure—during infancy or in utero. In *Cribsheet*, I talked about a study in which pregnant and breastfeeding moms were exposed to either a lot of carrots or none. Those who ate a lot of carrots had children who enjoyed carrots more later in life.[6] In fact, we have a lot of other evidence like this, showing that flavor exposures in utero and during infancy do seem to affect how much infants and children like different tastes.[7]

And even more relevant for long-term outcomes, we have evidence that flavor exposures in childhood impact consumption in adulthood, even if the available flavors change. A lot of this evidence actually comes from economists! A body of literature in economics studies people who moved to a new area of the country or the world between childhood and adulthood. They asked whether people continued to favor the foods of the area where they grew up, even if the foods most available to them as adults are different.

One important paper on this topic studied people in India and looked at those who moved from a region where the main carbohydrate is rice to one where the main carbohydrate is wheat, or vice versa.[8] The results showed that people are very loyal to their childhood carbohydrate. If you live as an adult in a mostly wheat region, rice is expensive. The people in this study were poor; in many cases, they were getting fewer calories than recommended per day. Nevertheless, those who grew up with rice were willing to pay a premium for it.

We see a similar—although perhaps, for long-term health, less important—phenomenon with coffee and mayonnaise, both of which have historically differed across regions in the US.[9] If you grew up with Maxwell House, you're loath to switch to Folgers, even if you live in a region that is Folgers heavy. A similar thing happens with Miracle Whip versus Hellmann's.

In a sense, none of this should be surprising. Many of us remain partial to our childhood snacks, our parents' cooking, the flavors of home. I cannot be the only one who was told repeatedly by a partner about a particular amazing dish their parents cooked, only to find it lacking in the realization.

So it does seem that, somehow, what you feed your children is going to matter at least for what they *eat* later, even if the links with health are less obvious. Which leads us to the next question: Practically, how should you go about creating the diet you want for your child?

CREATING THE DIET

The premise here is that you have a diet you are aiming for.

The truth is that some diets are easier to achieve than others. Most kids enjoy traditional "kid" foods—pasta, mac and cheese, nuggets, hot dogs (not all kids—my brother Stephen, for example, refused foods like ice cream for his whole childhood—but a lot of kids favor these foods). If your goal is something other than this—to get your kids to eat very complicated or spicy foods, for example—you are in for more of a challenge. And it's going to be easier with some kids than others.

One piece of good news, if you are reading this as a parent of an elementary schooler, is that relative to toddlers, your older children are likely to have less "food neophobia" (fear of new foods). This behavior peaks around age four and declines from there, so you may find that your eight-year-old is more open to new things now than she was at three. Less good news is that as children age through the early school years, evidence suggests their diet worsens—in one study, fruit consumption fell by 40 percent between third and eighth grades, and vegetable consumption by 25 percent. This probably reflects less parental diet control.

When you do have control, how can you affect your children's diet? This, fortunately, is a space where research does provide some guidance. We have a variety of evidence on how to push children toward particular foods. I will note that most—not all, but most—of this literature focuses on getting children to eat more fruits and vegetables. This is probably both because of the general perception that vegetables and fruits are healthier than other foods and because, for vegetables in particular, many kids seem to be resistant to eating them.

So how *do* you research your way into a more veggie-heavy diet (or, by extension, into whatever particular diet you want)?

A first principle: Exposure matters. Repeatedly offering a vegetable to your child and having the child taste it seems to improve their liking of it. We can see this with younger children, as in a study run in a preschool center in which forty-one children were repeatedly offered tastes of a vegetable (red peppers or "squash coins") that most of them didn't like at the start.[10] At the first vegetable exposure, the average rating was somewhere between "yucky" and "just okay." But after six exposures, the average was somewhere north of "just okay"—moving toward "yummy." More striking, at the end of the experiment, kids were eating *way* more vegetables; the average intake went up from 7 to 30 grams. The authors argued that it was not necessarily enough to have a kid try something *once*; they need to try it a few times.

This literature on vegetable exposure is large, and has some nuance. For example, for younger children, exposure seems to be sufficient even for getting them to eat bitter vegetables (example: Brussels sprouts). For older kids, though, exposure helps with non-bitter vegetables, but for bitter vegetables, researchers show better effects with what they call "associative conditioning," or what I call "dip."[11]

One example of a study like this comes from a middle school in

Houston where a group of seventy-eight children was divided roughly in half and studied over the course of a semester-long nutrition class.[12] All the kids were repeatedly exposed to vegetables during the class, but forty of them were exposed to vegetables along with peanut butter and thirty-eight were given only the vegetables. At the end of the semester, the kids who got the peanut butter with their veggies increased their liking of vegetables more and consumed more of them.

Other studies use other dips. One example that I have to say I find nauseating is a case where researchers paired Brussels sprouts with sweetened flavored cream cheese. Not for me, I'd say, but it did increase vegetable consumption among three- to five-year-olds.[13]

The thing about these studies is that they do emphasize repeated exposure—either with or without dips—and occasionally resort to rewards to encourage kids to try foods. The key seems to be the *repeated trying*; it just takes time for kids to develop a taste for new flavors. If they don't like daikon radish the first time you offer it, don't give up forever (I mean, if it's important to you that they eat daikon radish). Try it again, maybe with some peanut butter, some ranch dressing, or—dare I say it—flavored cream cheese.

This literature emphasizes that the *way* food is presented—the order, for example, or the relative amounts—and the way parents react to food rejections can matter a lot.

Much of this evidence comes from institutional contexts, where it is possible to control portions. For example, experiments in school lunches have shown that if you give children a smaller entrée portion, they eat more vegetables.[14] Maybe kids eat their little bit of mac and cheese first, but if they are still hungry, they'll consume some veggies.

In thinking about your home food service, this school-level experiment might lead you toward a more authoritarian version of dinner—as in "You can't have seconds on pasta/have dessert/watch TV until you finish your vegetables." But the broader view of the data suggests otherwise. Prompts like this may increase the consumption of foods in the short run, but also seem to decrease long-run liking of a particular food.[15] Basically, telling a kid "If you eat your carrots, you can have ice cream" seems to prompt them to think carrots are not appealing.

You want to privilege vegetables without forcing them. A simple way to see this insight is to say that if you are hungry, and there are vegetables, you'll eat them; if there is also pasta, you'll eat that first. One way to accomplish this *is* probably a smaller entrée portion. Another way—and, honestly, this is what we tend to favor in my home—is to do vegetables first. If dinner is at six, we'll sometimes do raw vegetables at five or five thirty. Or the vegetable will go onto the table first, and then the entrée a few minutes later.

Do I sometimes lie and say the entrée isn't ready yet? I'll never tell.

The second piece of this presentation is the reaction to food rejections. What do you do if your child refuses to eat the dinner you cooked? When thinking about this, it is worth remembering that kids are wily, and they really, really respond to incentives. Maybe one day they say they do not like the dinner you've prepared, so you make them nuggets instead. They learn that this is a way to get nuggets. Pretty soon, you are making two dinners every night.

What to do about this? One option would be to simply refuse to provide anything beyond the family dinner. For most healthy children, occasionally skipping dinner is not a big problem, so there isn't anything terrible about this policy. However, some parents (read: me) find this a bit difficult to follow through on. At some point we cribbed a family policy from something cookbook author Mark Bittman wrote about his children, and introduced a standard backup meal. Ours is hummus and raw vegetables. This is something the kids are willing to eat, but do not like so much that they always want it. It's also something we'd be fine with them eating frequently. So in my house, you can always eat hummus and raw vegetables for dinner if you choose to. In the end, I'd say it comes out about once every three weeks, typically when I make an effort to serve fish.

A final, evidence-based note relates to forbidden foods. This is the flip side of the encouraged-food coin. As we are encouraging our children to eat vegetables, we are often also attempting to *discourage* other foods—most notably things like soda, candy, sugary foods, etc. The simplest way to discourage foods is to forbid them. Indeed, I know a number of people who pride themselves on having children of four or five who have *never had cake*. In a brief period in which our family lived in California, so many families had these rules that my son's preschool had a strict no-cookies-in-lunches policy, which the parent association attempted to religiously enforce. (Pro tip: Graham crackers are the most cookielike crackers.)

These restrictions can be a little complicated, though. Experiments have shown that children will gravitate toward restricted foods when allowed to have them, even if they didn't initially prefer them. In other words, the restriction itself seems to make a food more enticing.[16] There may be a happy medium between a diet consisting exclusively of candy and one in which your kid has never eaten cake.

This evidence provides a lot to think about. It won't all be relevant for your family, but I bet at least some of it is. In the last part of this chapter, I'll talk about how you might pull this together into a more structured "family food policy." But first, let's talk schedule.

NOT *WHAT* TO EAT, BUT *HOW* TO EAT

The whole discussion above focuses on what your children will eat. But that's not the only meal decision. Yes, what they eat is important—but what about *when* they eat, and with whom? Specifically, what about *ominous music and drum roll** THE FAMILY MEAL?

For proponents, the family meal takes on enormous significance.

If you do not come from a family who ate a family meal like this, the devotion can seem extreme. I was discussing this with a colleague at some point, and she explained how challenging it has been to get used to her husband's family's devotion to eating together. "You HAVE to be at the table at seven! They get very upset. It's kind of weird."

Family dinner is a significant undertaking. If you want to eat together every night at, say, 6 p.m., you need to be home long enough before that to produce the food to eat. Every day. If you choose to do this, it will be a huge part of how you and your kids experience the day. In a way, it's not surprising that people are either devoted or skeptical; from the standpoint of one experience, the other may seem bizarre.

All this means that a large part of this decision for you may come from what you are used to, or what your parents did. However, it *is* a big decision for your family, so it's worth visiting the evidence. A survey of almost 100,000 kids in grades six through twelve looked at the correlation between family dinner frequency and all kinds of outcomes.[17] Relative to those kids who had family dinner 0 to 1 times a week, those who had family dinner 5 to 7 times a week were much less likely to use alcohol or tobacco. They were half as likely to be depressed, less likely to have eating disorders, and had more school engagement. On virtually every metric the researchers could measure, these kids were doing way better.

These results are echoed in other individual studies and in review articles.[18] For adolescents in particular, family meals are associated with much better academic and socioemotional outcomes.

The key thing, though, is the phrase *are associated with*. These studies can show a correlation between family meals and good outcomes, but they struggle to show that those relationships are causal. And it's clear that other aspects of the family drive at least some of this relationship. We can see that by asking what happens when we adjust for other variables.

For example: In that survey of 100,000 children, researchers studied both academic motivation and antisocial behavior. The data says that if we just compare levels for kids who have family meals to those who do not, those with family meals are about twice as likely to have high academic motivation and to avoid antisocial behavior. But once the researchers adjust for other differences across families, like measures of communication and support, these differences are smaller.

And even that may not be enough. The researchers do not see everything about the families, and there is a concern that if they could see even more details about family dynamics, they'd see that family meals have even less of an effect.

That it's such a big deal schedule-wise to have family meals is precisely part of the problem—in an ideal world, we'd have some *random* variation in whether families have dinner together, but given the complicated logistics, it's hard to imagine that it's random for anyone.

Of course, you may be asking, "Can't we run a randomized trial of this, where we randomize families into family meals or not?" The answer is yes, and a couple of small randomized trials have been done. One recent one was called the HOME Plus study (where HOME stands for "Healthy Home Offerings via the Mealtime Environment"), which recruited about 150 mostly low-income families in Minnesota and developed an intervention that encouraged the treatment group to eat healthier foods and have more family meals.[19]

This intervention showed some small impacts—a reduction in sugar-sweetened beverage consumption and a tendency toward less weight gain in the treatment group—but it notably *did not* impact the frequency of family meals.[20] It is simply difficult to change behavior around family meals precisely because adding family meals requires a significant time investment that many families do not have. A friend of mine explained to me recently that her family therapist told her it was important to introduce a weekly family meal with her two children. She diligently followed the advice. Once. The meal was a mess—the kids didn't understand why they needed to be there and eat the food that she offered, and her husband thought the idea was ridiculous. It was a lot of work for her to coordinate, and in the end, no one liked it. It might have been possible to set up the idea of a family meal earlier in their parenting journey, but introducing a family meal into a setting where it wasn't the norm was unsuccessful.

So where does the evidence leave us? The correlation between family meals and positive outcomes for kids is so strong and so clear across the board that it is difficult to completely dismiss them as due entirely to other factors. (Although I think it is fair to say that my friend Ben's claim that your child will be a serial killer if you do not have dinner together is . . . overstated.)

It is worth considering that to the extent that there are benefits from family meals, these benefits may accrue in part because this is forced time together. But it isn't clear that this time has to be spent eating dinner for your family to experience the positive effects. It could be breakfast. Or an hour after school. Or at bedtime. What works for your family?

Family meals and food are a long game. It's helpful to outline your policies and think carefully about what you want your diet (and your kids' diet) and mealtimes to look like, but getting there is never going to be instantaneous. I'd like my kids to sit and eat dinner with us every night, but my five-year-old gets up from the table *all the time*. It's an accomplishment if he gets up a little bit less this week than last week. Similarly, you'll have weeks or months when your kids really only eat pasta and it's just too much effort to fight them on it. As with many things, keep your eye on where you want to go and acknowledge that it will be a journey to get there.[21]

The (Data) Bottom Line

- Our data on what "healthy eating" entails is very bad. Don't force chia seeds on your kids just because of some study!
- There *is* evidence that tastes are formed when kids are young, so if you do want them to eat something, exposing them to that food at an early age is a good idea.
- Repeated exposure to foods can increase kids' taste for them, especially if you combine disliked foods (e.g., veggies) with liked foods (e.g., dip).
- There are strong correlations between family meals and good outcomes for kids. But it is very hard to make causal statements, given other differences between families.

ADDING TO THE BIG PICTURE

Stepping back, there are two big decisions here. First, what (if any) rules will your family have about diet, and second, what will the structure of your meals be? In a sense, these are related. Planning to eat regular family dinners may influence your choice of foods, and vice versa. But I think it makes sense to think about them separately, at least at first.

On the first question, you want to think about the diet you would like your children to eat and what kind of structures you want to put in place to make that happen. How are you going to approach vegetables:

Required consumption? Encouraged consumption? If so, how? What about sugar/dessert: Never? Sometimes? Only in particular circumstances?

In my view, a Google Doc is a perfect place to keep this list. It's easy to change over time and easy to share with others.

The decision about family meals and general meal structure is even more complicated. As with sleep, this introduces real constraints. If you decide that, say, the kids will eat dinner at home at six every day with at least one parent or grown-up, this is going to constrain after-school activities and other adult activities. Not to mention the fact that food needs to be produced for these meals.

But there are a variety of solutions. One parent I talked to explained that what was important to her was her kids having a sit-down meal with an adult every night. It wasn't possible for that adult to always be her and, indeed, rarely did two adults manage to make it to the same meal. But they worked it out so one adult (sometimes the long-term nanny, sometimes a parent) was there at every dinner.

Maybe you want to do two family dinners a week, or just one. Maybe family dinner is impossible, but family breakfast is something you can do.

The key things are to figure out what is important to you and how you want your meals to look and, if you have a partner, to get on the same page about these considerations. And think carefully, also, about splitting the work. If you both agree family dinner is a priority, you should probably both contribute to it (or you should at least consider that possibility).

As you think through this planning, let's acknowledge that family dinner can be a challenge. Meal planning for the entire family, possibly with many picky eaters to work around, is annoying. Resources like meal-planning apps, meal kits, and even meal delivery services can help with this. But there may also be value in giving yourself a break. Not all family meals need to be Instagram-ready. It is okay to eat pasta a lot, or bagel sandwiches. My kids eat pancakes for dinner at least every other week.

This is part of setting the priority. Deciding that family dinner is important to you may actually mean giving a little on food creativity. And that is just fine.

Helicopter, Chicken, Tiger, Ostrich

Which school of parenting do you adhere to? Are you a tiger mom, pushing your kids harder and harder at violin/piano/volleyball/math/coding? Are you a helicopter dad, constantly checking that your children have their homework done and remember their gym shoes and and and and . . . ? Are you a free-range-chicken parent, letting your children roam around the neighborhood on their own? Are you an ostrich parent, sticking your head in the mud and pretending everything is fine?

Okay, I made that last one up. But if this were a different kind of book, I'm sure I could pitch us on it.

Most of these parenting labels are used somewhat pejoratively. Few of us would self-identify as helicopter parents (or the latest incarnation, the "snowplow" parent), and outside of Amy Chua, most are probably not advertising their tiger-mom status. But they are widely used parenting labels, and as with any identity creation, one may feel the pressure to conform to one or the other.

Much of this book is about making your own parenting decisions. So it will perhaps come as no surprise that, in my view, you should fight the idea of labels here. Parenting is, in the end, about what you *do*, not what you call it. You can pick elements from various parenting philosophies and mash them together. This is true in your child's early life, as well—you can be a parent who breastfeeds until your child is two (drawing on attachment parenting) and still sleep train (firmly outside the attachment parenting space)—and it's perhaps even more true as your kids age.

But you do have to make choices, and inside this discussion is a very important set of Big Picture questions:

- How much scaffolding are you going to provide for your child?
- How much involvement will you have in their day-to-day?
- How much physical freedom will they have to come and go from your home, and at what age?
- What expectations do you have in terms of independent life skills, and when?

You'll notice these questions say nothing about extra math homework or competitive violin or any of the other traditionally "tiger parent" decisions. The media has a tendency to lump these together. Either you're a tiger parent who stands over your child at every moment *and* pushes them through worksheet after worksheet, or you allow them out on their own and look over their homework on occasion. The idea that you could prioritize independence but also engage after-school tutoring is inconsistent with these molds.

But the goal of the "economist-style" approach here is to focus on *individual decisions*. In doing this, we can separate decisions that are presented as a simple binary. You can give your kid physical freedom and still require them to practice the piano every day. The poster mom for "free-range parenting," Lenore Skenazy, helpfully points out in her book that despite her free-range instinct, she still once spent a summer making her elementary schoolers do piles of worksheets every day.[1]

Having acknowledged that these labels are separable, I want to preserve this chapter for these questions about independence. (There is much more to come about homework, extra school, and extracurricular activities in the last part of the book.)

When we focus on independence, we are really talking about two main approaches, which I will call helicopter versus chicken. To be concrete, think about the morning routine with a ten-year-old.

Here's option 1:

Daron wakes up when his alarm goes off at 6:50, and gets himself up and dressed. He comes down to breakfast and makes himself a scrambled egg and toast. He eats breakfast until 7:20 and then brushes his teeth. He checks that he has his homework and whatever he needs for soccer after school and then walks the three blocks to school.

And here's option 2:

Daron wakes up when you shake him awake at 7:00 (sleep is good, kids need it); you grab his clothes for him and put them on his bed so he knows to get dressed. He comes down and you've set up breakfast for him. He eats, then you remind him at 7:20 that he needs to brush his teeth. He does. Meanwhile, you check that his homework is in his backpack and that he has his soccer shoes. You get his jacket set out and ready to go. At 7:30 you go up and get him and let him know it's time for school, and the two of you walk there together.

In some ways, looking at these, you might think that option 1 (which I'd say is closer to the free-range setup) seems "better." But if you go with option 1, unless your kid is some kind of wizard, he will forget his soccer shoes or homework about 25 percent of the time. Sometimes he might forget to set his alarm and oversleep. Then what do you do? Do you run the shoes to school for him? Do you bring in his homework? Do you wake him when the alarm doesn't go off?

And reflecting on option 1, are you really comfortable with your ten-year-old child walking to school alone? What about using the stove to make eggs? Obviously, your skillet will be a mess.

There is a wide range between these two extremes—from complete independence to effectively total dependence. And honestly, good (successful, happy) parenting can appear anywhere along these axes. You may end up taking the view that your child's job is to do well in school and focus on their extracurriculars, and that your job is to help that happen. And if that means making their breakfast for them so they can get a few extra minutes of sleep, that's a reasonable trade. This is a version of helicopter parenting, yes. It may also be the parenting style you are happy with.

My point is not that one of these is better, but that you want to choose where you are on this continuum deliberately and with a sense of the evidence (more on the data to come). In practice it can be easy to fall into providing even more scaffolding than you really intend to.

Let's say that nominally you intend for your seven-year-old to dress himself for school: shirt, pants, socks, shoes. And let's say that every day when he's doing that you say a few times, "Hey, do you have your socks?" It's a throwaway. It's not an intentional support. You're busy with his three-year-old sister. You just happen to mention socks—in passing!—since often he doesn't seem to have them. You are confident he is getting dressed independently.

And then one day you're out of town. The family is late for school. Your wife calls—she's kind of mad. "He is supposed to dress himself! We were late because he forgot his socks—twice!" And you realize those throwaway comments—those are scaffolding. Actually, he's not fully getting dressed by himself. Yes, he's putting on his pants and shirt and he's even putting on his socks. But he isn't *really* taking responsibility.

Encouraging independence requires leaning into it, and especially with younger kids, it can be really, really hard. At some point both my kids decided they wanted to cook for themselves. Great, right? They were four and eight. It is not an exaggeration to say I thought I would lose my mind. They were so, so slow. *Agonizing.* I could have done it a million times faster. And so messy. Finn would crack eggs and then wipe his hands on the counter (dried egg white basically needs to be chiseled off, in case you were wondering). In some ways it was worth it, and I knew—I KNEW—that learning to cook pasta would be great for them. But the patience required was almost beyond me (I mean, it *was* beyond me, but I took some breaks).

As hard as it is to encourage, the value of independence is not hard to see. In our current environment, the need for more of it has started to take on a slightly hysterical tone. Many authors have argued the point that (relative to, say, my generation) more recent generations are less independent and capable.[2] They argue, among other things, that if we scaffold our kids too much, they will not be able to fend for themselves. In our attempts to help them succeed, we are setting them up to be failures.

These less capable kids are less able to deal with themselves when, the argument goes, they go to college. It could be a short step from shaking your ten-year-old awake to shaking your eighteen-year-old awake. But when they leave home, you won't be there to do that. When they get their first apartment, they'll have to eat Subway for every meal because you never taught them to fry an egg.

When I went to college, one of my first emails home to my mom asked her to ship me batteries *because I could not figure out how to purchase them.* At this time in my life I was a person who had achieved the goal of getting into Harvard and, perhaps more to the point, could literally see CVS from my dorm room window. I did figure out independence in the end, but not before my mother shipped the batteries (thank you, Mom).

What does the data say? Is there really anything wrong with helicopter parenting? And on the other side, is there any value to it?

PARENTAL INVOLVEMENT: THE GOOD

In the global scheme of things, parental involvement is associated with better child outcomes, in school performance and elsewhere. We can see this, for example, in one very old study of British children, published in 1980.[3] This study reported on data from about 250 seven- and eight-year-olds, and studied the relationship between maternal "coaching" (in this case, listening to the child read aloud) and reading ability in children. They found that kids whose mothers coached them were better readers, even controlling for a separate IQ measure.

We worry, of course, that parents who coach their kids in reading are different in other ways, but we see evidence supportive of this finding from randomized trials as well.[4] The evidence seems to point to the conclusion that it *is* possible to teach your child to read better in the elementary school years.

The possible value of more highly involved parenting goes beyond this specific skill. Focusing on high school students, a recent study has shown that parental involvement is associated with better grades and school performance.[5] This effect seems to go beyond what you'd predict based on mediators like TV viewing and homework time, so it seems that parental involvement is valuable somehow.

This effect is confirmed in meta-analyses in which more involved parents are shown to have children who do better in school.[6] At least some of these studies focus on younger children—those in elementary or middle school, the focus of this book.

In these meta-analyses, the authors try to separate out what type of parental involvement is most important. This is difficult to do, especially since these are largely not randomized studies and parental behaviors tend to cluster together. But to the extent that they draw conclusions, these studies point to the value of parental attitudes and encouragement, *not* specific homework help. That is, it's good to make clear what is important and be involved in supporting it, but not to make your kid's Greek myth diorama for them after they are in bed. Not that any of us would do that, right? RIGHT?

Most of these papers focus on academic achievement—in no small part because it's easy to measure—but there is also some evidence on interventions designed to increase parental involvement in other areas. One example focused on young teens in a housing project, and was designed to increase parental knowledge of sexual activity and other risky behaviors.[7] The authors found that more shared knowledge between parents and children decreased these risk behaviors, and most notably increased condom use. This is obviously less specifically relevant for elementary school–age children, but we can imagine parallel types of shared knowledge being relevant.

Bottom line: The data confirms what you'd probably expect—being involved with your child's life is, overall, a positive.

PARENTAL INVOLVEMENT: THE BAD

Okay, so more involved parenting is good. You want to be supportive of your child's academic and other goals, to monitor them, to have shared knowledge about what they do, and so on. It's an easy hop from here to even more involvement, because children will not do things as you would. They are, after all, children. You can support your kids by telling them academics are important; maybe you can support them even better by checking to make sure their homework is in their backpack. And what about interfacing with their teachers? If they are struggling to study, or there's an overwhelming amount of homework, perhaps it's your job to reach out to their teachers to figure out how you can help.

This is starting to veer into true "helicopter" parenting behavior, and in this area the research does raise some concerns. These concerns seem, primarily, to arise when we look at college students. Studies have argued that kids whose parents are very heavily involved (especially when the kids are actually *in* college) have less autonomy and are less engaged with their peers.[8] This work suggests that kids who are parented in this way are more likely to experience anxiety and even abuse pain medication.[9] One study of three hundred college students showed that students who perceived their parents to be overly involved helicopter types were more likely to be depressed.[10]

These results are worrisome, but it is hard to know what to take from these studies, since in most cases the parenting styles are reported by the children. In that last study of three hundred college students, the key thing was that the students *perceived* their parents to be overly involved. This suggests the problem may be a mismatch between how much involvement young adults want and how much they are getting. A telling counterpoint comes from a study that shows that helicopter-style parenting is associated with negative outcomes for college students only if they also perceived their parents not to be "warm."[11] One way to read this is that if you like your parents, having them involved is good; if you don't like them, not so much.

Beyond this type of evidence, the other information we have on this comes, largely anecdotally, from college administrators. Undergraduate deans report classes full of students who haven't ever woken themselves up with an alarm or interfaced with a teacher about a late assignment.[12] They cannot navigate the world of college on their own, and their parents remain constantly in touch—by phone, text, email—to monitor them.

Is this a problem?

In my view, this depends on what you are trying to achieve. Which is perhaps a useful overall frame. If your plan is to remain heavily involved with your children forever—helping them navigate college, graduate school, their first job, their second job, their marriage, etc.—that's a coherent plan. But if at some point you hope to have them fly on their own—and, I will confess, I do hope this for my own kids—you will need to let go at some point.

College could be a natural time to do this, but it's also fairly late. And it is, frankly, a lot to expect kids who have never managed anything on their own to all of a sudden do everything. And when you're there, on the other end of the phone or computer, available at a minute's notice, it's easy to fail to follow through on the letting-go plan.

High school is another natural time, but it's hard then, too, when kids get busier and when achievement matters more for their future. If you wait until junior year to try to enforce your child waking themself up on their own, you risk them missing a math test that really matters for them in the long term (or feels like it does). This, too, may be hard to follow through on.

I see the challenge of newly creating this behavior with older children as the strongest argument to encourage autonomy in the early years. If your third grader takes responsibility for their homework, and learns the consequences of forgetting it, that may be a hard lesson for them, but it's not junior year of high school. They will still do fine in the third grade. If your fourth grader is supposed to wake themself up and they oversleep and are late for school, that may mean they miss something they care about doing—quiet reading time, or some morning activity—but it's not a key educational goal.

In my travels, I have talked to many a parent of a high school senior who confesses—sometimes sheepishly—to still making breakfast for their child. "He works so hard," they say. "I just want him to get those few more minutes of sleep." I get that! And perhaps we may agree that all of a sudden springing the challenge of breakfast-making onto a seventeen-year-old in the fall of their senior year seems somehow mean. And yet that is what is going to happen if and when they leave your house!

They will have to navigate getting up early enough to find breakfast, or stocking granola bars so they can eat on the way to class, or whatever it is. You are not putting off the fact that they'll have to do this, just *when* they have to start doing it. All I'm saying is that if you do put them in charge of breakfast at the age of eight, this may not come up. By seventeen, they'll have it under control.

The (Data) Bottom Line

- More involved parenting seems to have some benefits in terms of children's achievement . . .
- . . . but on the flip side, survey data seems to suggest that over-involvement may lead to anxiety later.
- There's probably a happy medium, but it's going to depend a lot on your personal preferences.

ADDING TO THE BIG PICTURE

My own thinking about independence in kids has been heavily influenced by Thomas Phelan, so I'll nod here to his book *The Manager Mom Epidemic*, which I found hugely useful in considering how to implement more personal responsibility for my kids. I recommend you read the whole book, but I will highlight one key idea here: total responsibility transfer.

When someone in the family (a kid or an adult) is responsible for some task, they are *fully responsible* for it. This means they are responsible for planning to do it, doing it, and experiencing the consequences if they do not do it. If your kid is given the job of remembering their soccer shoes, they are responsible for thinking about how they'll make sure they remember, remembering, and, if they forget, deciding how to address the problem. If it is their job to make breakfast, they do everything (within the bounds of physical safety).

A similar logic extends to physical freedoms. If your child is allowed to play in the backyard, then they are allowed to do it. They are allowed to decide whether to do it and when, and if you think it's too cold or too hot or too rainy or too buggy, that's just too bad. In the end, it's their choice.

When you add this to your family Big Picture, it may help to think about categories.

First, there's physical freedom: How much physical autonomy do kids have, especially outside the house? Can they be outside in the neighborhood alone? How far from the house? Can they walk home from school alone? What about street crossings? Can they bike to the park with their friends? Do you need to know where they are at all times?

Second, there is the category of personal responsibility for their physical well-being: What parts of their life are they in charge of? Waking themselves up? Getting dressed? Cooking some subset of meals? Do they set up their own lunch (if they bring lunch to school)? Do they do their own laundry? Do they decide when it's time for a shower?

Finally, there's the academic responsibility piece: To what extent are they responsible for navigating homework and other school-related issues? Are they in charge of deciding a time to do their homework and doing it? Or maybe you work together on when to do the homework, but they are in charge of remembering to bring it back. I'd put extracurricular responsibilities in this category, too. If your kid plays an instrument, who decides their practice schedule? Do you stand over them while they practice?

Underlying all these decisions is your child's age. The answers to all the previous questions are going to be very different if your child is five versus if they are ten (and not all ten-year-olds necessitate the same approach). When you work through the responsibilities piece of the Big Picture, you'll need to revisit it with some regularity.

Part III

The Data Studies

I f you've worked out your family's Big Picture logistics, and you've got a system in place for decision making, in principle you're prepared for anything. You have decided what is really important for your family, and you can use that as your guiding light to navigate even the pretty unexpected child-related terrain.

In many ways, up to this point our approach has paralleled the first year of a business school curriculum. When I taught introductory microeconomics to MBA students, I focused on Big Picture tools and topics. I tried to help my students see how understanding a basic concept like "demand elasticity" was key to good decision making, even when the question they faced was rarely "What is the demand elasticity at my firm?"

There's another set of business school classes that come later. These classes focus on examples, often called case studies. Students study the experiences of actual firms, in actual business situations. They look at what the firms did right (or wrong) and try to glean some general lessons from the evidence. They learn, ideally, how firms actually implement the big-picture ideas and tools that are developed in the more fundamentals-oriented classes.

These cases are not meant to tell students exactly what to do. There was a very famous case about the struggle for dominance between VHS and Betamax, two home video cassette formats, in the 1980s. This case is still taught *not* because today's MBA students are likely to find themselves embroiled in a fight to dominate the video cassette marketplace, but because the facts of the case illustrate some important principles that are relevant to more contemporary decisions. (Spoiler: VHS won.)

You have now arrived at the case study portion of this book. More accurately, it's the data-study portion. It's true that in principle, you'd be fully equipped to make your parenting decisions based on your Big Picture and the tools, and there will clearly be questions that only you face, for which the experience of others is not helpful.

But there are a number of areas that many parents think about, and where there is a shared body of evidence. Just as all firms should not have to make the same mistakes Betamax did, all families should not have to dig through the basic evidence on school-entry ages to make a choice about when their child should start school. The "data studies," for the most part, will not *directly* apply to any particular child, but they provide a starting point for family choices.

The data studies in this book focus on four areas: school, extracurriculars, socioemotional struggles, and entertainment. In each of the sections that follow, I'll try to start by giving an overview of the kinds of questions that might come up in this area and talking about where data will help and where it won't. There are a lot of questions that come up for parents where there simply isn't any evidence to draw on; it may be useful to know that before you go down those rabbit holes.

I'll then go through some of the places where we do have evidence that might help in your decisions and talk through what the data really says, where the central lessons are, and where the holes remain.

And finally, at the end of each section, I'll return to at least one concrete "example problem" that families might face in these domains, and talk through how to use the approach advocated in the earlier sections, possibly along with the data here, to make a choice. Chances are, these example problems aren't exactly yours (except at the end, where I'll talk about the right age for a phone, which, let's face it, is a problem for everyone), but by seeing how one might approach them, you can draw some parallels.

So pull out your packet of Harvard Business School cases, brush up on your Betamax history, and let's get started.

School: Overview

Let's do some math. Your child will spend, say, 8 hours a day at school for 180 days a year for 13 years. That's 18,720 school hours (give or take a few snow days). When you look at it this way, it's not hard to see why, for many of us, decisions around school seem incredibly important. Which school? When to send them? Should we supplement with some kind of extra school? If there is a choice of schools, how to evaluate them?

The right thing to do is not often obvious. And it's not like ordering breakfast, where, if you make a mistake, you get a do-over tomorrow. It feels like an incredibly important choice that you only get to make once, and with no background or expertise. Good luck! Welcome to parenting.

But it's worth remembering that while school is a big thing, it isn't *everything*. Even during their school years, your kids will spend more waking hours outside school than in it (and way more hours if you factor in sleep time!). You aren't a 1940s British aristocrat (I'm speculating) and therefore you're probably not dropping your six-year-old off at boarding school. If you choose a school that doesn't work, you *can* revisit that choice. This isn't as flexible as breakfast, but it's not infinitely inflexible, either. It's worth making decisions around school thoughtfully, but it's also probably not useful to give those decisions more attention (and fear) than they really deserve.

The range of questions parents have about school is broad.

Some are widely shared. Should I hold my kid back and start them in kindergarten at an older age? (I already went through that one at the start of the book.) Should I try to lottery into the charter school in my city, or stick with my neighborhood public school? Is private school worth it?

Some are more idiosyncratic. Should I send one of my kids to private school even if I don't plan to send the others? My first grader hates homework—should I tell them they can skip it, or talk to the school, or tell them they have to do it anyway? My daughter is struggling to read and I think her teacher isn't approaching it right—do I go to the school, or do I engage a tutor (and would tutoring even work, anyway)? How are we considering racial or ethnic diversity in the school, and does it make a difference if my child will be in the majority or minority group?

In the case of schooling, there is some good news on data. Specifically, that we have some.

Education in general and schools in particular are popular topics in economics, and in social science more broadly. One key reason is that this is a hugely important policy issue. The US government spends about *$700 billion a year* on public schools. At the same time, outcomes are not always great, and there is a lot of bemoaning the fact that we are falling behind other countries (Western European nations, Japan, South Korea, etc.) in student learning. This debate has raged for decades.

This interest has led to data, sometimes to very good data. As I'll talk about later in this chapter, we do know something about what makes a good school, about the value of charter versus neighborhood public schools, a little bit about private schools. We know something about school-entry ages, and even a bit (although less) about homework and other "extra" schooling. In most or all of these areas, we have evidence that comes from compelling research, research that does a good job of zeroing in on the impact of education, as separate from the impact of family background.

At the same time, this is a good place to be clear on what the data doesn't help us with. I'd draw out two very large limitations.

First, nearly all the evidence I'll talk about in the data studies that follow is going to focus on test scores. As a parent, there may be outcomes you care about for your child other than test scores—for example, how happy they are at school, how confident, how supported. It's not that these features necessarily *aren't* delivered by schools that also do well on state or national tests, it's just that we don't really know, since they are hard to measure (sometimes we do measure "family satisfaction" with schools, but that isn't quite the same thing).

Whether your child will be happy at a school should clearly be part of your decision to send them there, but it isn't a part you should look to the data for.

A second issue is that most of the evidence—especially around school choice—tends to focus on environments of policy interest, specifically worse-performing school districts and vulnerable populations. If you are lucky enough to live in an area with many well-regarded public schools to choose from, it's less clear that this data applies to your personal situation.

This issue is even more important when we come to private schools, and to questions about choosing between them. If you're in a position to choose between two well-regarded private schools, and you're evaluating, say, their relative performance in the statewide robotics competition, there isn't any systematic data to help you. Similarly, if you're choosing between private schools with different philosophies—for example, Quaker versus Montessori—data isn't going to save you there, either.

And finally, if you're looking for evidence on homeschooling or "unschooling" (a philosophy that de-emphasizes any formal schooling at all), you won't find it in data-based sources. The choice to engage in these nontraditional forms of schooling is so idiosyncratic that it's virtually impossible to separate out the other characteristics that come along with this from any impacts of schooling.

This doesn't mean these choices—which type of private school, whether to homeschool—aren't important, just that you won't be able to draw on data as part of your decision process.

On the following pages, I'll talk through three data studies: on school choice, on homework and tutoring, and, finally, on the controversial question of how kids learn to read and which way to teach reading is the best. A fourth key piece of the schooling question is school-entry age; we covered that in the introduction.

In the last section, I'll work through a specific decision problem—similar to what I did with school-entry age at the start of the book—which will (ideally) illustrate how one could bring these tools together.

 ## SCHOOL CHOICE: PUBLIC, PRIVATE, CHARTER

The most basic question: Which school?

How you are likely to think about this depends heavily on where you live and, by extension, where you choose to live may be impacted by the schools.

When Penelope was three, Jesse and I did a cross-country job search. She wasn't in formal school yet, but she was old enough for us to recognize that school was coming down the line, and investigating the various school situations was a big part of our job search. A main takeaway from this process (other than that Jesse was familiar with the term *cafetorium* and I was not) was that the landscape was hugely different across areas.

We visited places where the decision was simple: the public school district was excellent and everyone seemed to live within walking distance of one of two great elementary schools. And on the flip side, we visited places where the public school district was very troubled, and the choices seemed likely to be either charter school or private school.

At the same time, if private school is among the options on the table, there are very significant budgetary considerations. At some point I had a conversation with a fellow mom about the fact that choosing to send a child to private school might mean moving to a smaller house—how should the family think about that trade-off?

When you're facing this choice, where does the data come in? It will be helpful to think about two questions. First, are some *kinds* of schools "better" than others—should we always favor charter schools, or private schools? And second, does the data say anything about what makes for a good school in general—is there anything concrete you can look for when you sort through the options? I'll take up both of these in the sections that follow.

WHAT THE DATA SAYS: SCHOOL TYPES

There is a huge body of academic literature on education, not to mention a plethora of think tanks and other policy organizations that focus on schools. You might have thought that with so much research and policy interest, we'd be able to easily answer the question of what kind of school is best.

But it isn't that simple. You cannot evaluate whether private schools, for example, produce better outcomes than public schools by comparing kids who go to the two kinds of schools. Private school attendance is associated with many other features of families. So a simple comparison is unlikely to yield anything of value.

Even a seemingly simpler comparison—say, comparing kids who go to a neighborhood charter school to kids who go to the public school in the same district—is complicated. For example, the parents who seek out the charter school may well be different (perhaps more invested in their children's educational success?) than those who do not. It may be these differences that matter, not the schools themselves.

What to do? The ideal (as always) is to use some type of randomization. If you randomly assigned some kids to charter schools, for example, you could be more confident in drawing causal conclusions. Turns out, at least in the case of charter schools, we can do precisely that by using school lotteries.

How does this work? Let's start with a simple example.

Lynn, Massachusetts, is a city a bit north of Boston with a relatively low-income population and a public school district that historically has not performed well.[1] In the early 2000s, a charter middle school—run by a charter school chain called KIPP—opened in Lynn. Initially, not that many students wanted to go to the school, so they took everyone who showed up. After a couple of years, though, they got more students than they could take—200 applications for 90 spots, on average.

Massachusetts has a number of charter schools and they all adhere to a state rule: if you have more applicants than you can take, you have to decide who to take using a lottery. (If you want to see how this might work, you can see it on a much larger scale—New York City—in the excellent documentary *Waiting for "Superman."*) There are various ways to run such a lottery, but the key thing is that it's *random*. Some kids are randomly chosen to be offered admission, others are not.

The students that do not get offered admission typically (not always, but often) remain in the public school system.

But this means we have a set of kids—specifically, those who entered the lottery—some of whom are randomly chosen to go to a charter school and some of whom are not. By comparing them later, we can see whether the charter school kids do better or worse than those who remain in public school.

In this particular example—studied by researchers from MIT—the students who ended up in the charter school had considerably better test scores than those who lost the lottery and went to the public school. The charter school students' math scores were about 0.4 standard deviations higher than the public school students' scores. This number may not have a lot of meaning, but if you think about it in terms of IQ points, it's equivalent to about six points on a standard IQ test.

This paper is just one example of a "school lottery" paper. In Massachusetts alone there are a lot of examples. Similar types of lotteries for school vouchers (which can be used to pay for private school) can let researchers understand something about the comparison between private and public schools. Equally important, these lotteries are truly random: they are often publicly randomized, and this gives us confidence in interpreting the results causally.

This example also illustrates some of the more complicated aspects of using these lotteries to learn about questions of school quality. A particular issue is what economists call the LATE Critique (LATE stands for "local average treatment effect"). The issue, in slightly broader and less technical terms, is that this type of experiment tells us the effect of charter schools for children whose families are interested in charter schools—that is, for the people who entered the lottery. People have levied criticism against studies like this for *not* reflecting the effect of charter schools for a randomly chosen child (the effects could be larger or smaller; it's not obvious).

A closely related point, perhaps more relevant for individual family choices, is that these studies are specific to the places they are done and to the alternatives that the "lottery losers" face. We'll see a little bit of nuance about this in the data to come, but it's worth keeping in mind—broadly—that these studies tend to be focused on low-income urban school districts with poorly performing public schools.

These are important caveats to everything I'll say from here. But with them, we can ask: What does the literature find, in general? Is the overall evidence on charter schools in line with the KIPP example in Massachusetts? And what does this same method tell us about private schools?

(I should say that this is by no means the definitive book on the politics and policies of school choice, and in the appendix on page 265, I suggest a few pieces of further reading for those of you who really want to nerd out on this topic.)

The KIPP-Lynn school results are not alone. Studies of charter schools in many cities—e.g., Boston, New York—tend to find large positive impacts on test scores, on the order of 0.2 to 0.3 standard deviations.[2] These studies tend to focus on charter schools that follow what is called a "no excuses" model—a long school day, strict but clear discipline policies, frequent teacher and student feedback. They also tend to be located in poor-performing urban school districts, where the alternative to the charter schools are underperforming public schools.

This last point is important. In one summary paper that combined data from 113 charter school lotteries, the authors found that the overall effects were positive but actually much smaller than the results we see when focusing on Boston or New York alone. Rather than being 0.3 standard deviations, they were more like 0.04 to 0.08.[3] It turns out that some of what is behind that difference seems to be that charters are simply much more important when the backup school is worse.

In the following graph, the authors of this study show this using data from Massachusetts. They graph the *effect* of charter schools (i.e., how much test scores are improved by winning the charter lottery) on the vertical axis. On the horizontal axis is a measure of the test scores of the

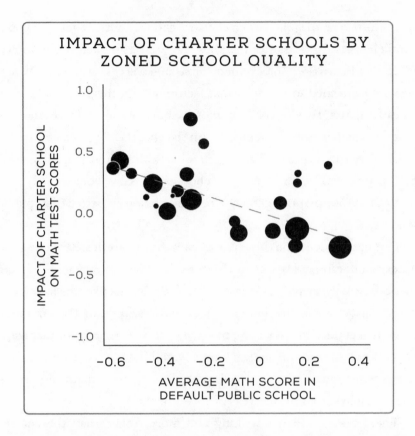

IMPACT OF CHARTER SCHOOLS BY
ZONED SCHOOL QUALITY

school where the students would end up in the absence of the charter. The circles represent different studies—circle size gives you the sample size—that estimate the impact of charter schools. What we see is that in places where the default public school—where the student would likely go if they lost the charter lottery—has worse test scores, charter schools really increase test scores. In places where the default public school has higher test scores (more to the right on the horizontal axis), the impact of going to a charter school is neutral, or even negative.

In a sense, this shouldn't be surprising: the alternative matters. From a parental decision-making standpoint, this suggests that one factor (just one!) in whether you consider a charter school should be what the alternative is. How good is your local public school district?

It's also true that the better charter school results do tend to come from charters that follow one of these no-excuses models—epitomized by chains like KIPP, Achievement First, and Success Academy. When authors have tried to identify what factors within this framework specifically matter, they've come up mostly short. Some evidence suggests that intensive tutoring is helpful, but in the end, the biggest factor seems to be that this type of charter school is more often placed in low-performing areas where the other school options are worse.

What about private schools? Are they obviously better than public schools?

Our best evidence on this comes, again, from lotteries. This time, the lotteries allocate not spaces in charter schools but monetary vouchers that can be used to pay for private school. Programs like this have been run in a number of cities, like New York and Washington, DC. And they do seem to find some moderate positive effects, especially for Black students.[4] One study in Milwaukee found overall faster growth in math test scores for students who won a voucher lottery, with math test scores increasing by 1.3 points per year of enrollment.[5]

These results are less striking and more fragile than the charter school results. Some studies have found that vouchers have significant *negative* effects.[6] Again, the issue seems to arise in part from the alternative. In this case, a more significant issue than the quality of the public school district is the quality of the private school options. School vouchers are not especially generous, and in most cases are sufficient only for less expensive private schools. Beyond this, private schools that want to participate in voucher programs tend to be those that need more students; but being undersubscribed isn't a great sign for their quality.

From the standpoint of parental decision making, I'd argue that these results are less useful than the charter school evidence. The voucher circumstances simply feel less relevant to the decision making of many parents. And these results do not really answer the question of whether private schools are, on average, better than public options. Put differently, if you have the resources to attend a competitive and well-funded private school, it may or may not be the right choice, but you shouldn't rely on this evidence to tell you if it is.

I want to pause here to acknowledge the issue of race in these conversations about schools. Schools with lower test scores tend to disproportionately serve Black and Latinx students. These students are more likely to be in underfunded schools that have lower test scores. One implication of this is that charter schools, or school voucher programs, tend to be disproportionately positive for students of color. As a country, we grapple with both the legacy and the current reality of racism, especially anti-Black racism. Access to lower-quality schools is different from police violence, but it's part of the same structurally racist system. Beyond the individual choices that parents make about schools, any conversation about school choice must engage with this reality.

And in engaging with this reality myself, I must recognize that others will have more to say on this. Whole books have been and will be written on these issues, many of them by writers of color. There is data on some of these questions—much of it highlighting differences in resources available across schools—but there is also historical context necessary to better understand this. In the appendix (page 265), you can find resources to go deeper—much deeper—into these questions.

WHAT THE DATA SAYS: SCHOOL CHARACTERISTICS

It's one thing to compare types of schools in general. But there is a more fundamental (and, from a data perspective, harder to answer) question:

What makes a "good" school? Let's say you are going to tour a bunch of school options. What can you look for to know which ones are the best?

The data tells us some interesting but not, perhaps, decision-relevant things. For example: Kindergarten teachers really matter. John Friedman, one of my closest work colleagues, and his coauthors showed this in a 2011 paper. They found that kids with a more experienced kindergarten teacher not only did better in kindergarten (which seems obvious) but also had higher earnings in their late twenties.[7]

In a related paper, the same authors showed that having a higher-quality teacher in school in general (i.e., not just in kindergarten) increased college attendance and earnings in adulthood, and lowered the chance of teen pregnancy.[8]

Okay, super, it's good to have good teachers. But this is a pretty hard thing to figure out on a school tour, never mind that by the time your kid gets into a school, the teachers might have changed.

More practically, something that comes out of these papers and many others is the importance of class size (i.e., how many students per teacher in a classroom). A large number of studies have demonstrated that smaller class sizes raise student achievement in both the short and longer term.[9] This *is* something you can evaluate, and it probably does differ across schools. Private schools do tend to have smaller class sizes, although there's variation even within school type.

Beyond this, at least one paper has attempted to go into the weeds of what makes some charter schools work well, and argued that more instructional time, more comprehensive teacher feedback, and more tutoring are key to success.[10] Instructional time is easy to observe, and it may also be possible to learn a bit more about how teacher feedback is managed—is there a system of accountability for student performance?

Finally, there may be value in considering outputs as well as inputs. When researchers look for what makes a good school, they tend to focus on test scores. That's something you see directly, so you may want to start there.

Putting this all together, completing a version of the table below may help you be explicit about some of these comparisons when you are investigating school options. Seeing them all in writing can let you visualize the trade-offs. You may have one school with smaller classes but less clear teacher feedback or worse test scores. Seeing this information all together isn't going to make your decision for you, but it may be a start.

It is worth remembering that there are a lot of outcomes you may care about more as a parent. Are the kids happy? Is there enough recess? Is the school diverse? Do their values align with ours?

In my case, the aspect of my children's elementary school I value most is its focus on community, on being a positive member of society and giving back. There is no spreadsheet column for this. You'll need to reflect on considerations like this on your own; school-specific information may help, but the research-based data probably will not.

SCHOOL NAME	_____ (SCHOOL 1)	_____ (SCHOOL 2)	_____ (SCHOOL 3)	_____ (SCHOOL 4)
AVG. CLASS SIZE (K-5)				
STUDENT/ TEACHER RATIO				
HOURS OF INSTRUCTION PER WEEK				
TEACHING FEED-BACK SYSTEM, FREQUENCY				
TUTORING OPTIONS				
STATE TEST PROFICIENCY SCORE				

The (Data) Bottom Line

- In relatively poor-performing school districts, charter schools deliver (on average) better learning outcomes.
- Test scores tend to be better in schools with smaller class sizes and frequent and informed teacher feedback.
- When comparing schools, look for some outcome data: test scores, proficiency rates. It's not everything you care about, but it may be helpful.

 SCHOOL AWAY FROM SCHOOL, OR, DO I NEED TO SIGN UP FOR KUMON?

American attitudes toward homework—and schoolwork outside of school in general—have ebbed and flowed over time.[11] In the early part of the twentieth century, homework was thought to be an important part of learning. By the 1940s, however, it was falling out of favor as unnecessary. Then the 1950s brought Sputnik, and a feeling of losing to Russia, and a ramping back up of homework. This declined again in the 1960s and 1970s, only to return in the 1980s with a general realization that test performance in the US was falling behind that of much of the rest of the world.

It is notable that many of these changes over time are driven not by some exciting new research finding or realization, but a feeling of global competitiveness. Of course, it's not obvious that the reaction exactly mirrors the reality. The more recent iteration of these concerns focuses on how we are falling behind Asian countries like Japan and South Korea, where children do more out-of-school work. The reality is that at least some kids in South Korea are spending hours every day at places literally called "cram schools." Even if we all agreed that this was ideal (and many people would not), it is a stretch to suggest a few more math worksheets in kindergarten is equivalent.

Are we currently in a pro- or anti-homework moment? I'd say it's a bit complicated. On the one hand, there seem to be more extra-school enrichment options than ever. There is a veritable proliferation of Kumon and Russian School of Math (RSM) locations, and various copycat versions. In New York City, at least some parents are signing up their four-year-olds for test prep to get into the "right" kindergarten programs.[12]

On the other hand, some more "progressive" schools are now consciously moving to a no-homework policy. I was speaking recently to a friend with a child about to enter kindergarten. Even though she lives in one of the country's best school districts, literally down the street from the public elementary school, she was still contemplating private schools that focused on the principle of no homework until middle school, or even beyond.

Her criteria are not obviously in conflict. You could want to avoid a school that assigns homework on the principle that you want more control over the out-of-school work your children do. But it all combines to paint a nuanced picture of current attitudes.

As a parent, though, we probably want to focus on the concrete. There are really two issues here. First, how do you think about school-based homework—is it something to embrace or not? And second, how should you approach additional non-school-based work (if at all)? The second of these is more obviously a choice, and it's more separable from other decisions like where to live and what school to attend. But I'll start with the first since it's in many ways a bigger and more interesting question, and it feeds into the second. I'd also argue that it *is*, to some extent, a choice. Like my friend, you could look for a school or school district with a more limited approach to homework. And even if your child does have homework in the early grades, you might be able to push back on it.

But should you? What does the data say?

WHAT THE DATA SAYS: HOMEWORK

There is a huge and highly contentious body of literature on the question of homework. There are defenders of homework, writing articles with titles like "A Teacher's Defense of Homework."[13] And there are enthusiastic haters, with books like *The Homework Myth: Why We Give Our Kids Too Much of a Bad Thing*[14] or the 1999 *Time* magazine cover story titled "Too Much Homework! How It's Hurting Our Kids, and What Parents Should Do About It."

Both sides have arguments that (I think!) are valid in theory. On the pro-homework side, there are a few key points.[15] First, homework may reinforce in-school learning. If you're learning the multiplication table in school, it may be helpful to practice at home. It's just more time spent on a task, and you do not necessarily have that time in school. Related to this, more complicated homework assignments may push kids to develop problem-solving skills on their own that are harder to teach in a classroom context. A final big piece is the possibility that homework encourages development of noncognitive skills by requiring students to be organized and remember to do their homework and return it to school. (There are other possible benefits as well, including parental engagement.)

On the anti-homework side, we see arguments that student time is being wasted on piles of busywork, that homework is taking away time from free and imaginative play or time with family. Or, possibly, sleep. Homework may teach students to hate school and to resent learning. And it may be unfair if it favors higher-income students whose parents have more free time to, say, build their solar system diorama with them or carefully review their math assignment.

It is simply very, very hard to evaluate these questions. It is challenging to observe and measure many of the outcomes that are implied by the arguments above. Noncognitive skills and love of learning are both extremely difficult to capture in data. And we cannot rely on instinct. Both pro- and anti-homework arguments around these outcomes seem plausible. I can see why it would be useful for kids to learn early how to remember to do something and follow through on it. I can also see why twelve pages of double-digit multiplication problems would lead someone to conclude that math sucks.

(Beyond this, the value or harm on these dimensions will depend on your child. A child who is already skilled in executive functioning may benefit less and be harmed more; vice versa for one who needs more scaffolding.)

We can at least attempt to study achievement directly. Does homework improve performance in school or on standardized tests? Answering this would help us evaluate many of the pro-homework arguments—both the rote memorization value and (maybe to a lesser extent) the problem-solving value could show up in better school and test performance.

Even this is hard for the standard causality reasons. If you compare children in classrooms that assign homework with those in classrooms that do not, it's very hard to know whether it's the *homework* that matters or some other factor. Some studies do look at the relationship between reported time spent on homework and school performance at the student level, but these are, if anything, more problematic. It isn't even obvious whether the effects from an analysis like this are biased up or down. On the one hand, students who are more serious about school may spend more time on homework; on the other, those who struggle may need more time. It's hard to know if you'd over- or understate the causal effect.

It seems like it would not be very challenging to run a randomized controlled trial on this—for example, assign some classrooms to have homework and others not to, or assign homework to some students and not to others. And in fact, there are some randomized studies, although not nearly as many as you might expect, and they are generally small. For example, one study published in 1990 started with four fifth-grade classrooms and assigned two to a "homework" condition and two to "no homework." The authors found that the students in the homework condition had higher test scores later, although with only four classrooms in the study, it is challenging to draw strong statistical conclusions.[16]

The limits on the homework evidence make it difficult to be confident in any conclusions. However, combing through two big reviews—one in 1989 and a follow-up in 2006—it is hard to avoid observing that the evidence consistently points to homework having a positive effect on school performance.[17] Across a wide variety of study types, with varying types of biases, we see evidence of this positive effect.

The effect sizes are generally moderate, and they are much larger for older kids than younger ones. That is, there is more limited evidence that this matters for kids in the six-to-eight range, but the effect seems to grow as kids work through middle school.

This all focuses on the binary homework-or-not choice; a related question is, how much homework is enough? Homework amounts seem to have gone up over time. One article cites an increase in homework for kids ages six to eight from an average of 52 minutes a week in 1981 to 128 minutes by 1997.[18] This question hasn't been subject to much scrutiny, and on its face it seems like it would matter a lot what you were trying to achieve with the work. If the goal is to memorize multiplication tables, more practice might be better. If the goal is to reinforce work habits (remembering to take the homework home and bring it back in), this could likely be achieved with a more limited amount of time.

And of course, it's obviously the case that the value of homework will depend on what type of tasks the students are doing. This is heavily emphasized and, again, is hard to study. A homework assignment of keeping a reading log is very different from completing workbook pages; both may be good, but they aren't the same. There are some "best practices" in homework—it should be productive and integrated, for example—but it isn't clear that everyone follows these (in fact, they surely do not).

The somewhat scattered nature of this discussion reflects, I think, the character of this debate. A thoughtfully designed homework program probably *could* enhance learning for many or most kids, and in practice, most of the data shows that homework has positive achievement impacts. But whether there are downsides—and if they are avoidable—is less clear. To the extent that this is a key issue for your family, it may make sense to learn more about any school's homework policies—how they think about homework, how much you can expect, do they welcome any family input, etc.

WHAT THE DATA SAYS:
BEYOND SCHOOL HOMEWORK

School homework is one thing, but what about "extra school"? What about math enrichment, Kumon reading practice, after-school science lab?

In spite of how other parents—or, say, the internet—make it seem, the US actually has nowhere near the focus on out-of-school learning that other places do. In South Korea in 2006, parents spent the equivalent of 2.6 percent of the GDP on private tutoring. Spending for the whole formal education sector was only 3.5 percent![19] This "shadow education" system exists throughout much of the world, in Asia in particular.[20]

And there is some of this in the US, of course. But for the moment, most out-of-school tutoring in the US is still more focused on remediation than acceleration. As a parent, you might consider it for either reason. Does it work?

Basically, yes. In a sense, we do not need detailed studies of after-school tutoring programs to know that one-on-one instruction can enhance achievement. Lots of basic education literature has shown this works in helping kids at a variety of levels.[21] This is likely part of the reason that smaller class sizes tend to enhance student performance—students individually have more time with their teacher.

We can, of course, dig a little into the data. The results of one quasi-experimental study in Luxembourg are shown below. In the study, 122 students were provided with in-school tutoring and 122 of their friends were not.[22] The authors looked at their grades before and after tutoring. The students who got tutoring improved their math scores more (the authors saw the same thing for performance in English, Latin, and French).

Turning to specific approaches, there are a few small studies that have looked directly at Kumon (a franchise of tutoring locations focusing on reinforcing skills through practice) and evaluated its impact on

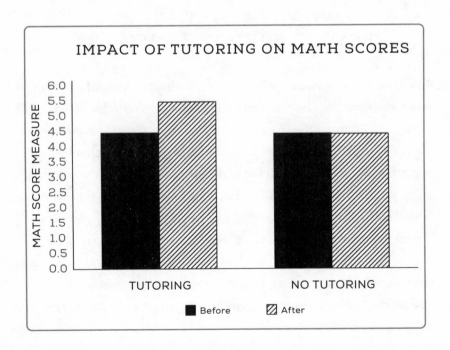

math performance. The results are largely positive, suggesting that the program improves kids' ability to calculate fast, in particular (not surprising given the programmatic focus on calculation fluency).[23] Of note is at least one study that suggested a Kumon-like program could help identify and promote students with strong mathematical ability who came from disadvantaged backgrounds.

This study raises an issue that pervades these discussions and that occupies much of this literature: the role of out-of-school tutoring in perpetuating inequality. In the areas of Asia where there is significant spending on additional teaching, that spending is concentrated among children with wealthier and better-educated parents.[24] SAT tutoring in the US—admittedly well outside the age-range focus of this book—tends to be more common among higher-income families.[25]

When we ask exactly *who* is hiring a private tutor in New York City to prepare their four-year-old for the gifted-and-talented test at public school entry, we will not be surprised to learn it is families with more resources.

From the standpoint of parental decisions, it seems clear from the data that some achievement gains may be obtained by "extra school." If you send your kid to improve calculation speed at Kumon, they will probably come out with the ability to add numbers faster.

This is different from claiming that this matters in the long run. I once spoke with an extremely professionally successful man who explained he had refused to memorize the multiplication tables on principle (I didn't fully understand the principle) and instead had effectively worked out his own personal version of algebra so he could visualize the answers. His system would be a Kumon failure, and also probably tremendously inefficient, but with presumably some value to his long-term reasoning skills.

Extra school also comes with an "opportunity cost": more school means less time for something else. In writing the sleep chapter for this book, I reviewed some data from South Korea, where teenagers were sleeping an average of 6.5 hours a night, largely due to out-of-school work. That's not enough, and if going to the Russian School of Math means your ten-year-old doesn't get a full night of sleep, it's not clear the tutoring will help them "get ahead." And the possible role of stress and anxiety from having to do well in both school and "extra school" is something we don't fully understand in young kids.

Similar to the world of extracurriculars, it can be easy in some circles to feel that you are constantly getting behind with "extra school." That feeling is a terrible reason to sign up for out-of-school tutoring. If your kid is dying to do some math enrichment, maybe give it a try. But keeping up with the Smiths, whose kid is enrolled in a five-day-a-week math boot camp, is probably not worth it.

The (Data) Bottom Line

- School homework is a contentious topic, and hard to study.
- On the whole, the data suggests that some homework can enhance learning, although this likely depends on the design.
- Extra school and tutoring do seem to increase test performance, albeit at the cost of other uses of that time.

 BOOKS AND READING

There are a lot of big learning moments with an elementary schooler—the basic points where your kid suddenly knows something they didn't before—but I would venture that none of them feel quite as magical as the point where they learn to read. It can feel like overnight you go from slowly sounding out "H-A-T" to reading "The boy is in the toy store with his mother."

For many parents who like to read—and probably even many who do not—this excites us in part because we cannot wait for our children to love books. When Penelope was learning to read, in the frustrating moments, I repeatedly explained to her that once she knew how to read, she would *always* be able to find something to do. She didn't appreciate this at the time, but later admitted I was right. (At least that is how I remember it; anyway, I *was* right.)

I've included this discussion in the section on school even though not all kids learn to read in school, and (more important) reading is also recreational. An important parenting question for many of us may be, "How do I encourage my child to read outside of school, outside of what is strictly required?"

But there are also questions that interface more directly with schooling, especially around learning to read. How do kids learn? When do they learn? Most practically, how should they be taught? Are some methods of teaching reading "better" than others?

WHAT THE DATA SAYS: LEARNING TO READ

Among my favorite book genres is histories of nineteenth-century polar expeditions (spoiler alert: it's super, super cold and a lot of people die). Jesse and I share many interests, but not this one. The last time I read one of these books and tried to tell him what was happening, he retaliated by explaining the details of the book he was reading, which was—I'm totally not making this up—a history of the German Federal Statistical Office.

But for me, a close second to books on polar explorers are books on neuroscience, which is where I think it makes sense to start in understanding the question of how kids learn to read. Because before thinking about how kids *learn* to read, it is useful to think about how adults (or fluent readers in general) actually read.[26]

Of particular relevance is the question of whether you read by *recognizing* words or by *sounding them out*. If you're a fluent adult reader, you probably think that you read by recognizing words and just knowing what they look like. Basically, you perceive yourself using some kind of pattern recognition—when you see the word *read*, you recognize it as "read." You do not think of yourself as sounding it out. And for a word like *read*, this is likely correct. For short, common words, we seem to read through pattern recognition.[27]

(How do we know this? One piece of evidence is that for short words—say, under eight characters—the length of the word doesn't influence our reading speed. If we were sounding it out, this wouldn't be the case. Other evidence comes from brain scans that look at how the brain processes real versus imaginary words.)

But it turns out that although you do not perceive it, you actually also make use of a fair amount of phonics (basically, chunking words and sounding them out) inside your brain when reading. You do it fast! But that doesn't mean you don't do it. And it's the reason we can process words we haven't seen before, or imaginary words.

For example, here's a word I made up: *delumpification*. You can likely read this, in the sense that you could pronounce it. And beyond that, you probably can work out what it would mean (something like, "the process of removing a lump"). But this isn't because you recognize the word! Implicitly, your brain is sounding it out in pieces it knows: *de / lump / ification* (perhaps—our exact knowledge about how this type of word gets chunked isn't perfect).

Understanding this process, and in particular understanding the sense in which even fluent readers rely on sounding out to read, has implications for how kids learn to read. Notably, it is key to the great debate over teaching phonics versus "whole language" reading.

Traditionally, reading has been taught through the use of phonics—kids learn the sounds of letters, then how they fit together (the consonant-vowel-consonant words), then common exceptions ("if there is an *e* at the end, *a* says its own name"; "ou" says "oww," etc.), then weirder things (the silent *k* and so on).

If you're familiar with them, think of the Bob Books. They start with just four letters (*a, m, s,* and *t*) and the first book in its entirety is: "Mat, Mat sat, Sam, Sam sat, Mat sat on Sam, Sam sat on Mat, Mat sat, Sam sat." The next book introduces more letters (*c, d*), and so on.

Phonics has been used (successfully) for decades, probably hundreds of years. But at some point, some people suggested it might not be the best approach. Beginning in the late 1960s, a movement (credited to, among others, linguist Noam Chomsky) suggested that it might be better to teach reading with a more "whole-language" approach.[28] In particular, this movement argued for forgetting about phonics and immersing children in language and stories with the expectation that they would, effectively, learn pattern recognition to read words.

To simplify somewhat, there were a couple of arguments in favor of this. One is that phonics is boring. That "Mat" story from the Bob Books? No five- or six-year-old will find it exciting. It's a chore. Similarly, drilling on the millions of exceptions in the English language is tedious. *Why on earth is the* k *silent?* A whole-language approach skips right to better stories—not Harry Potter, but at least something that's not quite so pedantic. So maybe it holds kids' interest better.

The other point this movement made is that when adults read, they read through pattern recognition, and if that's where kids are headed anyway, we might as well start there. The whole-language approach got some traction in the 1980s and 1990s; at some point, California public schools adopted a version of it, as did Massachusetts. As it turns out, however, ignoring phonics is *not* an appropriate way to teach reading.

For one thing, as mentioned earlier, adults reading by pattern recognition alone is wrong. Even fluent readers are using a form of sounding out to read many words. So chunking words and putting them back together is a key tool. This suggests that we ignore it at our peril.

But we can also see the failure of this whole-language approach in experimental data. A team of researchers at Stanford showed this in a clever experiment in which they invented a new script and attempted to teach it to undergraduates. The script had English sound correspondence, but the letters looked different.[29] Some undergraduates were encouraged to learn using a phonics frame (basically, to work out which squiggle corresponded to which sound) and others were encouraged to use a whole-word approach (memorizing which picture corresponded to which word). The students using the whole-word approach initially did better, but once more words were added, they were unable to keep up; phonics facilitated the reading of a larger number of words with a smaller number of symbols. A large number of studies show that phonics-based reading instruction is more successful than whole-language reading.[30] Some people have even argued that the California adoption of this whole-language approach was responsible for a precipitous decline in test scores in California in the 1980s and 1990s, although this is subject to some debate.[31]

In the end, phonics has returned, and this is almost certainly what your child's school will use. (It's also probably how you should teach them to read, if you choose to do it yourself.) If you find that your child's school has adopted a whole-language approach, you should ask *a lot* of questions.

There is some push for what people call "balanced literacy," meaning that basic phonics instruction is combined with more interesting story reading.[32] This adopts some of what is "fun" about the whole-language approach—you can quickly move beyond the Bob Books—but the main focus stays on phonics as the central learning tool.

So, when will this all happen? When is your kid actually going to learn to read?

I talked some in *Cribsheet* about reading among very young children. You can certainly find products that tell you your baby can learn to read. They can't! Science has proven it.[33] Please, please do not try to teach your baby to read (it will frustrate and disappoint you, they probably will not like it, and it will not work).

Toddlers and preschoolers also (in most cases) cannot read fluently. Kids of two and three years old will often start doing some pattern recognition—recognizing their name, or the M in the McDonald's arches, or a particular logo. This is great, and it's great to encourage it! But it's not reading. Some very young children do learn to read fluently, but it's unusual. With an older three- or four-year-old, you may be able to start doing some early phonics, and certainly a four-year-old can understand the idea of letters. This may especially be true if they have an older sibling who is learning to read. (One thing to note here is that there is often a lot of focus on learning the *names* of the letters, but this is actually far less important for reading than the letter *sounds*.)[34]

Most kids learn to read—to put letters together into words and read somewhat fluently—sometime between first and third grade. We can see this in data.

The following graph shows the evolution of reading skills based on data from the Early Childhood Longitudinal Study, a study that tracked a cohort of students who were in kindergarten in 1998.[35] Students in this cohort were evaluated on their reading skills in kindergarten, first grade, third grade, fifth grade, and eighth grade. At each time period, they got a score that indicated their proficiency at each reading skill. These skills start at letter recognition and go all the way up to evaluating the students' comprehension of complex nonfiction texts.

I focus here on the evolution of students' reading abilities early in their school career—from kindergarten through the end of third grade. When the kids entered kindergarten in the fall, most of them (about 70 percent) could recognize letters, but only a small share (about 30 percent) could recognize beginning sounds of words. Virtually none of them could recognize sight words or comprehend words in context (this last milestone would be close to reading simple texts).

By the start of first grade, letter recognition and beginning-sound recognition had advanced, but still only a small share of kids could recognize sight words or really read texts. This skill enormously advanced during first grade. By the spring of that year, 80 percent of the cohort could recognize sight words and about half could read in context.

By the end of third grade, virtually the whole cohort was reading fluently, although still only about a quarter of them were comprehending texts at a high level. This skill comes later in the data, toward the end of fifth grade and especially by eighth grade.

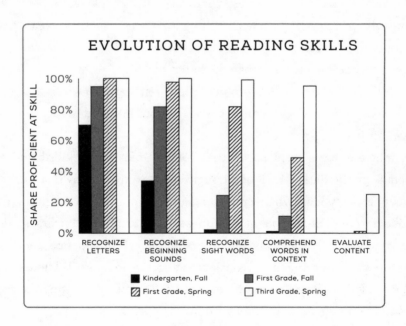

Note that this varies a bit across languages. English is harder to read than a language like Spanish or Italian, since the latter have effectively complete letter-to-sound correspondence, whereas English has a lot of spelling exceptions. As a result, Spanish and Italian speakers learn to read faster. Languages with characters rather than letters (like some East Asian languages) are much harder—they require more of the whole-language approach by definition—and take much longer to read fluently.

Based on the data in the previous graph, we see that by the third grade nearly all the children can read somewhat fluently, and a good share are starting to be able to better understand what they read—to move from "learning to read" to "reading to learn." And then the question becomes: Can you get them to *like* it?

WHAT THE DATA SAYS: LOVING TO READ

Much ink has been spilled on the question of how to get your kids to like to read. An Amazon perusal reveals plenty of book-length takes—*Raising Kids Who Love to Read, Resistant to Reading: Tips and Tricks, How to Get Your Screen-Loving Kids to Read for Pleasure*, and so on. To a large extent, these books focus on a category of kids they label "reluctant readers"— basically, kids who aren't really into reading for fun.

Kids can be reluctant readers at any age, but it's also worth noting that as kids age, they tend to read less for pleasure. It's not that surprising— as more time is scheduled for homework and activities and kids get more access to technology, reading may take a back seat.

The books dedicated to this issue have two central messages. First, if you want to encourage your kids to read for pleasure, it helps to explicitly make time for this. You may want to say, for example, "Our family is going to take this 45-minute block on a weekend afternoon to all read together." Generally, the idea would be to pitch this as "free" reading time—you can read anything you want: catalogs, baby books, a serious novel, whatever. (More on the general issue of content choice to come.) It's not a punishment, it's a form of entertainment. Like family movie night, but with books.

There are various obvious times to do this—before bed, free time on weekends, early morning before it's wake-up time. My kids do a lot of their reading at breakfast (our family rule is you can read at breakfast and lunch but not dinner, which makes it seem like a treat). As you think about this, though, you do want to go back to the family Big Picture. Devoting the pre-bedtime period to reading could crowd out other things—other family time, extracurriculars, sleep, family dinner. And again, having your kid love to read may or may not be super important to you. So be deliberate!

The second key (and perhaps blindingly obvious) message of these books is that kids like reading better if they are good at it and if they understand what they are reading. Closely related to this is the observation that understanding the *context* of what you're reading is extremely important for absorbing it.

One nice study demonstrating this was published in 1989 in the *Journal of Educational Psychology*.[36] The authors took a set of elementary schoolers in Germany and tested their comprehension of a story about soccer; the story was provided both in audiobook and written form, so this was really a test of their verbal comprehension abilities, not reading specifically. The authors categorized the children in two ways before the test. First, they used a generic verbal IQ test to classify the kids as high or low aptitude on verbal skills, including general comprehension and vocabulary. Second, they used a multiple-choice quiz to assess the students' knowledge about soccer; they classified the students as either experts or novices on the topic of soccer.

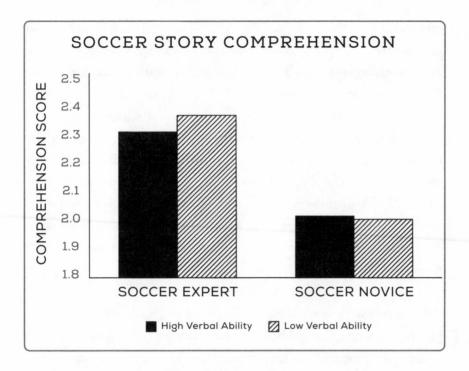

What the authors found—see one of their results in the above graph—was that comprehension of the story (measured in a large number of ways) was much better for those kids who were soccer experts, and this effect swamped any effect of general verbal aptitude. Basically, the kids with low verbal ability who knew a lot about soccer got a lot more out of the story than those with high verbal ability who did not know much about soccer.

Contextual understanding is hugely important for reading comprehension. And, by extension, for enjoying reading. If your kid has no interest in polar bears and no knowledge of polar bears, they are probably not going to enjoy reading a dense scientific treatise about polar bears.

And not every kid has the same set of interests. Various studies have shown that when kids are given a chance to choose what they read, it improves their interest in reading.[37] There are a large number of (mostly school-based) interventions designed to encourage kids to read. The exact methods vary, but they tend to share the feature that they let kids choose the books they want to read and then encourage kids to talk about the books (thus providing more content and engagement).[38]

Flexibility in reading choice is really important. Yes, your kid is likely to have to read certain books for school—that's inevitable and probably good for them. But if you want to pitch reading as entertainment, to have a "family reading time" or bedtime reading—you need to be prepared to let them pick what they want. You may have loved *A Wrinkle in Time* as a kid, but you shouldn't force it down your child's throat if they'd rather read *The Land of Stories*.

Some good share of the time, your kid is probably going to pick books that are below their maximum reading level. This is also okay. Entertainment reading time is not for pushing oneself to the maximum. You yourself are probably not going to read James Joyce for recreation.

Finally, this likely calls for some flexibility in book genre. Increasingly people are recognizing the value of graphic novels for engaging both reluctant and happy readers.[39] For a couple of weeks in the fall of 2019, the bestselling book *overall* in the US was a graphic novel called *Guts* by the absolutely awesome Raina Telgemeier. Okay, so it has pictures. But it's still reading. A similar point can be made for intermediate books like the Diary of a Wimpy Kid, Dog Man, and—I hesitate to mention—the Captain Underpants series.

No matter what you do, even with dedicated reading time and book choice, some kids just like reading better than others. This is also true of adults. This is perhaps one of the many times in parenting we should step back and remember that our kids are their own people and some things are out of our control. It is a hard lesson.

WHAT THE DATA SAYS:
TECHNOLOGICAL ADVANCES

The basic mechanics of reading haven't changed in hundreds of years, but the past decades have seen a substantial change in reading technology. This gives rise to the possible use of technology—computer-based tutoring, apps—to teach reading or help struggling readers. I would describe the evidence of its usefulness as mixed.

There are some small studies that look at the use of iPad apps to teach phonics to very young children. A representative example is a study that randomized 48 children ages 2 to 5 into a treatment where they got 30 minutes of iPad-based literacy instruction each week for 9 weeks.[40] The study found improvements in letter recognition and other literacy skills. So perhaps there is some scope for app-based learning. It's possible some of the benefits are about novelty; if kids do not typically have access to screens, lessons on an app may be a treat (at least initially!).

On the other hand, most of the evidence on computer-based tutoring in reading for school-age children suggests relatively little effect.[41] Some individual studies do see impacts, but the overall picture is fairly negative.[42] One reason may be that computer-based tutoring is used as a substitute for in-person tutoring, which is pretty clearly more effective. Kids may learn better from a computer than from nothing, but having a person do the instruction is definitely preferable.[43]

A second recent development is e-readers (Kindle, Nook, etc.). I'm talking about the type of device that literally attempts to replicate books—not the Kindle Fire, which is basically a tablet, but a little books-only Kindle. Is this better or worse for learning to read, or encouraging kids to read, than a printed book?

Basically, it's neither. Kids like e-readers fine; they don't seem to be much better or worse than regular books, which makes sense, given that they are not really that different.[44] One thing kids do like— and this gets back to the issue of choice—is that books can be more immediately delivered to an e-reader, and there is more choice at your fingertips.[45]

Finally, let me give a brief mention to audiobooks. I will confess to being extremely partial to these as a parenting strategy. Both my kids have serious motion sickness and, as a result, TV in the car is totally verboten. At some point, we discovered audiobooks, and it completely changed the car experience. I know some people like to talk to their kids in the car. I really applaud this engaged parenting, but it's not for me. I like to talk to Jesse or think, and having two kids happily in the back listening to audiobooks and not vomiting works for me.

It turns out that our kids like the audiobooks so much, they'll listen to them during downtime as well. But at some point I started to worry: was audiobook time too passive? Was it no better than TV?

I am pleased to report that this is wrong. Audiobooks actually seem to increase student interest in reading.[46] But more than that, they may actually help kids *improve* their reading abilities.[47] As kids work to move from "M-A-T" to "Jack and Annie climbed the rope ladder to the tree house," they benefit from hearing how fluent reading should sound, and audiobooks can help with this.

And kids can listen to audiobooks with much higher reading levels than they can read, which may keep their interest and motivation. (But beware: They can also listen to things that are slightly too advanced content-wise. My kids share an Audible account, and one day, at four, Finn explained to me that he was listening to Percy Jackson, which we had bought for Penelope. He told me Penelope helped him with it. ("Don't worry," she explained when I sought her out, "I only let him listen to the chapter where they fight Medusa.")

The (Data) Bottom Line

- Phonics-based reading instruction is best supported by the evidence.
- Most kids read by third grade, but their understanding of context continues to grow over time.
- Kids are more likely to enjoy reading if they read about topics they are interested in (okay, we didn't really need data there), and as a result, there is value in letting them choose their books.
- New technology:
    - Computer-based tutoring: not as good as in-person tutoring.
    - E-books: the same as regular books.
    - Audiobooks: help with story comprehension.

Application

One Child at Private School

How to pull all this together? You need to combine a decision-making approach with the data. Take the big-picture framework and the information from the data studies, and put it all in one place.

Start by framing your question. In the school space, there are many, and your questions are likely unique to you. But just as in the case study approach, we can learn from seeing how others have worked through their decisions, even if they are not *quite* ours.

One common school question is whether to hold a kid back from kindergarten entry, which I discussed in the first part of the book. Here I'll work through a more idiosyncratic choice: how to think about whether to send just one of your children to private school. Here we go.

You've got three children. Brandon, in seventh grade, is doing great at your (very good) local public school. He loves his friends, is getting decent grades, his teachers like him. It's all good! Your third child, Dalton, is a happy four-year-old at a pre-K program that you like.

The problem is the middle child, Kendra. She's a bright kid, but second grade has been a disaster. She hates her teacher and you cannot help but think the feeling is mutual. Her written work comes back full of red slashes where she "forgot to put a period in." Even though you know she can multiply two-digit numbers without a problem, her teacher is still having her work on single-digit subtraction. You've spoken to the school administrators, but they shrug it off—there's no obvious gifted program to help out. Kendra's starting to hate school.

There is a good private school 20 minutes away. And you start to wonder: Would it be a good idea to apply?

FRAME THE QUESTION

First, frame the choice. Most directly, the question is "Should my kid apply to this school?" But I think perhaps a better way to think about the initial framing is "Is this feasible for our family, and what would we need to learn to figure that out?"

In practice, this feasibility probably has a few pieces.

Money and Fairness: Private school can be expensive. It's worth working through a budget carefully. Would paying for private school mean giving something up, and if so, what? In this case, the issue of money is wrapped up in the issue of "fairness." What if Brandon and Dalton want to go to private school, too? Are you in a position to pay three private school tuitions? If not, are you comfortable with the (perceived) inequity between your kids?

Pickup/Drop-off: School logistics are always complicated, but adding a new school to the mix will not make it easier. In this example, we're talking about moving from a local, perhaps walkable, public school option to a school someone will need to drive to for drop-off and pickup. Who will do it? Otherwise, is there a bus? Would taking that bus require your child to get up at 5:30 a.m. to catch it?

It's worth thinking through the details here, rather than just assuming they will work out. Many a household argument has been had over the question of who is going to be late for work to do school drop-off in traffic.

Beyond the issue of feasibility, this is a time to think about whether this is the right solution to this problem. Are you broadly happy with Kendra's school, but just hate this one teacher? Guess what? Private schools can also have a few crummy teachers. Even if you're not resource constrained, this is a big move, a big change—do you really think it will make things better?

FACT-FIND

Assuming you do want to explore sending Kendra to private school, the next step is evidence gathering.

The biggest piece of evidence you need here is some way to compare the schools. How will you know if the private school is "better," either in general or for your child specifically?

The data in this chapter can be a little helpful here. We know that the standard outcome-based way to measure school quality is with test scores, and that in general, small class sizes, experienced teachers, and frequent teacher feedback are important.

Now's the time to do some due diligence on test scores—both in Kendra's current school and in the private school option. Get some information on class sizes. Find out how much feedback the school administration is giving the teachers. Ask about teacher background and experience. You might also look into homework. If you're unhappy with the homework approach in the current school—too much busywork, not enough thinking—find out what the private option does. Will this become closer to what you're hoping for?

There is also some non-data-based information you'll likely want to get, the most important being whether your kid likes the private school. In this example, Kendra is eight. She's plenty old enough to visit a school and at least give some thought to whether it has a good feel. If she visits for a day and you have to drag her out kicking and screaming because she loves it so much, that's probably informative. It's not decisive—my kids kick and scream out of Dave & Buster's but that doesn't mean they need more time there—but you can learn something from this.

There's also the "feel" of the school as perceived by you. One of my colleagues once told me that her husband hated school as a child, and a central goal for him with their children was to have the kids love school. He was much more concerned about this than about whether the school was going to push them as hard as possible to achieve. It's difficult to be specific on this last piece. But it's useful to acknowledge it's there, since doing so may help you incorporate it into a discussion without just resorting to "I have a gut feeling."

FINAL DECISION

A final meeting is in order. This is not likely to be a decision you can make without talking it through in person. There's a question about to what extent Kendra should be involved in this meeting. There are a lot of questions—logistical, monetary—to which you probably do not want her to be privy. However, part of the value of this process is to separate those out. You shouldn't have arrived at this step unless you felt this plan was feasible. Indeed, you shouldn't have arrived at the previous step, in that case. Now the question on the table is whether this is a good idea, given what you've learned about the schools and how Kendra feels. At a minimum, she should have a voice.

FOLLOW-UP

How you want to follow up here depends a bit on what you decide. If you decide not to switch Kendra's school, it seems useful to revisit the question, perhaps next year. One year of a terrible teacher is a fluke, but multiple years could be further evidence the school isn't the right fit for her. Or maybe you want to leave off revisiting until some transition period—middle school, for example.

If you do switch, I'd argue it still makes sense to revisit the decision. You can go back—this could be a grand experiment that ultimately fails. Private school is expensive and the logistics are complicated, and it would be a shame if you stuck with it even when everyone felt it was not working.

Extracurriculars: Overview

One afternoon, when Penelope was eight and Finn was four, I was chatting with a colleague while waiting for a meeting to begin. We were discussing our kids—his eldest was just a bit older than Finn— and we got onto the topic of extracurricular activities. I'm aware this may have been a mistake.

It turned out that his kid was doing dance, piano, violin, tennis, chess, extra math enrichment, and voice lessons. There may have been more. At some point I felt the panic rising and may have blocked it out.

I think of myself as a fairly confident parent; I try hard to think about my choices and be happy with them. But in that moment I felt, quite simply, distantly behind. Yes, my kids play violin and my son was doing a soccer clinic on Sundays. But it was nothing compared to this schedule. What if my children were missing out on some great passion? What if Finn was really an amazing dancer and I never gave him a chance? When would there be time for all these activities, anyway?

It was lucky the meeting started, or I suspect I might have run out in a panic to start scrutinizing where more activities could fit in the family schedule.

I don't think I am alone. In this age of modern parenting, extracurriculars can feel like an arms race. It's not just the number of activities;

it's also the intensity. The kids who are doing 3 hours of gymnastics a day in the second grade. Travel hockey. Three different wind ensembles for the clarinet player. Not just playing chess, but *chess tournaments*. There is something deeply demoralizing about scrolling through your Instagram to see you friend's five-year-old with a chess trophy while you play a board game called Wash My Underpants with your kids. There are no Wash My Underpants tournaments, and we lost the instructions, so I doubt we are playing correctly, anyway.

But doing intensive extracurriculars can also feel like too much. As I was writing this, someone sent me a quote from Twitter: "I'm next to a family at my son's gym who are talking about how ridiculously over-scheduled their lives are doing kid stuff that their kids don't want to do. If only there were a solution."

Of course, there is a solution: quit. And yet at the same time, if you do quit, is that depriving your child of some crucial life skill or some chance at some great success, better college admissions, a more secure future? If you let your child quit piano because they hate it, are you teaching them they can just quit stuff that they don't like? That seems somehow like a bad message.

Breathe. Breathe. Breathe.

The choice about extracurriculars is ripe for deliberate parenting. Piling on more activities because you're panicked that your child is falling behind isn't a good idea, nor is quitting just because you cannot take the amount of whining about practice time. This is a place to step back and think about what works logistically and about *why* you make the choices you do.

Much of this section will focus on data studies that might be helpful in thinking through the benefits (or costs) of various activity choices. But I think it's useful to start by framing the discussion. In particular, when I was thinking about these issues, I reached out to a number of parents to ask how they thought about extracurricular activities. And I learned that this wasn't a very well-posed question. There are a lot of reasons for your kids to be involved in activities that supersede any of these investment concerns.

First, many, many people told me that extracurriculars were, essentially, a form of childcare. You need after-school coverage for your kids, and one option is chess, or squash, or soccer, or dance. Rather than being a logistical burden, this is a logistical benefit.

Second, nearly everyone I talked to said their kid took swim lessons "so they will not drown."

Third, for many families, religious instruction is an essential part of their out-of-school activities.

In a sense, I want to put all these aside and focus on the more complicated choices that arise when extracurriculars go from being after-school childcare or drowning prevention into more of an "investment" mode. For most of us, this happens much more as our kids get older.

Your four-year-old goes to a once-a-weekend soccer clinic. But if your ten-year-old wants to play soccer, all of a sudden there are three practices a week and all-day weekend tournaments. Your five-year-old practices the violin for 5 minutes a day, a few days a week. But if they stick with it into middle school, all of a sudden there are two weekly ensemble meetings and the expectation of another 45 minutes a day of scales and practice.

My impression is that this has changed somewhat in the past thirty years. As a kid—even an older kid—I remember doing many, many activities but almost none of them in a very serious way. But there has been a slow creep of pre-professionalism into kids' activities. One of my close friends, Hilary Levey Friedman, has written a fascinating book on this (*Playing to Win*), all about the sociology of these changes. Suffice to say, it's harder to be an activity dilettante than it once was.

Whether we like it or not, many extracurriculars in the modern day are a real commitment. Given this, there is value to thinking carefully about the pros and cons of getting involved.

At the outset, one con is extracurriculars interfering with the Big Picture you imagine for your family. If your family plan is to eat dinner together most nights, this may simply limit the possibility of extra activities. If your Big Picture involves one weekend day devoted to family—to religious services, perhaps, or simply to family-only activities—then that will also create limits.

It may be tempting to ignore your Big Picture in the moment, when either your children are pushing you to do something or you're feeling the pressure of falling behind. Don't give in! You developed the Big Picture for a reason. If a firm changed their mission statement every time they felt the wind blowing a different way, they'd likely fail. That doesn't mean your Big Picture should never change to accommodate the varying needs of older children, but it should be a deliberate choice, not something you decide on a whim.

If something fits inside your Big Picture, though, then you want to think more. What are the reasons to do it? When I surveyed parents about why they chose the activities they did, a few things came out:

- Benefits for the body or the mind: sports for exercise, music lessons because of "something about math," chess for spatial reasoning, arts to make you creative, and so on.
- Social benefits: teamwork to build character, value of a new social environment, overall communication of values.
- College admissions: I think this explains itself.

But parents also expressed some reservations here, worries that maybe their reasoning was not grounded in very good evidence. Or that they'd missed some important trade-off. Sports may be good for fitness, but what about concussions?

These claims can be evaluated with data. There is at least some evidence on all these questions to inform these choices.

Oh, and I should say there was one other thing that got quite a lot of mention: the kids enjoyed the activities. This is a good reason to do them! It's not definitive—your kids may enjoy activities that ultimately do not work for your family—and there may be reasons to encourage them to do things even if they do not always enjoy them. But it matters, for sure.

One bad reason for doing activities, I would argue, is to realize your own unfulfilled dreams. Pushing our children to do things we wish we had done, to achieve vicariously through them—this seems unfair. It's easy to say, but this can be hard in the moment. I always wanted to play the violin well; I never had the dedication to actually do it, and my one year of lessons ended poorly. I do worry, sometimes, that I'll push my children harder in this because I wish I had done it. I try not to, but who knows how successful that is. Parenting: not for the faint of heart.

So let's dive in. What does the data say extracurriculars *really* do for your child? As with the last section, we'll start with some key pieces of data, and then bring it back in to an application at the end.

 THE BODY AND THE BRAIN

When I asked parents about their choice of outside school activities, a common response was something like "I make them do sports for exercise and fitness, and music because it's good for the brain." But to what extent do sports really improve fitness? And is music actually good for the brain? And while we are on the topic of the brain, let's pause to think about whether the first of these goals is getting in the way of the second. In particular, sports may be good for the body, but does the possibility of concussions mean there's a trade-off with the brain?

WHAT THE DATA SAYS: THE BODY

There is a lot of research on youth sports and physical health. Most of it focuses on three questions, which I think, conveniently, are probably among the key ones for parents. Does participation in sports prevent obesity? Does it promote exercise? And is it the key to a lifetime of healthy physical activity?

Most of this "body" discussion focuses on sports. Few parents are probably thinking of activities like music and chess as contributing to physical fitness. In my travels I did come across an article observing that chess grandmasters lose a lot of weight during chess tournaments,[1] but under a bit more scrutiny, it seemed like that might be more because they are too nervous to eat when competing than that playing chess burns calories. I think it is safe to say chess might be a good idea for your kid, but not for its physical fitness benefits.

We begin with obesity. Childhood obesity is a growing problem in the US (and elsewhere). The CDC estimates that about 18.5 percent of children ages six to eleven are obese (meaning their BMI is above the 95th percentile on a growth chart).[2] Will playing sports change this?

Before even getting into the data on this, it is worth saying that the basic biological facts make it somewhat unlikely that this matters a lot. In particular, exercise doesn't actually burn that many calories relative to variations in diet. A 60-pound child playing an intense, competitive soccer game for an hour will burn about 280 calories.[3] An hour of baseball would be half that, at best. One soda, a bag of chips after practice, an extra dessert—and those exercise calories are gone (this is also true for adults; it doesn't mean there aren't benefits to exercise, just that its links to weight are complicated).

So it would be surprising (I think) if we saw huge causal effects of playing sports on weight. And indeed, we do not.

Of course, by this point in the book, you shouldn't be surprised to hear that there are *correlations* between obesity and sports participation. Take an example of a study of about six thousand inner-city kids, some who play sports and others who do not.[4] Girls who play sports are less likely to be overweight or obese; for boys, the results are more mixed. But digging into it, you can see clear evidence of selection. Girls who cheerlead are much less likely to be overweight. Boys who play football are much more likely to be overweight. The overall picture points to differences in choices of sports, but probably *not* treatment effects of the sports themselves.

This study is representative of other findings. The correlation between sports participation and weight is mixed in the data.[5] One study notes that kids who participate in sports eat more—more healthy food, but also more junk food. Again, pretty small changes in food intake will negate the calorie loss from even fairly significant exercise.

The correlations between sports and obesity are mixed in their directions, but it's clear that such correlations are hard to learn from. It is not even obvious whether the correlations will be too big or too small. Usually we worry that for "good" behaviors like exercise, if we just compare people who do the activity with those who do not, we'll overstate how beneficial it is. But that's complicated here—for example, kids who are bigger may be more likely to decide to play sports like football where size matters. Because of this, you might actually *understate* the weight loss benefits of sports.

Several school-based interventions look at short-term impacts of sports. This includes a larger one in Switzerland, and a few others.

Generally, these programs show small improvements in areas like body fat and general health, but these are not sustained after the programs end.[6] This suggests that continued improvements in these measures may require continued investment. Short-term interventions may not be the same as long-term changes in physical activity.

In 2013, three economists writing in the *Journal of Health Economics* approached this long-term question by exploiting the fact that US states differ in the amount of physical education required in schools.[7] They argued that the amount of mandated PE is determined largely randomly across states, but if schools required more minutes of PE each week, kids would end up exercising more. These regulations affect students throughout their time in school, so they represent a long-term change in exercise.

These authors found that more PE time lowered obesity for boys in particular. The effects were moderate. An additional hour a week of PE lowered obesity rates by about 5 percentage points (which is large), but only in fifth graders, the oldest group in the data. This may reflect the overall higher rates of obesity in older kids, or the fact that by fifth grade, the students have been exposed to extra PE for more years. Girls did not show much effect at any age. Bottom line: more physical activity probably has some effect on weight, but it is small.

In contrast, the effects of school sports on *exercise* seem to be much more significant.[8] We can see this, for example, in the long-term follow-up of that Swiss study that examined increased physical education in some schools. When the researchers came back a couple of years later, they found that the reductions in fat were not sustained, but the kids in the intervention schools had better aerobic fitness (they had them run—the intervention kids were faster!).[9]

Summary papers on youth sports—not school sports, but those outside of school—echo these results.[10] Being involved in these sports has clear impacts on physical activity, with less clear spillovers to obesity. In the end, diet is much more important than exercise for weight.

Evidence like this Swiss study suggests that gains in fitness may be sustained over some period of time—at least a few years—but what about the long term? One reason you might want your kid to be involved in sports is to encourage a lifelong exercise habit.

Really good, really convincing evidence on this would require long-term follow-up of kids who were *randomly* allocated to different levels of sports participation. For example, you might imagine following up on the children in that study of school PE variation across states. Unfortunately, we do not have anything that approximates this in the data.

What we do have are a couple of studies—mostly in Scandinavian countries—that look at the relationship between adolescent sports participation and physical activity in young adulthood. A representative example is a study from Norway that surveyed people a number of times between the ages of thirteen and twenty-three.[11] At each survey, they were asked about physical activity and participation in "sport clubs." The authors found a significant degree of persistence over time. People who did more sports as teenagers were also more likely to be involved in exercise activities as adults.

Also representative of the literature, this seems to be truer of boys than girls, and the effects are larger for children who joined organized sports at younger ages.

Even reflecting on the large number of similar studies, I'd describe this evidence as suggestive at best. The fact that kids who exercise turn into adults who exercise could be true for a lot of reasons. My younger brother was running 5K races at age five, and he turned into an adult who runs a 2:37 marathon and once attempted a 100-mile race. But this likely reflects an overall general insanity, not that the races he participated in as a child were influential.

It is perhaps frustrating that these "body" topics focus so heavily on weight, with a lesser focus on aerobic fitness. For one thing, it is well known that BMI and other obesity measures are by no means perfect summaries of how "healthy" someone is. And at least for some of us, encouraging our children to be physically active is part of teaching them about how to have a healthy body and lifestyle—probably one that does *not* involve obsessing over specifically how much they weigh.

Beyond this, parents I talked to—especially some with children who had developmental delays—cited activities like dance and gymnastics as important in promoting balance and coordination, and in developing gross motor skills. There are physical therapy–related reasons to think this might help, but little direct evidence. (I did find some literature on dance therapy, but the methods were not sufficiently compelling to bear describing here; suffice to say, it doesn't seem like a magic bullet.)[12]

As with most topics in this book, the data helps us in some areas, but not all.

We do have some evidence on injuries. I'll get much more into concussions in the section on the brain, but kids *can* get injured playing sports. Estimates suggest that there are about 2.6 million ER visits for sports-related injuries each year, and a third of children will get a sports-related injury during their elementary, middle, or high school years.[13] You can't protect your kid from everything, and the fact that they might sprain an ankle may just be the cost of doing business. More worrisome are injuries that reflect overuse—these are more common in kids than adults, since kids are still growing—injuries like ACL tears, "Little League elbow," and stress fractures. Kids who play very intensive sports will hopefully have trainers looking out for them.

But there may simply be a limit to how hard kids should be pushing themselves physically. In researching this, I came across an article titled "Should Children Be Running Ultramarathons?" An ultramarathon is typically 50 or even 100 miles. Some of them are run in the desert, or at high altitude.[14]

The article's conclusion, to paraphrase, was "probably no."

WHAT THE DATA SAYS: THE BRAIN

"Music lessons make you smarter. Kids who play an instrument are better at math." It is almost certain you've heard this somewhere.

It's always hard to know precisely where ideas like this come from, but in this case, one clear contributor is scientific literature on the "Mozart effect." In 1993, three researchers at UC Irvine published a provocative paper in the journal *Nature* that purported to find causal evidence that listening to classical music improves IQ scores.[15]

The authors did a very simple thing. They took thirty-six college students and had them each do three spatial reasoning tasks—scores on these tasks can be translated to IQ test scores. Before each task, the students took a 10-minute break and were exposed to one of three conditions: 10 minutes of Mozart (Sonata for Two Pianos in D major, if you are curious), 10 minutes of a relaxation tape, or 10 minutes of silence. They randomly decided who listened to what, and in the end, they compared the performance of the students who listened to Mozart to the other two groups.

What was most surprising about the results was their *size*. Converted to IQ scores, the data suggested that listening to Mozart, rather than either relaxation or silence, increased IQ by 8 to 9 points! This is an enormous effect—almost a full standard deviation. If that's what you get from just listening to a few minutes of music, imagine what you'd get from *playing* it. At least, that's one interpretation.

This finding was novel, provocative, exciting. The effects are enormous. It's not surprising that the study was published in *Nature*. But it is always smart to be cautious about effects like this. Data can be tricky, and false positive results do happen. One should perhaps be extra cautious about results like this that are so surprising.

And indeed, subsequent attempts to replicate this have not shown the same effects. A 1999 paper summarizing the follow-on literature argues that the true effects are less than a quarter of the size of the original, not reliably statistically significant, and limited to one particular task (a spatial reasoning task involving paper folding and cutting).[16] Moreover, the literature suggests that it may not be Mozart per se, but any kind of enjoyable or exciting music that improves ability on this task.

If you're trying to get your kids a bump in test scores by piping classical music into the car on the way to school, it's unlikely to work out quite as you hope.

But there is a second, much larger body of literature that simply relates kids' participation in music instruction to school performance. The basic fact is that kids who play an instrument or take music lessons in general tend to do better in school.[17] This effect is long term and seems to grow over time: kids who play instruments do better in high school even after you hold constant their grades in elementary school.[18]

But this isn't the same as saying that music instruction *causes* them to do better, and it's even further from saying what some people have suggested to me, which is that playing classical music improves math performance because the two are somehow synergistic in the brain.

To be confident about these kinds of impacts, we'd want to see randomized data. There is a bit of this—mostly from school-based programs that introduce music education.[19] One summary paper notes five of these experiments: three showed modest positive effects on school achievement; two showed no effects. Given the bias toward publishing positive effects in a case like this, this strikes me as not a fantastic ratio.

On the other hand, we *do* know that playing an instrument causes changes in the brain. Some of the more interesting studies of brain plasticity—the idea that what happens in the brain is affected by what you do—focus on musicians.[20] The brains of violin and piano players look different, for example, perhaps reflecting the more coordinated use of the two hands in violin versus the two hands working separately on the piano keys.

It can be tempting to put a lot of weight on these brain studies, to conclude that they mean that music matters in a particular way, but in fact *everything* we do changes our brain. We have other studies showing that spatially connected areas of the brain are strengthened by playing *Tetris*, for example. Noting that playing the cello increases white matter in some part of the brain is not the same as saying it is singularly good for math test scores.

In the end, I think it's likely that nearly all the links between music and academic achievement are selection—specifically, other differences in family background or personality between kids who play music and those who do not—rather than some treatment effect of music. This is different from saying that there isn't some value in having a kid play an instrument (more on social groups to come), but if you are looking for musical education per se to improve math test scores, I'd look elsewhere.

The same is likely true of most extracurriculars. If you dig deeply, you'll find all kinds of correlations. Kids who do drama, music, art, chess club—they probably all do relatively well in school. But you're not likely to find anything in the data to point to causality there.

Concussions

We cannot leave a discussion of the brain without visiting the evidence on concussions.

As a child of the 1980s, it is hard for me to believe how much our thinking about head injuries has evolved. When I was a kid, I do not remember ever discussing concussions. (To be fair, I wasn't the world's greatest athlete and you do not get concussions in cross-country running. But my brothers did lots of sports!) When I learned to ski, there was no helmet in place. The idea, I think, would have been seen as ludicrous. And forget bike helmets.

Concussion concerns are now everywhere, and probably for good reason. The most oft-discussed culprit is football. Concussions in football are common and have, in the past, probably been too frequently ignored. Repeated concussions, playing with a concussion, and getting a second concussion on top of the first all have quite bad consequences for the brain. Autopsies of former professional football players have consistently shown evidence of traumatic brain injury, evidence that would be consistent with violent trauma, and that in at least some cases seems to have influenced behavior off the field.

Most of the discussion of this is in the context of the NFL, but there is a serious debate in some circles about the ethics of youth football, with some towns and school districts raising the minimum age requirement for play. But not everyone agrees with this—there are arguments that these concerns are overblown, and that a worry over injuries and concussions will mean fewer kids in sports, which may be a loss to them for other reasons.[21]

We can start with the basic question: What is the big deal about concussions? Are they really something to worry about?

Broadly, yes. A variety of evidence suggests that concussions—especially repeated concussions and those that happen in succession before earlier ones have healed—*can* have long-term negative effects on health.[22] These consequences include cognitive problems and mental health issues. This doesn't mean that every concussion leads to serious health issues. Many—the vast majority—have no detectable long-term consequences. And it's hard to know what makes one person's experience worse than another, partly because our understanding of what makes one concussion worse than another is not especially good.[23] If you've ever had a concussion, you probably relate to this. It's really hard for even the best doctors to predict what it will be like.

What we do have is reasonable evidence—much of it from football players—that repeated concussions can leave detectable marks. Brain changes appear even in nonprofessional football players.[24] There seem to be some effects related to how long players have been involved in the sport—football players who started playing at younger ages have more problems than those who started older—which may reflect the fact that more time playing means more concussions, or it could reflect larger impacts of concussions in younger brains.[25]

Putting this together, I think a nuanced reading of the data would say that concussions are something to be careful about, and if your child does have one, the most important thing is to react appropriately—with rest, no activity resumption until they are better, etc. (You may also want to keep in mind that it's possible to overreact to a single concussion. The vast, vast majority of kids who get a concussion will be completely fine.)

So accepting that concussions are a concern, where does that leave youth sports? Are there particular sports you'd want to avoid?

Yes, it is true that football is a significant concussion culprit. But it is not alone. The following graph shows estimates of concussion rates by sport for 2012–2015. This data is based on injury reports collected from a nationally representative group of high schools.[26]

Not surprisingly, football has the highest concussion rates: about 9 concussions on average for every 10,000 athlete exposures (that's 10,000 games, practices, etc.). But soccer—especially girls' soccer—is nearly as high. Boys' soccer, boys' wrestling, and girls' basketball also have high rates of concussion.

Researchers (full disclosure: this next paper is by my dad) analyzing a fuller sample of college sports also pointed to soccer, football, and wrestling as high risk. To these they added basketball, lacrosse, and ice hockey. Low-risk sports include running, baseball, tennis, and—lowest risk of all—swimming.[27]

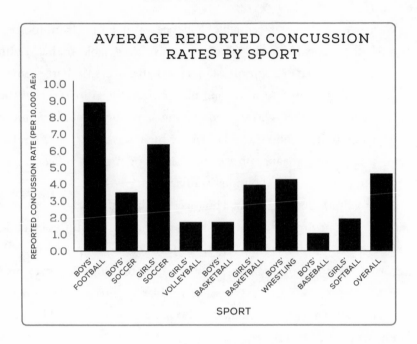

The fairly consistent finding that soccer has a high concussion risk may be somewhat surprising, given that soccer is primarily played with the feet. The issue seems to be heading; the force and angle of repeated heading may produce concussions and concussion-like experiences.[28] More serious soccer players, as adults, show some of the same neurodegenerative effects as football players.[29] As with football, there is some disagreement in this space; some researchers have argued that the structure of the studies is biased toward finding neurological problems in soccer players in particular.[30] It's an evolving area, and I suspect it's not likely to be fully resolved anytime soon.

Where does all this leave you as a parent? I've had conversations with parents who wouldn't ever let their children play any concussion-risk sports. Some of these parents had a mental (or physical) list of off-limit sports. There are others who are happy to let their kids, say, play soccer until they introduce heading, or ice hockey until kids start to body check (bash other kids into the walls or to the ice). And still others have decided that this isn't their primary concern, that they are comfortable with soccer or football or other sports, as long as concussions get careful attention if they do arise.

Any of these stances seem reasonable. But, as always, *talk* about it. Here data may help frame a discussion with your child. Let's say your eleven-year-old has played soccer since they were five, but now you have decided the risk of concussion from heading is too great, and you want her to focus on swimming or track or tennis. Depending on your child, you may get a lot farther by showing her some of this evidence and talking about your concerns, then coming up with a plan together, rather than imposing a ban on soccer with little explanation. After all, it is her brain, so she should probably have at least some say in it.

The (Data) Bottom Line

- Youth sports seem to have some small impacts on long-run sports participation, but no evident effects on being overweight or obese.
- There is no good evidence that learning to play music actually enhances brain function.
- Concussions are serious, and some sports (football, girls' soccer) carry more significant risks for concussion than others.

 # CHARACTER-BUILDING THROUGH EXTRACURRICULARS

When she started kindergarten, Penelope asked to play the violin. (When I later asked her why—after she had learned it was actually a lot of work—she said she had seen an older kid with a violin case, and thought the case looked neat.)

Befitting my slightly tiger-parent tendencies, I found her a teacher immediately. Jesse was a bit skeptical. He and I had both taken a number of years of failed piano lessons. Presumably he was remembering, as I was, the experience of an exasperated teacher listening and saying, "Did you practice *at all* this week?"

"She can try," he told me. "But if she wants to quit, we're not going to force her to keep going."

But then one week, he happened to come with us to the music school where her lessons were held, a large (for Rhode Island) complex about 10 minutes from our house, which on Saturday mornings was filled with kids taking lessons, participating in ensembles, playing in the orchestra. He took one look at the groups of middle school students sitting around in the hallway tuning their instruments and announced, "She can never quit."

What he saw in that moment—I think—was the way this activity could deliver a social group, an identity, outside of school. He saw a set of peers that might be a crucial escape during a time—say, middle school—when almost no one feels like they fit in. He saw a place Penelope could build confidence in her ability to do something, could strive to achieve something separate from academics.

He didn't see a path to Carnegie Hall or even, apropos of the last chapter, a path to better grades. What he saw was a path to Penelope finding her place, to being happy.

I think this is sometimes missed in the current "pre-professional" extracurricular environment. But in fact, the idea that out-of-school activities can deliver socioemotional benefits shouldn't be ignored. There could be possible impacts on anxiety or depression, or on general happiness, and, extending it, possible effects on the nebulous "character" that people link to, say, Boy Scouts.

Do extracurriculars make you happy?

WHAT THE DATA SAYS:
SOCIOEMOTIONAL BENEFITS

The evidence on this question largely comes from psychology and sociology.

I will be honest: economists are traditionally somewhat skeptical of the other social sciences. Chalk it up to cross-field academic jealousy, or disagreements about methods, or whatever you want; the fact remains, we do not always get along. Socialized as I am inside the world of economics, I'm not immune from this skepticism, even if some of my best friends are sociologists and psychologists (hi, Hilary and Jane!).

And it is true that there are important concerns about estimating causal impacts of extracurriculars on child outcomes. Families whose children do more extracurricular activities tend to be different in other ways—wealthier, for example, and better educated—which are hard to fully control for. However, in this case, the *framework* brought to these problems is especially useful. Specifically, I would call out two approaches.

The first is something called the developmental-ecological model of development, which owes its origins to a researcher named Urie Bronfenbrenner, who wrote on this beginning in the 1970s. Bronfenbrenner was a psychologist, although some of the follow-up empirical work on extracurriculars is written in the realm of sociology.

To greatly paraphrase, the theory posits that children (and people in general) are shaped by their environment, including their immediate "microsystem" environment (family, peers, etc.) and the "macrosystem" (the country, global politics, and so on). To think about how children develop in any domain, then, you need to think about the experiences they have and who they have them with. Under this theory, it is inevitable that the activities kids engage in will influence their emotional development.

The second theory is on belonging, originated (in large part) in a 1995 paper by Roy Baumeister and Mark Leary called "The Need to Belong."[31] The paper presents a case for the importance of belonging—feeling that one is part of a group—in terms of influencing emotional well-being and cognitive processes.

So putting these together: People care about belonging—it makes them happy and better functioning—and who you interact with matters for your development. I think this is probably obvious from our lived experiences. Feeling like you fit somewhere really matters. I vividly remember the first time I really felt like I belonged in a social group. (It was at a camp where I did math all day. Yes, I know, don't judge me.) It was a transformative experience for my confidence, for my sense of self. I'm guessing this is resonant for many of you (maybe not *specifically* the math camp part).

The combination of theory and lived experience suggests that these experiences may well matter for happiness.

There is a huge amount of correlational data showing that extracurriculars are generally associated with good socioemotional outcomes for kids. This includes, for example, data from Michigan showing that students who were engaged in activities (sports, drama, etc.) in middle school were less likely to exhibit risky behaviors like drinking when they were in high school.[32]

A 2012 review paper focuses on fifty-two studies published between 2005 and 2010. The results are not uniform, but in general they seem to point to better social adaptation, less depression, and fewer risk behaviors among kids who do out-of-school activities.[33] Researchers have even dug into the question of whether you can do too much—are "overscheduled" kids less happy? Broadly, the correlational data seems to say no— even kids who engage in more than 20 hours of activities a week show better outcomes than those who do none.[34] (This is different from saying that you get *more* benefits from doing more, which the data doesn't support—thank goodness.)

But of course this data is all correlations. Even with our strong prior belief that this matters, it's hard to draw sound conclusions from these results. We worry, as usual, that kids who do extracurriculars differ in other ways. In this case, we should probably also worry about "reverse causality"—if a kid is depressed or socially anxious, they may be less likely to engage in activities, so it's the mental health issues that cause the lack of engagement, not the other way around.

Helpfully, there is some randomized data on extracurriculars coming out of Finland. The Finns actually did an experiment where they incorporated extracurriculars into the school day at some schools and not at others. It's not a perfect experiment for speaking to our current lived experience, in part because the results of putting activities *in* the school day may be different, and in part because the Finnish context may be different, but I'd argue we can still learn something.[35]

The study showed that the "integrated school day" (this is their term) had good effects on socioemotional health for kids. In the following graph I show the effects of the program on four behavioral health measures; the treatment group score is solid (these are the kids who participated in the extracurriculars), and the control group is in stripes. In all four measures, a higher score is worse—it reflects more problems—and since the program is randomized, we are confident that *before* the program, the two groups were equal. Afterward, they were not.

The most striking results are on "internalizing behaviors"—depression and social anxiety. Kids in the schools that got the integrated extracurricular programming showed lower scores on these scales—in other words, less depression and social anxiety. They were also slightly better on adaptive behaviors. Interestingly, they did not show better scores on externalizing behavior, which you can think of as "acting out." This result echoes some of the correlations as well. Extracurriculars—sports in particular—sometimes appear to worsen, or at least not improve, external behavior problems. If you're a fan of professional sports, this will not shock you.

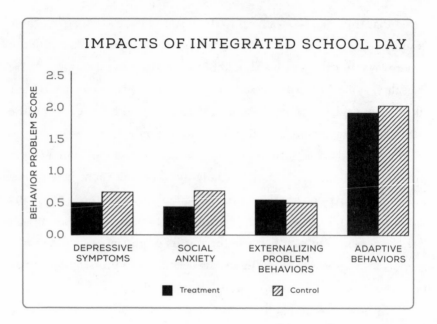

IMPACTS OF INTEGRATED SCHOOL DAY

Putting this randomized evidence together with the huge number of correlations we see in other papers, non-school extracurricular activities do seem to have some socioemotional benefits for kids.

A natural follow-up question is whether some activities are "better" than others. Here our evidence is a bit less complete, in part simply because fewer papers focus on just one extracurricular activity. In practice, most of the evidence is about sports, and we do see that kids who engage in sports show less social anxiety and better adaptation.[36]

A few scattered studies are specific to other activities. For example, one from 2015 focuses on character development in the Boy Scouts and shows that on some measures, like "helpfulness" and "cheerfulness," boys who are active in the Scouts improve more over time than those who do not.[37]

But by and large, it seems like the benefits accrue independent of what you are doing. Notably, the Finnish schools in the randomized study mentioned earlier offered a wide variety of activities (team sports, cooking, music), and the authors of the study did not suggest that one was obviously "better" than another.

In thinking about the choice of activity, it may be useful to circle back to the theory, and in particular to the theory on the influence of peers. We *know* that children's peers matter in general; this is especially true in adolescence. The correlations in the data—even putting aside causality—tell us that the kids who are doing extracurricular activities tend to be less depressed and anxious and engage in fewer "antisocial" behaviors. When your kid engages with peers in these activities, their peer group (at least in this particular part of their day) is positively selected on these dimensions.

These positive outcomes do not, however, imply that your child needs to engage in hours per day of pre-professional ballet dancing or volleyball to reap the socioemotional benefits. The Finnish study showed improvements in mental health from a fairly light-touch intervention, which, effectively, introduced clubs at school three days a week. Most of the correlational evidence on this focuses on kids who do, say, a few hours of an out-of-school activity per week.

So don't feel the need to overdo the extracurricular activities. But do consider them. You may find a happier child, even if Carnegie Hall or the Junior Olympics remain stubbornly out of reach.

The (Data) Bottom Line

- Participation in extracurricular activities does seem to deliver some socioemotional benefits. This may be a result of an increased feeling of "belonging."
- Your child does not need to engage in pre-professional levels of engagement in these activities to deliver these benefits.

COLLEGE ADMISSIONS

I will be honest: I am reluctant to even write this section. For one thing, I do not want to acknowledge that my children will ever leave me to go to college. Finn's future plan (as of this writing) is to live in my house and open a restaurant using all my cookbooks. Sign me up.

But also, there seems something faintly wrong about making elementary school (or even middle school) decisions with college in mind. A lot of things happen between when your child is seven and when they are eighteen, many of which will influence their path. Making choices about after-school activities for a six-year-old because you think extracurriculars will help them get into your flagship state school? That's a lot of pressure on your kid. So a piece of me wants to end here, and say that I will leave college for another book (actually, lots of books have been written on how to get your child into college).

But among some parents I spoke to, there was a suggestion that concerns about college play a role in extracurricular choice. Should they?

First, it is useful to break down what "this might help with college admissions" really means. It could mean two things: The first is that your child might literally be recruited to college on the basis of the activity. The second is that engaging in this activity could make them a more well-rounded and appealing applicant.

WHAT THE DATA SAYS: RECRUITED ATHLETICS

Is your child likely to be recruited to a top school on the basis of their extracurricular achievement? Most universities do a fair amount of sports recruiting. Even very academically oriented schools admit a surprising number of students each year to fill out their team rosters for football, tennis, swimming, lacrosse, etc. And for these students, it's true that their participation in a sport is key to their admission to college. Effectively, coaches will identify athletes they want and work with the admissions office to get those students admitted. For an even smaller number of these select students, there may be a break in tuition in the form of sports scholarships.

But this is a really, really small number. In a given year, about 280,000 five-year-olds play youth soccer in the US. There are about 500 NCAA Division I soccer teams, each of which fields maybe 25 players, so about 8 per college year. That means about 4,000 students per year will play Division I soccer. Not all of those athletes are "recruited," of course, but even if they were, that would mean about 1.5 percent of youth soccer players end up playing Division I soccer. This is likely a huge overestimate as well, given the number of non-American players on these teams.

If you think you'll use soccer to, say, get into an Ivy League school, you're down to even smaller numbers. Perhaps 150 students a year will be recruited to play soccer for Ivy League teams.

Obviously, these calculations do not, in fact, mean your child has a precisely 1 in 2,000 chance of playing soccer for Yale or Princeton. What I think they illustrate is simply that these probabilities are so small—and so uncertain!—that it may not make sense to consider them when making choices during elementary school.

WHAT THE DATA SAYS: BEING WELL-ROUNDED

What about the idea that engaging in extracurriculars is key to being a well-rounded and appealing candidate for college admissions?

This is extremely difficult to evaluate since, for reasons that are probably obvious, colleges tend to be a bit tight-fisted with the criteria they use for admissions. Clearly, nonacademic pursuits play some role, but it is hard to know precisely what. At the same time, this is a rapidly evolving landscape. Even if we understood precisely what matters for admissions now, we obviously can't know what will matter in 2033 when your now five-year-old is applying.

Most of what we do know about admissions decisions comes from published interviews with admissions officers, which are limited, but not impossible to find. In 2009, Leslie Killgore wrote an excellent article for *The Review of Higher Education* in which she reported on interviews with admissions staff at seventeen elite universities.[38]

By and large, the admissions officers were clear that academic performance comes first in their evaluations. Outside of athlete recruitment, any type of extracurricular activity takes a back seat to schoolwork. When they do get into extracurricular activities, Killgore sums up the general picture with the following observation: "An admissions officer at one Ivy League college notes, 'My feeling as an evaluator is that I want to see that in some way, shape, or form a student has developed a genuine interest and has pursued that interest and has had an impact. And has learned and changed because of that experience.'"

In other words, they are looking for evidence of some focused out-of-school engagement (which, at least according to some of the quotes in the article, could be work or family responsibilities rather than organized clubs or sports).

Looking at this from the standpoint of an elementary school parent, I would say at most—AT MOST—it suggests having an eye on extracurricular activities when your child is headed toward high school. But again, this is so far in the future and so uncertain that it falls into the realm of things we should try not to think about. There may well be good reasons to enroll your child in ballet or gymnastics or trumpet. But you should not do it because Stanford's orchestra is traditionally short on trumpet players.

THE SUMMER

Logistics are the bane of summer for many parents. Good news! Part II of the book will help, and a good task management system can rescue you.

However, the questions do not stop at logistics. Let's say camp is part of your summer plans. You've got to make a choice about which camps you actually want your child to attend. Should you really care about whether they go to one camp or another? Is there something profound that kids are supposed to get out of the summer that they'll miss if you do not think this through?

There are—obviously—limits to what we can imagine learning here. If you're looking for some secret formula to tell you whether lacrosse camp or tennis camp is causally linked with being a more successful adult, you'll be sorely disappointed. But the data can be part of the conversation.

In the case of the summer, the data helps us with two things. First, there is a tremendous amount of evidence on the value of specialized (usually, but not always, sleepaway) camp for certain groups of kids. Extrapolating from this may actually help structure some of your thinking on what benefits you might imagine for your kid.

Second, we can look into the dreaded "summer melt" of reading and math skills and the question of just how worried you should be about it.

Before getting into this data, let's acknowledge the very significant financial considerations here. Camp can be very, very expensive. The day camp in your town may be a good deal, but eight weeks at Sleepaway Camp FancyPants in Maine is definitely not. It is useful to review this, but when you get to choosing, the financial piece will have to come first.

This may be an opportunity to have some conversations about financial issues with your children. Kids can understand that resources are limited. It's a hard set of conversations to have, but it may be healthy to simply explain that some options are out of reach.

It may also be an opportunity to start working on financial literacy with your kids and including them in thinking through financial trade-offs. I spoke to one mother whose son really, really loved a summer music camp that was just on the edge of what they could afford. They worked together to think about how they could make it possible for their family—are there scholarships, for example, or are there other activities they could cut out to make this happen? Kids can understand this earlier than you might think, and they can be part of the solution.

WHAT THE DATA SAYS: SUMMER CAMP AND THE VALUE OF BELONGING

Perhaps the largest research study of the impact of camp on kids involved 5,000 kids at about 80 camps (30 percent day camps, the rest sleepaway). After the camps ended, the campers (and their parents) were surveyed about their experience. Ninety-two percent responded yes when asked whether camp "helped me feel good about myself"; 70 percent of parents said their child's self-confidence improved.[39] There were all kinds of other positive results, too: improved independence, self-esteem, etc.

Sounds great, right? There are just two problems. First, it's a bit hard to learn from a study that surveys people after an experience like this and just asks them if they liked it; among other problems, the people who respond to your survey are a lot more likely to be those who were happy with their experience!

Second, this study was financed by the American Camp Association, a group that provides a lot of helpful services to camps and parents but is not exactly nonpartisan on this subject. Does this necessarily mean that the study is wrong? Of course not. But just like studies of, say, the health benefits of chia seeds that are financed by the chia seed industry, we may want to approach this with a degree of skepticism.

But these results are echoed by other—less partisan—evidence, most of which focuses on children with health issues. One example is a 2005 study of thirty-four children with cancer who attended an oncology summer camp.[40] At the end of camp, the participants reported feeling more similar to their camp peers than their school peers, and there was a resulting improvement in "psychosocial" outcomes—self-acceptance improved, loneliness declined.

We see similar results for kids with many other conditions, including diabetes (this result goes back to the 1970s),[41] visual impairments,[42] obesity,[43] and general pediatric medical issues.[44] In all these cases, attending a camp with children who had a similar condition seemed to increase campers' self-esteem and self-acceptance. In the case of obesity, there was also some weight loss associated with camp attendance.

These results extend to kids who may feel isolated for other reasons. In particular, there are some studies of the socioemotional effects of kids attending an academic summer camp for "gifted" children (i.e., they took a test to get into the camp).[45] One paper interviewed kids at the start and end of a three-week camp experience. One of their main outcomes was measures of "self-concept": Basically, do you feel confident in who you are, what you like, and what you are good at? Are you comfortable in your own skin?

The authors found improvements in social self-concept (feelings about the ability to be comfortable socially) and emotional stability. They also looked to see if the children decreased their sense of academic self-concept, on the theory that maybe the self-comparisons would work in the other direction on academics, but found no change.

(In the spirit of transparency, I feel I should disclose here that I'm biased toward these results since a camp like this was pretty much the only saving grace of my otherwise awful middle school experience. And it did, indeed, improve my "self-concept," if only briefly, before it was crushed again by the true horror that is eighth grade.)

This literature really focuses on kids who are "marginalized" in some way—especially socially—and it seems clear that they benefit from a social grouping concentrated with kids "like them." In a sense, this seems pretty similar to what the data says about the social benefits of extracurricular activities. Camp is another way to provide a social group outside of school.

Is there a lesson about choosing a camp here? My read is probably yes, if your child is struggling a bit socially. Camp may be a chance for them to experience a different peer group, to realize the world is bigger than the social dynamics of their classroom. It isn't clear that the camp needs to be specialized in some way; it may be enough to simply introduce a different set of peers.

A Note on Sleepaway Camp

Sleepaway camp is its own special thing. For some people, this was a central formative experience in their lives. For others, it was an opportunity to have someone write on your bed with shaving cream and do some crafts in the woods. Most of the literature I've cited about the benefits of camp does focus on sleepaway camp, so there is clearly something about the immersive nature of this experience that may reinforce some of the benefits.

But it's also scary to send your kid away to camp! For many parents, this experience will be the first time their child is away for an extended period, and for many kids, this is the first prolonged period away from their parents. It's hard not to wonder how your kid will survive without you.

And indeed, things at camp will not exactly replicate your household. Among the academic papers I read in writing this book, one of my favorites was a 1969 analysis of toothbrushing behavior among ten- to twelve-year-old boys at summer camp.[46] The authors found that toothbrushing was rare, even with reminders, but that if toothbrushing was made a requirement for swimming, the boys were more likely to do it. (The behavior returned to its previous low level when the swim contingency was removed.)

So, your kid may not reliably brush their teeth. And I think we can surmise that they'll probably eat more junk food than you allow, and stay up later.

Will they also be sad and homesick? It seems to depend a bit on the kid. A body of literature in psychology focuses on whether kids are more likely to be homesick if they have poor parental attachment, but it doesn't seem to find much.[47] Most kids miss home to some extent, and homesickness does vary across kids, with younger children and those who have not been away before suffering more.[48] Some people argue that this is good practice for going to college and living alone, with the implicit suggestion that if your kid is never away, they'll have even more trouble adjusting to these steps later in life. But that's really all speculation. Beware: This literature has a whiff of "mom-shaming" to it. There is a lot of focus on the various ways you can mother badly and leave your kid insecurely attached.

There are plenty of evidence-based ways to deal with homesickness in kids (practice time away from home, counseling at camp, supportive caregivers, explicit coping instructions).[49] If you're really worried about this, but you still feel sleepaway camp is important for your child, try to find a camp that provides good support.

WHAT THE DATA SAYS:
SUMMER SCHOOL

Near the end of the year, a sign typically appears by the exit at my kids' school with a message about the dreaded "summer melt."

"Did you know kids can lose up to a full grade level in reading over the summer?"

"Summer is for Reading! Do you have a reading plan?"

And so on.

Math is not neglected. As early as kindergarten, we went home for the summer with a packet of first-grade math prep, and a promise of a gumball if it was returned completed. (Spoiler alert: You can get the gumball even if you do not complete the packet.)

Why all the focus on this? The source seems to be a push in the 1980s and 1990s to recognize "summer learning loss." The big player in this research is a Duke University psychology professor named Harris Cooper, whom we actually met earlier, in the chapter on homework. This guy is every kid's worst nightmare. He has built his (very successful) career on the idea that homework is great, and you've got to do it over the summer, too.

In a 1996 review article titled "The Effects of Summer Vacation on Achievement Test Scores," Cooper and his coauthors looked at how academic skills evolve during the summer.[50] They found evidence supporting the idea of summer melt: kids have lower test scores at the start of the new school year than at the end of the previous one. This seems to be more true in math than in reading, and with things like calculations and spelling than with more problem-solving-oriented skills. (Read: It's easy to forget the multiplication tables over the summer but harder to forget how to think.)

Summer learning loss has become a policy issue because it seems to affect some groups more than others. More specifically, low-income students seem to lose more over the summer than their higher-income peers. Some of the literature from the 1980s and 1990s focuses on the possibility that this summer period is *the key* to understanding why low-income students fall behind in school.[51] Maybe any one summer isn't so important, but adding this inequality together over a whole school career may mean large differences in total learning. (During the COVID-19 pandemic this issue became increasingly salient as kids were out of school for a much longer period. That episode is still too recent to learn from.)

The more recent evidence on this isn't as stark as the earlier data. In 2019, a researcher using testing data on 3.4 million children—a much larger sample than previously available—argued that although there is evidence of summer learning loss, it is relatively small and doesn't affect everyone.[52] The data here is useful because it comes from consistent, computerized assessments; kids were tested before school ended in the spring and then when they returned in the fall. And since these tests were given frequently, researchers could actually measure out *months* of learning, and precisely estimate how many "learning months" were lost over the summer.

The results showed that there was, on average, some summer learning loss. For example, between kindergarten and first grade, the average kid lost about 1.5 months of learning over the summer. This loss was a bit larger in older grades, up to even a little over two months between fifth and sixth grades. But this average masks a huge range. For the kindergarten-to-first-grade transition, kids ranged from a *loss* of four months to a *gain* of two months. This is a huge difference—now imagine it magnified over many years of schooling.

Overall, the data showed that 60 to 75 percent of kids lost some learning during the summer (this implies that 25 to 40 percent of students gained some learning). In line with the earlier data, the authors found that lower-income students lost more learning, but this effect was very small. Less than 1 percent of the variation in summer learning loss is explained by socioeconomic factors. This doesn't mean that these factors aren't important, but they seem less important than earlier studies suggested.

The author of this paper actually found that what is most predictive of summer learning loss is school-year learning *gain*. That is, the size of the gain from the fall to the spring of the previous year predicts the size of the loss over the summer: the bigger the gain, the bigger (on average) the subsequent loss. How to interpret this is not completely clear. In looking more closely at the evidence, I think it reflects noise in the test measurement.

These tests aren't perfect; as with any testing tool, sometimes kids have a good day, sometimes a bad day. There's construction noise, their toe hurts, whatever. On average, this washes out. But for an individual kid, an especially good day in the spring will be reflected in a seemingly large gain from the fall. But since it was a surprisingly good day, there is no reason to think it would be repeated the next fall, so it will look like a big loss over the summer. But really, it's all just the good spring testing day. The reverse is true of kids who have a bad testing day in the spring.

(Technically, we call this "regression to the mean," and from the standpoint of understanding what happens on average, this is irrelevant. But please excuse my nerd-out. Thanks.)

To return to the question at hand: Is there summer melt? Some, yes. Is it something we should be actively panicking about? Probably not.

What if you are panicking about it even though I just said not to? Or what if instead of worrying about summer melt, you want to encourage summer gain? This could reflect a worry that your child is behind in some area, or a desire to advance them ahead.

Perhaps not surprising given the conclusions about "extra school" in chapter 8, it does seem like summer school or summer tutoring can move kids forward (this seems to apply both to remedial school and where the desire is to push for more advancement).[53]

Yes, you can use the summer for reading prep or math advancement or other skill development. But it's possible that you'll decide summer is better suited for socioemotional development, or learning to build a fire, or fending off coyotes in the woods. These are different skills than you learn in school, but they aren't obviously less valuable.

For example, there are coyotes roaming my Providence neighborhood all the time; all the math worksheets in the world aren't going to deal with that problem.

The (Data) Bottom Line

- The evidence suggests summer camp can promote a "sense of belonging" among kids, especially kids who are more isolated in various ways.
- Most kids who go to sleepaway camp are homesick, but this is more extreme in the first year than in later years.
- Summer melt is a real thing: kids lose some learning over the summer. Tutoring can help maintain (or advance) their academic skills, but at the cost of time spent doing other things. There are always costs.

Application

Sleepaway Camp

Your eldest, Amanda, is in third grade. One day, she arrives home from school and announces that Pamela from her class is going to sleepaway camp this summer, and she wants to go, too.

In your head: *Absolutely not, you're still way too young to be away from me at all.* As a single parent, you keep your kids close.

Out loud: "Hmm, let's talk about it later. Can you help me set the table?"

You hope she will forget. She does not. She raises the question again a week later. "Have you decided about sleepaway camp yet?"

You bring it up with your two closest friends—is this an insane idea? One of them comes back with "Wow, she's so young!" The other says she spent the entire summer away at camp every summer starting after third grade, so it seems like the perfect time to her. Plus, it was "very formative." Whatever that means.

Maybe there would be some value? Time for the decision process.

FRAME THE QUESTION

The basic question here is pretty simple: Should Amanda go to sleepaway camp? Wrapped up in this, though, is a more detailed set of logistical and other questions.

One question is budget: Can you afford this? A second is time and logistics: Can you fit this in this summer? How many weeks would be ideal? Do you want to think about the entire summer, or just a few weeks?

In addition, at this stage it likely makes sense to engage Amanda and ask her to really think about whether this is something she wants. A nine-year-old is old enough to participate here. If camp is financially feasible and logistically possible, sit Amanda down for a discussion. Invite her to a meeting. Make an agenda! Help her understand what camp would involve—being away, sleeping in a bunk, whatever—and try to figure out if she really wants to do it. Maybe look at the camp's website together.

The goal of this process should be to figure out, first, if camp is something Amanda really wants to do when faced with the reality of it. And second, to better understand what kind of camp, how many weeks, where. As you will learn in the fact-finding step, there are a million camps—you need some parameters to choose one, or you'll go insane.

FACT-FIND

For this choice, the main evidence gathering you need to do is to determine which summer camp is the right one. There are so many! They range from "regular" summer camp (hang around outside, eat marshmallows, canoe) to math camp to music camp to art camp etc., and within these broad categories, there are a million variations. And once you've picked a few, there is further information to gather: Tents or cabins? How long are the sessions? Is the camp coed?

We know one big value to sleepaway camp is that it gives kids a sense of belonging, a new social scene. How important this is for your child depends a lot on your particular kid. If one of the benefits for Amanda is a new social environment—if she is struggling socially at school, or feels like she doesn't fit in well—one of the considerations should be what kind of social group *will* she thrive in? Is there a way camp can facilitate this?

Or maybe this is the furthest consideration from your mind, and you see this just as an opportunity for some good old-fashioned outdoor fun time.

As a social scientist, my only other advice for this choice is to (as much as possible) try to talk to parents of current and recent campers to learn more about the camp. The key is not just to find out if the kids like the camp—indeed, since mostly you'll get connected to these people through the camp, they will generally be very positive. I think the biggest value is to find out if the other parents and kids are "like you." Does it seem like an environment they value will work for your family?

On top of the camps themselves, there is a bit more logistics gathering to do here, too. Can you make the exact camp session dates work? Is there space? (When my daughter first asked about this, it was January; turns out, a lot of camps fill up in October. Oops.)

FINAL DECISION

Maybe you're down to two camps, or maybe one has emerged victorious. It's time for a last chat with Amanda. Look at the details with her. Talk through the logistics. Does she really want to do this? Will it be fun? Is it better to wait?

Make the choice, and pull the trigger (or not!).

FOLLOW-UP

Remember to revisit! If Amanda does go to camp, find a time in the fall to discuss how it went, with a little distance. Does she want to go again? To the same place? A different place? More time, or less? Pro tip: Don't have this conversation on the way home from camp.

And if she didn't go, find a time to follow up anyway. Maybe she wants to go next year?

Feelings: Overview

In the academic literature on what's best for kids, there is an overwhelming focus on test scores. You'd be forgiven for thinking, then, that society's main focus is producing optimized test-score machines wrapped in small-people packaging.

School performance is top of mind for many parents; we want our kids to do well academically, if for no other reason than it creates more opportunities for them. But it is also pretty clearly true that this is not the only thing we want for our children. I remember having a conversation with a close friend about his son, who was two or three at the time. The friend remarked that before his son arrived, he thought he would be very focused on academic achievement. But faced with the reality of this little person, he said, "I just want him to be happy."

I just want him to be happy.

If your kid *is* happy, it is easy to take it for granted. Of course they're happy; they're a kid. And once you take this for granted, it's natural to start focusing on other things—let's call them "performance metrics." However, the moment your kid is not happy—and I don't mean, like, mad that you took away dessert, but actually struggling—this other focus tends to melt away. Hearing a kid explain that they have no friends, or that someone is bullying them, or that they are too weird for school can be so much worse than anything academic.

The flip side of "Is my kid happy?" is "Are they making others happy?" Is my kid nice? Are they thinking about and supporting other kids? I don't want my child to be bullied, but I also very much do not want them to be the bully.

Data-based analyses tend to focus on test scores because *this is what we can measure.* We have reams of data. We can compare over time, we can run our fancy regression models, we can make claims about causality. When it comes to feelings, to "socioemotional" outcomes, it is harder to measure what we care about even for one child, let alone on a broad scale we could analyze formally. Figuring out if kids are happy and nice is a bit like Supreme Court justice Potter Stewart's iconic definition of obscenity: "I know it when I see it." Which is different from being able to define it on a survey.

But all is not lost. Within the past thirty years, and especially within the last ten or fifteen, there has been more academic work focusing on these topics. And while the data will not be perfect (it never is, anyway), there is enough to say something on at least two fronts.

First, how do we raise kids to be nice, to effectively interact with others? And second, how do we raise them to be confident, to be happy? I'll note in the second set of questions that the focus isn't—shouldn't be—on how to raise kids who are popular. You can forget about that. Kids will be who they are socially for the most part; the question is how to help them be confident and happy in their own skin.

 ## INTERACTING WITH OTHERS

"How was your day, Mom?"

"Um, okay. I'm having some conflict with someone and I'm really,

really mad about it. I kind of lost my temper and I wish I hadn't done that."

"Maybe I can help!"

"How?"

"Okay, so when you feel like you are going to yell, start by closing your eyes and taking a deep breath. In . . . out. And then ask yourself, 'Will it make things better if I yell? Will that help?'"

Welcome to third-grade socioemotional development, 1988 versus 2019. Penelope and I have a version of this conversation about once every three weeks. She is absolutely chock-full of suggestions for ways I can lower interpersonal conflict in my life and better control my emotional reactions. In the teacher notes home from my children's school, the socio-emotional curriculum gets similar space to math or social studies.

This is, at least in my impression, new. I went to a school very similar to Penelope and Finn's, and yet I remember very little formal instruction around these topics (this is probably why I am so awful at them). Yes, people were reminded to be nice to each other and not hit, but it wasn't especially well enforced and, much more important, no one really thought about providing any *tools* to do this.

It's hard to know what prompted this shift. As an economist, I'm drawn toward market-based explanations. Maybe the economic return from these people skills has increased in the market, so there is more value to developing them. There has also been a clear shift in cultural attitudes toward mental illness and treatment; the stigma associated with both has significantly decreased. There are more conversations about the value of mental health. Or maybe people just realized it is good to be nice to other people. All seem plausible.

Of course, once you acknowledge that these are valuable skills to develop, you should then ask whether we know anything reliable about how to develop them. In practice, I'd separate this into two questions. First, we can ask what we know about developing these skills at the individual level, where the discourse really focuses on *empathy*. How can you help your child develop an understanding of how other people are feeling? And second, we can ask what we know about developing good social environments for larger groups—is there evidence on what works to prevent bullying, or to improve prosocial behavior in classrooms or elsewhere?

Both have data! Let's see what it says.

WHAT THE DATA SAYS: EMPATHY

In order to develop empathy, kids need to have a "theory of mind." Basically, they need to be able to understand what other people are thinking and feeling. As far as we can know, this develops in stages over the first years of life.

The first step in the path is to *recognize* emotions based on facial expressions. Jesse used to play a great game with Penelope called "emotion faces," which involved making and recognizing faces for different emotions. In one study, researchers found that by the age of three, about 55 percent of children could recognize emotions; by five, this was up to 75 percent.[1] (Studies like this rely on presenting kids with various pictures and scenarios and asking questions about them.)

As kids age, they get more sophisticated. By the age of five, kids can start to *understand* emotions. They begin to comprehend, for example, why a story where a kid loses his ball or his cupcake would connect to a picture of a boy with a sad face. By seven, more kids can understand the idea that there may be a distinction between felt emotion and expressed emotion—I can be smiling but really feeling sad. And by the age of nine, kids have a better sense of ambivalent emotions; that is, the understanding that someone can be sad and happy at the same time.

These last two components are especially relevant for having empathy in social situations. It's pretty valuable, in thinking about the elementary school experience, to recognize that someone can seem to be laughing with you when, actually, their feelings are hurt.

In a broad sense, all kids will go through some version of this evolution, but of course they'll do it at slightly different ages, and they'll do it more and less successfully. Some people—adults as well as kids—simply have a better understanding of theory of mind than others. A highly developed theory of mind can improve the quality of social interactions; that is, your ability to interact with others.

Clearly, some of the cross-person variation in this is innate. But like many skills, it also can be learned. Children whose parents model this type of thinking tend to be more skilled at it. Studies of this argue that when mothers use more mental-state language, their kids also seem to have a better theory of mind.[2]

Of course, it's hard to know whether this is causal. The way parents talk to their children is related to a lot of other characteristics. Beyond that, if you think there is a genetic component to this (which seems at least plausible), you'd expect this relationship even if maternal modeling was irrelevant.

However, some of the more sophisticated evidence does seem to support causality. One study observed eighty-two mother-child pairs at multiple time periods over the course of a year.[3] At each of the three visits, mothers were asked to explain the contents of a picture to their child, and they were scored (in part) on the extent to which their explanations focused on the mental state of the people in the picture.

The researchers found that the children's theory of mind was related to their mothers' use of mental state language and that the timing was suggestive of causality. That is, mothers' use of mental state language predicted future theory of mind, but not past or current. In addition, the relationship remained even when adjusting for a wide variety of demographics and for the child's earlier theory of mind scores.

Perhaps even more compelling is experimental evidence showing directly that this can be taught to children. In one study, researchers recruited ninety-three children between the ages of five and eight. To start, the kids were tested on their emotional understanding (basically, how sophisticated their theory of mind was). Then all the children heard nine vignettes. Two groups of children were randomized into treatment—one treatment involved the experimenter explaining the ambivalent emotions of some of the characters; the other treatment involved the child answering questions and explaining these emotions. A third group was the control group; they were asked factual comprehension questions about the stories. At the end, all the children were tested again on their understanding of emotions.[4]

The researchers found that both of the treatment groups significantly improved their emotional understanding relative to the control group, suggesting that thinking through emotions in particular storytelling contexts may help develop more general understanding.

In a similar study, seven-year-olds read stories and afterward were either engaged in conversation about the emotions in the stories or asked to draw pictures of those emotions. The group that discussed the emotions showed improvements in emotional understanding relative to the children who just drew pictures of them.[5]

Combined with the evidence within families, this suggests that theory of mind can be taught to some extent. More than that, it gives a sense of one way to do this—namely, by talking through the emotions in example situations. Books are obviously a great place to look for these examples, and as texts get more sophisticated, there is more to unpack with your kids.

My personal favorites here are the Ramona Quimby books, which manage to perfectly capture the emotions of childhood without grating on adults. Many a good conversation has been had in my house about poor Beezus and the way Ramona has—usually accidentally— embarrassed her.

WHAT THE DATA SAYS: BULLYING, VIOLENCE, AND PROSOCIAL INTERACTIONS

We can think of this emotion-learning as an individual task, but it relates to a broader question of how we can improve *group-level* functioning. More specifically, how do schools and parents create classrooms that are inclusive, that are nice?

This has become increasingly salient as mental health problems, including depression, anxiety, and others, have risen in teens. We are simultaneously focusing more on developing empathy and coping skills and dealing with the fact that mental health seems to be worsening under (perhaps) social and academic pressures. Access to social media probably isn't helping this (more on that in the next chapters).

The basic question is: How can we limit bullying on the one hand and increase prosocial behavior on the other? Perhaps not surprisingly, there are a large number of school-based programs that aim to improve these behaviors.

One of the earliest anti-bullying interventions was run in forty-two schools in Norway in the 1980s.[6] The core components of the program involved school-level changes (rules, staff discussion, a "Bullying Prevention Committee"), additional supervision and intervention with students who were bullying or being victimized by bullies, holding class meetings on bullying prevention, and involving the broader community.

The evidence from Norway points to a successful program. There was a large reduction in bullying after the program, both as reported by the aggressors and the victims. Ancillary benefits included increased student comfort with recess time and an improvement in the "social climate" of the class.

This type of evidence is quite encouraging, but not all interventions are similarly effective. A 2010 meta-analysis summarized about forty anti-bullying interventions. The interventions themselves differed a lot, as did the methods of evaluation, and the results are mixed. Some interventions showed large improvements, others showed nothing.[7]

The meta-analysis determined that these interventions seem to work better with older children, and that more intensive programs are more effective. Intensity relates to in-school components, but also to whether there are parent meetings and playground supervision. Firm discipline also seems to be key. The analysis also found that studies using a randomized design showed smaller effects than those that just compared kids before and after the intervention. This could be interpreted as an indication that the before/after designs are flawed (after all, we do tend to prefer randomized data), but it may also reflect the particular types of schools where randomized trials have been run.

Some individual programs—largely modeled on the older Norway intervention—do seem to show more consistent results. One example is a Finnish program called KiVa, which focuses on grades four through six and involves 20 hours of lessons over the course of a school year. The lessons focus on the role of a group, empathy development, and strategies to help others. There's role-playing, discussion, and even a computer game.[8]

A large-scale evaluation of this in Finland, across almost eighty schools, showed reductions in a number of measures of bullying and victimization. These results are echoed by those of a similar program in Italy.[9]

This evidence suggests that thoughtful, well-designed anti-bullying programs can have some impacts. But it also makes clear the importance of the "thoughtful, well-designed" piece. Not all programs have the same effects. Focusing on those with empirical support seems crucial.

Another set of programs goes beyond a specific focus on bullying and looks more toward pro-social behavior in general. Programs that target general violence prevention focus on the idea of playing well with others, etc. Among the most widely used of these in the US—full disclosure, this is what my children's school uses—is a program called Second Step.

The Second Step program shares many features with successful anti-bullying programs and also draws on empathy training. It's a comprehensive curriculum, designed to be taught in schools in the same way you'd teach science or social studies. There are units on empathy, problem-solving, anger management.[10] The program has a strong focus on the practical—literally asking, "What tools can you use in this situation?"

Here's an example, courtesy of Penelope: Hold up your hand, thumb across your palm, and fold your four fingers down. This is your brain. Sometimes you have big emotions—anger, happiness, sadness, frustration. Sometimes they can be so big that they can "flip your lid." Raise all four fingers high! When this happens, you can overreact, say things you do not mean, do things you wish you didn't. You've got to find a way to get things under control when you feel like your lid might be flipping. What strategies will work for you? Examples include breathing deeply, closing your eyes, or imagining a cotton-candy unicorn. If you do this, you can help keep your lid from flipping.

Much of the curriculum focuses on explaining and visualizing the issues in a way kids can understand, and encouraging them to engage with their *own* practical tools for how to address the problem.

At least some experimental support exists for the value of this program in school settings. One study of 741 third to fifth graders found "improvements in positive approach-coping, caring-cooperative behavior, suppression of aggression, and consideration of others," although notably, no change in disciplinary referrals.[11] Another, similar-size study showed improvements in aggression and better teacher-reported behavior scores.[12] And a third showed persistent reductions in physical aggression, although no teacher-noted behavior change.[13] Other trials in younger kids showed improvements in executive functioning.[14]

Some of the evidence is more nuanced. One of the larger studies of this—a sample of more than 7,000 kindergarten to second-grade students—found no average effects, although they did find that students who entered the school year with worse skills in these dimensions benefited more.[15]

The overall picture is one of positive, if somewhat modest, impacts, shared across a variety of age groups and outcomes. I should be clear that Second Step is widely used but is only one of a number of socioemotional learning programs out there; another popular one is called PATHS. And although the details differ by program, their basic emphasis is very similar: empathy development, problem-solving, dealing with big emotions.

What strikes me, again, in watching how these curricula unfold with my own children is how much emphasis there is on this type of coping as a *skill*. Something that has enough value that it should appear alongside what I think of as more fundamental skills like math and reading, and also something that people can learn. It's hard for me to escape the feeling that my elementary and middle school experiences might have been quite a lot better if there had been more focus on these elements of learning. Then again, perhaps it is not too late to learn from Penelope.

The (Data) Bottom Line

- Theory of mind and emotional control are skills that can be taught.
- It is possible to help kids develop empathy; evidence-based approaches focus on explaining emotional reactions in the content of stories.
- Anti-bullying interventions in schools show mixed results, perhaps reflecting differences in their design.
- Socioemotional curricula can help develop social skills in individuals and groups.

SELF-ESTEEM AND SELF-CONFIDENCE

The flip side of "I want my kid to be nice to others" is, of course, that you want other kids to be nice to yours. And you want them to be confident and happy in their own skin. You want your children to have enough self-confidence to believe in their value, and to be able to brush off some social slights.

This is something I struggled with as a kid. I was not an especially popular elementary or middle schooler, and on top of this, I cared tremendously what other people thought of me. I tried desperately to integrate with the popular kids. Once, in the sixth grade, I did briefly make inroads before I was dropped again. When I look back, I just wish I had not cared so much about what other people thought. When I think about my own parenting, this is always top of mind. How can I help my kids be confident in who they are?

It is worth flagging that some people feel that our current parenting and school climate puts too much emphasis on self-esteem. We are *too* interested in kids feeling good about themselves. This is exemplified by books with titles like *The Feel-Good Curriculum: The Dumbing Down of America's Kids in the Name of Self-Esteem*, which pitches the view that a focus on self-esteem has created a generation of "entitled, righteous, underachieving children."

A valuable underlying point here is perhaps that you can have *too much* self-esteem, and that it probably doesn't benefit kids to think they can do no wrong. Self-esteem grows from achievement, from mastering some skill that can't just be handed out. Still, there is a long way between that and underconfident, unhappy kids. Like the rest of parenting, it's a balance.

In thinking about what the data says on self-confidence, self-esteem, belonging, and resilience in the face of bullying, it's worth coming back to the data on extracurriculars. A lot of the benefits of extracurriculars and even of summer camp seem to come from self-confidence and self-esteem. Involving your kids in out-of-school activities may be a good buffer even if they are not struggling at the moment, because it gives them a place to focus if things get difficult at school, whether around academics or social engagement. Extracurriculars may be a place to find new friends, or a place to be successful when school is not.

But we can also get more specific in the data. Let's say your child is on the receiving end of the bullying or is the "weird kid." What do we know about addressing this? What does the data say about determining resilience in the face of bullying? And if your kid is really struggling, what do we know about interventions that work?

I should be very clear here that this data is not a substitute for therapy or intended to deal with very challenging socioemotional issues. Kids with anxiety or depression need professional help, and a trained therapist's toolkit goes far beyond what we can look into here.

WHAT THE DATA SAYS: RESILIENCE TO BULLYING

The dictionary definition of *self-esteem* is "confidence in one's own worth and abilities; self-respect." Basically, the feeling that you are good enough, that you are a person with value. Self-esteem is connected to self-confidence, but it's not the same thing. Viewing yourself as someone who has high "worth" is different from having confidence in your abilities. In a sense, we might think feelings of worth may be harder to achieve. I can develop confidence in my abilities by successfully doing observable tasks; but how do I feel good about my worth? We are likely to rely on others to convince us we are worthy; self-esteem is a fundamentally social concept.

It's a topic of considerable interest in psychology. One of the more interesting pieces I've read about this connected self-esteem to self-concept (which, you may recall from the discussion of summer camp, is a measure of having a strong sense of your strengths).[16] The authors argue that people who have a clear and stable self-concept are also more likely to have higher self-esteem. In contrast, they note that individuals with lower self-esteem seem to have a less clear, "less stable" self-concept. Colloquially, they feel bad about themselves in ways that vary over time.

Self-esteem relates closely to the idea of "resilience," or the ability to bounce back when bad things happen. If you think about what you need (as an adult or as a child) to successfully get through setbacks (whether they involve people being mean to you or other issues), the ability to shake it off is key. (In one very difficult period of my work life, I literally played Taylor Swift's "Shake It Off" at maximum volume in my office several times a day. Haters gonna hate.)

Perhaps the most difficult thing for any parent is the realization that you cannot protect your kid all the time. This applies to physical safety, of course, but also to social "safety." I am sure we would all sometimes like to go into our kid's classroom and get right in the face of the mean kid and scream at them. But this isn't productive or socially acceptable. (Seriously, do not do this; you have to settle for giving their parents the side-eye at drop-off.) You can talk to your kids about how to manage social interactions, and perhaps how to improve them. But at the end of the day, unless your child's experience is very, very unusual, there will be social setbacks.

And these setbacks *do* matter to kids. We have lots of survey data that suggests that bullying—through physical aggression or more emotional means—is harmful for kids, producing unhappiness, depression, and anxiety. It affects their self-worth.[17] One longitudinal study of seven- to nine-year-old children in Finland found that those who were more socially isolated were more likely to develop both internalizing (depression and anxiety) and externalizing (acting out, being aggressive, etc.) behavior problems.[18]

However, not all kids react to social isolation in the same way, and this is where resilience comes in. It is hard or impossible to control whether your child is popular. The real question is whether there are ways to buffer them if they are not. In the Finnish study discussed earlier, the authors found that the link between social isolation and behavior issues is modulated by friendships. Specifically, for kids who reported having some friends, the authors did not find that social isolation led to behavior problems. You do not have to be popular to be happy, but it is helpful to have some friends.

Other data suggests that families can play a similar role. We see this, for example, in a study of children in the UK in which researchers collected information on home environment, maternal warmth, and sibling relationships (all the kids in this study were twins, so they all had siblings).[19] Children in the study also reported their experiences with bullying.

The researchers then tried to measure the children's self-esteem and resilience. Basically, they estimated the relationship between self-esteem and the extent to which kids are bullied. Children who are bullied a lot but still have high self-esteem are labeled "resilient."[20] The researchers explore the relationship between this resilience measure and family characteristics.

Overall, they found that kids who lived in families with more maternal and sibling warmth were more resilient. Effectively, having a stable and happy home life seems to protect kids against the worst effect stemming from bullying by peers. Is this causal? That's very hard to say. There are a lot of other differences across families that may well relate to both positive home environments and resilience. I will say, however, that these results are both intuitively sensible and echoed in other work that shows that having stable family relationships helps protect against the long-term consequences of bullying.[21]

In a sense, you probably do not need data and evidence to say that coming from a stable family is good for kids' outcomes. Many other things we see in the world should convince us of that. But what I think is notable in these results is the interaction. It is not that kids from stable families are bullied less—that may be true, but it's not the focus of these results. Instead, when they are bullied, these kids seem to have fewer bad consequences in either the short or the long term. They can draw on another aspect of their sense of self. They are, in a word, resilient.

COGNITIVE BEHAVIORAL THERAPY

When I was in college, I worked as a light designer on a number of productions directed by my friend Sara Heller. Many years later, when I was a professor at the University of Chicago, Sara was a graduate student there, working on a PhD in public policy. (She's now a professor at University of Michigan.)

While at the University of Chicago, Sara produced one of the most striking pieces of social science research I have ever seen. The city of Chicago, like much of the US, has a tremendous problem with high incarceration rates. There is a whole body of literature about the policy reasons behind these numbers, but reducing incarceration rates within the current system has proved to be a thorny problem. We can see that the cycle of issues that lead to incarceration often starts quite young, with behavior issues in school.

Sara and her coauthors designed and implemented a randomized evaluation in two settings in Chicago—a high school and a juvenile detention center.[22] They evaluated a program called Becoming a Man, an intervention designed around the more general approach of cognitive behavioral therapy (CBT). To greatly simplify, CBT is a short-term, practically oriented approach to psychotherapy. Rather than focusing on underlying reasons for trauma or behaviors, it focuses on tools to change thinking patterns, to recognize stressful situations, and to change your approach to them.

In Sara's experiment, the program emphasized slowing down your thinking and evaluating whether an aggressive response to a situation was appropriate. Boys were brought together in groups to work on these skills. One activity involved a ball. One boy in a pair was given a ball, and the other one was told to "get the ball." In nearly all cases, they attempted to do so by force.

At the end of the activity the facilitator asked, "Why didn't you just ask for the ball?" Often, the boy who had the ball said something on the order of, "Sure, I'd give it to you, it's just a ball," and the one who was trying to get the ball indicated that it never occurred to them to just ask. The program focused on developing mental tools for the boys to recognize when they were facing a situation where, in fact, escalating to physical violence was unnecessary.

The program was enormously successful, especially given that it was a very light-touch intervention—not expensive, relatively short-term—and that it was implemented with a very high-risk sample. The researchers saw reductions in incarceration, improvements in school performance and attendance, and (when implemented in juvenile detention) reductions in recidivism (the kids who participated in the program were less likely to be reincarcerated after they were released). It is an elegant and thoughtful paper, a great piece of research with enormous implications for policy.

The work in Sara's program was done with a population much older than that considered in this book, and very high risk. But it reflects a broader pattern of literature on CBT-style interventions that show positive impacts in kids struggling with a number of different issues. Much of this work has focused on high-risk samples, with evidence showing that "trauma-focused CBT" has positive effects on children who have experienced very significant adverse events (abuse, violence). These effects extend to measures of changes in brain activity among participants.[23]

Research in this area has also shown impacts on improving anxiety and depression among kids struggling with more everyday issues like classroom bullying.

For example: One small study of bullied adolescent boys found that a CBT-style intervention reduced anxiety, depression, and the bullying that the children reported. The effects persisted even several months later.[24]

Studies have also shown impacts among younger children. In one case, researchers evaluated a particular program (the Cool Kids Program) designed to reduce anxiety.[25] They focused on a cohort of eight- to thirteen-year-olds with high anxiety scores, and found that the program reduced anxiety and depression and increased self-esteem. The program (like much of CBT) focuses on practical approaches to recognizing and managing anxiety, rather than delving into the underlying reasons for these feelings.[26]

In the data, CBT seems to work, on average, for anxious, depressed, or low-self-esteem kids. Obviously, it will not be for everyone, and if your child is struggling, it will almost certainly make sense to seek individualized professional help. What is reassuring here is that there may be help available.

The (Data) Bottom Line

- Self-esteem, anxiety, and depression can be impacted by peer experiences.
- A stable family life, including positive relationships with friends, siblings, and parents, can buffer negative peer experiences. Home can be a safe space.
- Cognitive behavioral therapy (CBT) shows some promise in addressing anxiety, depression, and low self-esteem in kids.

Application

Is My Kid the Mean One?

It is a call you do not want to get.

"Hello, Steve? This is Francesca. Julian's mom. From Matthew's class?"

"Oh . . . hello!" You struggle to remember Julian among the sea of third graders. The one with the dinosaur backpack?

"I'm sorry to call so late, but I'm afraid we have a bit of an issue. Julian says he's being bullied at school; the other boys won't let him play soccer at recess, among other things."

"Oh gosh, I'm sorry. That sounds really tough. Would you like Matthew to help?" You're momentarily proud that perhaps she's called because she thinks your kid is the kind of kid who will be helpful. This is fleeting.

"Well, actually . . . Julian tells me Matthew is the ringleader. I'm afraid he is the one who told Julian he was too bad at soccer to play with them."

Your heart sinks. You thank her for calling, say you'll talk to your partner and Matthew, and hang up. Is your kid the mean kid? And what should you do about it?

FRAME THE QUESTION

In this case, your instinct may be that step 1 is to haul Matthew downstairs and, basically, yell at him. How could he be the one bullying other kids? Have you taught him nothing? He's going to march into school tomorrow and invite Julian over for the weekend. For sure no dessert this week. You're considering canceling his birthday party in the face of this. *You are furious.*

Or, your instinct may be to assume Julian's mom is a liar, and to go railing to your partner about the injustice of it all.

Wait.

Both of these are early parenting style reactions. You're in newborn mode. You want to fix the problem RIGHT NOW. It's the green poop reaction. Clean it up, call the doctor, fix the problem.

That isn't going to work here. This isn't a quick-fix problem, even though it may seem like it in the moment. You do not know all the information here. The social dynamics of a third-grade soccer game may be more complex than you realize. It is possible that there is more to the story than Julian's mom is hearing. If you come in hot with Matthew, you risk damaging your relationship with him *and* not getting to the bottom of what is going on. If you assume Julian's mom is lying, you may lose the opportunity to nip something problematic in the bud.

The first step should still be to frame the question. With your partner, if you have one. (But probably not with Matthew.) My sense is there would be a few questions to answer here: What exactly happened? Is this a pattern of behavior? What can we do to fix this?

FACT-FIND

The most significant evidence gathering at this point is about the social dynamics of the third grade, something you probably hoped you had left behind when you, personally, moved up to the fourth grade. No such luck.

You're going to need to call Matthew's teacher, at a minimum. Do they know what is going on in class? Do they have the impression Matthew is bullying Julian or leading some kind of charge against him?

You might also crowdsource some information. If you know the parents of other kids in Matthew's class, you might ask them what, if anything, they've heard. Finally, although it is hard, you might call Julian's parents again, to try to understand the context a bit better. That initial conversation, when you were surprised and probably a little angry and defensive, may not have been the best time to figure out what is really going on.

And lastly, you probably do need to talk to Matthew now. But in a quieter, less angry moment. Let him explain what happened from his standpoint.

FINAL DECISION

What decision you make here depends a lot on what you learn from your fact-finding. Imagine you learn that there is a general issue with bullying in the third grade. In that case, it may be time for a meeting with the school, perhaps bringing in some of the lessons we covered in the last chapter on how to develop socioemotional skills in the classroom. Schools can be resistant to change, but not always. And if they are struggling with this issue, they may welcome some data-based approaches.

Or you might also learn the issue is Matthew. This isn't what you hope, but we do not always understand our kids as well as we think we do. It may be that you need to do some more focused one-on-one work with him—or have someone else do it—to get him to think more about how his actions matter. Admitting that you need to do this may be very hard. But better now than later.

Or, finally, you may learn that there's more to the story—perhaps Matthew is struggling in some ways you didn't realize. And that rather than being punished, he needs more help managing some complicated emotions. Some of the data from chapter 10 may help you think about how to proceed.

In all, you need a plan to move forward. And a plan for how to follow up with Julian's mom, and inevitably a plan for Matthew to follow up with Julian. Even if the fault does not lie with him or the incident is a bigger one than just their interaction, it needs resolution.

FOLLOW-UP

Follow-up here is pretty straightforward. If you find yourself in this situation, you will be dealing with it over the slightly longer term. Resist the urge to give up and forget about it. If you invest the time now, it's likely to pay off big-time in junior high.

Entertainment: Overview

If you think about the big pieces of your kid's day, we've hit a lot of them by now: sleep, eating, school, after-school activities. What's left, more or less, is leisure. What should kids do when they're not otherwise scheduled? A big part of this, of course, is the question of screens: both the passive, watching kind and the active, social kind.

Screen time strikes fear in the heart of many a parent. Screens have been vilified. Apocryphal articles report on parents in Silicon Valley—people who *work in tech*—who will not expose their children to screens. Screens change your brain, say the headlines. (Spoiler alert: Everything changes your brain.) Media and technology exposure is contributing to a teen epidemic of depression and anxiety. Enroll your child in a screen-free summer sleepaway camp. Send them to a digital detox program. *Put away your own phone, you are setting a bad example.*

It's not so simple, though, is it? Screens are not like cigarettes. Not all the messages on them are bad.

At school, perhaps your second grader has "Technology" (even if it is just iPad games). Starting in fourth grade, he's supposed to be able to type fluently. His homework is literally on the computer. One day when Finn was four, he asked me to get him something on the iPad, and Penelope (age eight) chimed in with "HOMER has been proven to raise reading scores by 74 percent!" HOMER turned out to be an app to teach your child to read. Even I was a bit swayed—74 percent does sound like a lot! Maybe I can just outsource this teach-my-kid-to-read thing to the App Store. Even passive television watching has cheerleaders. There's compelling research showing that exposure to *Sesame Street* actually raises school readiness.[1]

It can be hard not to feel like we are vilifying screen media *just* because it's new. When novels first became common in the eighteenth and nineteenth centuries, many of the same fears were raised. All those women sitting around, reading these imaginary stories rather than, say, the Bible or Plato. Too much escapism; women were left untethered to reality, so absorbed in their books that they were unresponsive. I have an image of nineteenth-century moms playground-shaming each other for reading *Madame Bovary* while one of their children snatches a stick from another and runs off with it.

This is a challenging area to navigate (like much of parenting). I'm going to show some data on the impacts of passive screens—TV, video games—and some about social media. Some of it is interesting, but it doesn't provide a lot of direct answers to the question of whether screens are "good" or "bad."

This is not because the data is incomplete or flawed—it is, but that isn't the central problem. The problem, instead, is that this question does not have an answer.

To think about these issues, we need to consider the core economic idea of "opportunity cost." In terms of money, this concept says that when you evaluate the true cost of something, you need to take into account the other possible use of those funds. When I evaluate whether to spend money on a fancy vacation, I need to consider what else that money could go to—what is the opportunity cost?

This also applies to time. If I spend time on one thing, a consequence is having less time to spend on something else. When I'm writing this book, that's less time to write academic papers—there's an opportunity cost. When your kid is using a screen, that is less time spent on some other activity. The question isn't whether screens are inherently good or bad, but whether in a particular moment they are inherently better or worse than other things.

It is possible for screens to be a perfectly healthy part of life. *If* you keep their opportunity cost in mind.

Thinking through your family's relationships with screens—yours and your kids'—is going to be super important. This book may help some, but I won't get much into examples. There are tons of other writers who have. Anya Kamenetz's *The Art of Screen Time* is full of realistic scenarios of how a family might go about this.

SCREENS: THE WATCHING KIND

According to data from the TV-tracking company Nielsen, the average American child between the ages of two and eleven watches 24 hours of TV a week; any video game or computer game time is on top of this.[2] Some data suggests these numbers have come down over time, although this information is notoriously difficult to collect.

Is this an appropriate amount? The American Academy of Pediatrics (AAP) is of the view that kids watch too much TV, but for school-age kids, unlike for very young children, they aren't comfortable putting a specific limit on TV time. The AAP and other sources warn of the dangers of television—obesity, poor sleep, bad school performance—but without much compelling evidence.

I've written about this before. You can find all kinds of correlations between TV watching and child outcomes, but it seems very likely these are driven largely by other differences across families and not by TV itself.

Some of the best evidence comes out of my own household (my husband wrote a paper many years ago about early television viewing and test scores, which I talked about in both *Cribsheet* and *Expecting Better*), but the data on which the (reassuring) conclusions are based is quite old now. It's hard to know whether we should draw strong conclusions about screen engagement in the 2020s from experiences in the 1950s.

This doesn't mean we cannot say anything here. But it does mean this is a good time to use the tools we've developed to *structure* this choice. The key to deciding your family's relationship with this type of media—TV, video games, streaming videos, movies—probably does not lie in some particular piece of data or evidence. Instead, you need to break down the decision in the context of your family.

I like to think about this in what I'm going to call a wall/content analysis; that is, separate out the impact of staring at a wall from the impact of what's on the wall. I will try to (conceptually) isolate the time impact of TV or video games from the content impact.

WHAT THE DATA SAYS: STARING AT THE WALL

If your child is staring at the wall, they are not doing other things. This may seem obvious, but I think it's perhaps an underappreciated aspect of the passive media discussion. When my kid stares at the wall, she's not doing homework, playing sports, playing outside on her own, reading, practicing violin, cooking, eating snacks, doing crafts, learning to code, etc.

Now, there are a finite number of hours in a day (specifically, 24). What this means, in the language of economics, is that staring-at-the-wall time has an opportunity cost. The cost of this time is the value it would have in the next-best use of it. If your child would otherwise be playing a sport, then the opportunity cost of the wall-staring time is whatever benefit they'd be getting out of that sport.

This crowding out of time that would be spent in other ways does seem like it can have downsides. Consider one study from Norway, which shows that boys who grew up with television access had lower test scores and were less likely to graduate from high school than those who did not.[3] The authors of this study argued that it was the crowd-out of time spent on schoolwork that was responsible for this; for instance, this effect was larger for boys from families with higher education, where the alternative use of time may have been more cognitively focused.

Other studies reinforce this, like one from France that shows that video game play per se is not associated with lower test scores, but time spent reading is associated with higher test scores.[4] In other words, if you were reading *instead of* playing video games, that could increase your test scores. But that you're not reading because you're playing video games as opposed to wall-staring isn't so important.

The time-substitution effects go beyond cognition. One of the most commonly cited downsides of TV watching is an increased risk of obesity. If we have a rough model of weight that is calories in, calories out— that is, if you consume more calories or burn fewer, you gain more weight—then we can see why there might be a link here, *if* the other use of the time spent watching TV would be sports or other physical play.

Having thought about the opportunity cost issues around wall-staring, a reasonable place to start your media planning is to ask: How much time in a typical day do I think it's good for my child to stare at the wall?

Your first instinct might be "none," but I think that's not obvious. Everyone needs a break sometimes. If your kid decided that every day before dinner, they'd take a half hour break to stare at the wall, you'd probably be fine with that. In fact, you might be thrilled—it's meditation! Also, you get a moment to yourself. It is perhaps easy to forget in the pressure of modern parenting, but not every minute of every day needs to be spent in optimizing your child. At the same time, the answer is probably not five and a half hours of wall-staring every day; this would leave relatively little time for other activities.

So, before we even get into content, part of your Big Picture conversations should probably include some "staring at the wall" analysis. If you plan to allow your children to watch TV or play video games or have other forms of passive screen time, the first question is, just logistically, where does this fit in?

WHAT THE DATA SAYS: TV AND VIDEO GAME CONTENT

Of course, the TV or video game screen on the wall is a lot more appealing to kids than the wall alone, and as a result, enforcing limits is more challenging. If you told your children you're going to limit the amount of time they are allowed to spend staring at the wall, you probably wouldn't get too much pushback. But if you put limits on TV time, many kids will express the wish for more.

(On the plus side, the fact that TV is fun means you can use it as a motivator and a way to keep kids quiet. The iPad has made long flights with children infinitely easier.)

This kind of resistance isn't unique to this part of parenting, though, so I'd venture you have prior experience with setting limits. The other big issue is that once you put a TV on the wall the kid is staring at, or a video game on the computer, or Netflix on the iPad, you start to worry about the content. Does it matter what they are watching?

The short answer: yes. Kids can absorb stuff from TV (not very small children, but most kids can by age three, and a school-age child certainly can). They could learn good stuff; evidence shows that *Sesame Street*, for example, is beneficial for promoting early cognitive skills.[5] I know from experience that children can learn some basic facts about polar bears (their skin is black, not white, FYI) from videos.

But they can also learn bad stuff, or get scared by what they watch. Many of us have stories of a time that we were mistakenly allowed to watch a movie or show that was too scary or too adult for us, and it stuck with us. (For me, this mistake was the movie *The Ring*, which, to be fair, I watched the year I graduated from college, but I still blame my mother for not saving me.) TV shows and movies can introduce themes we are not ready for our kids to know about. Ratings do not always help with this, because every kid is different.

In my family, Finn is notoriously unaffected by spooky and scary movies, but much more likely to get emotional at sad parts. Penelope hides her face at socially awkward moments but has no problem when, for example, the parents in *Frozen* die.

So, it is generally a good idea to pay attention to what your children are watching. If for no other reason than you do not want to be kept up at night by a child explaining they cannot go to sleep because the girl from *The Ring* is going to come through their TV and get them (IT COULD HAPPEN). In my household, we've found Common Sense Media to be an excellent summary source for age ratings.

But is it okay to let your kid watch violent television shows or play violent video games if they're comfortable and not disturbed by it? Or is this kind of violent content going to make them more likely to be violent?

To the second question: some people say "yes," and this answer reflects some facts in the data. On average, kids who play more violent video games are more likely to have behavior problems and engage in real-life violence.[6] Of course, that type of evidence has serious limitations. It's not clear which direction the causality goes—is it the violent tendencies causing some kids to like violent video games more, or is it the video games causing the violent tendencies? In addition, there is the basic problem that other characteristics of the kids are likely different—their family background, parental education, and so on.

More compelling evidence comes from laboratory experiments. One example is a paper published in 2000 in the (very prestigious) *Journal of Personality and Social Psychology*. In one of the many experiments in this paper, the researchers tested whether exposure to violent video games increased short-term aggression.[7] The experimenters had some participants play a violent video game (a first-person shooter game about Nazis called *Wolfenstein 3D*) and others play a similar but explicitly nonviolent game (a nature adventure game called *Myst*). After a period of play, all the participants engaged in a competitive reaction-time task where the goal was to press a button faster than a hidden opponent. If they lost, they heard a loud noise, at a volume level set by their opponent. If they won, they could set the volume of the noise their opponent would hear.

In reality, there was no actual opponent; the experiment just deceived people into thinking there was. The authors of the study measured aggression based on the noise level the participants set and, in particular, based on whether participants reacted to louder noises from their opponent by upping their own noise level. Put simply, did they retaliate more if they'd been shooting Nazis than if they'd been wandering through an enchanted forest?

Yes, yes they did. The retaliatory noise blasts were louder if the participants were playing the violent game. A few other laboratory studies have found similar results; basically, in the short period after exposure to this type of game, aggression levels do seem to be higher.[8]

Combined with the first data, some have taken this to say that video game exposure promotes violence in general. In reality, this seems to be a stretch. Short-term, laboratory-generated increases in aggression do not obviously translate into long-term changes in behavior.

And in fact, as this literature has evolved further, it doesn't seem like the violent content–aggression link is very important in the field. Longitudinal studies that try to link *changes* in aggression to video game play, holding baseline features of players constant, do not show any relationship.[9] Other studies have shown that when data can do a more complete job adjusting for differences across families, these links between video games and bad outcomes melt away.[10] On a related but not identical note, other studies have debunked claimed links between video game play and sexist attitudes.[11]

This doesn't disprove the laboratory studies on aggression. But it suggests that whatever link does exist isn't big enough or long-lasting enough to have an impact on real-world behavior.

It's also probably reasonable to think about content here in the same way you think about wall-staring time. TV or video game content can be explicitly educational. Studies have shown that math video games can improve knowledge of fractions.[12] (I know, fun! I'm downloading that right now.) There are plenty of apps that try to gamify basic skills, and it's likely the case that if you spend an hour playing a math video game, you'll learn more math than you would by playing an hour of a first-person shooter.

On the other hand, let's go back to the Big Picture. This break time you've built in—it's not obvious that it's the time you want to spend on math. The bottom line is that time playing entertainment-based video games is just that—time not spent on other things—but unless it's upsetting to your kid, the content itself is probably not something to worry about.

WHAT THE DATA SAYS: ADDICTION AND SLEEP

Before concluding that television and video games are largely benign, other than the opportunity cost, it's worth also visiting the possibility of addiction, and the effects of screens on sleep.

Video game addiction, in particular, gets a good bit of play in the media. We imagine kids who spend hours staring at their screens, sneaking game consoles into their beds, not leaving their rooms even to use the bathroom. If allowing even a bit of TV or video game play puts your child on this path, it's something to consider. Maybe some TV is fine, but a distracting and debilitating television addiction is clearly not.

On the one hand, some people do become addicted to video games and play them at the expense of virtually everything else. There are kids who become so absorbed in screens in various ways that they neglect school, friendships, and their family. This is undeniably unhealthy, and when it happens, some outside intervention is likely to be necessary.

On the other hand, this type of addiction is fairly rare. Aggregating across a large share of studies, one review article put the average share of "problem" gamers between 2 and 10 percent.[13] This is generally based on studies of kids who play video games regularly, so that share would be much smaller if you included all the occasional players, too. The vast majority of kids who play video games do not show signs of problematic game play or video game addiction and are generally unlikely to develop these issues.

When these authors push into better understanding what characterizes players who develop addictions or for whom game play becomes problematic, they find they are more likely to be boys.[14] They are also more likely to come from backgrounds with other disadvantages—more likely to be poor or from single-parent households.[15] Perhaps most notable, there is some evidence of the same psychological features that characterize other forms of addiction.[16]

This last point suggests that, at least in part, video games may simply be the catalyst, not the cause. In the absence of a console, maybe the same kids would develop symptoms of addiction to something else—Dungeons & Dragons, alcohol, pot. It also suggests—this shouldn't be a surprise—that some kids are more susceptible to these issues than others.

This feels like one of the many concerns in parenting that you should neither obsess about nor completely dismiss. Some kids will have a problem with video games. If you feel like your child is too engaged, choosing screens over humans too frequently, or showing symptoms of depression or obsession, you should act. On the other hand, this is unlikely, and certainly many kids can play video games without these consequences.

When it comes to sleep, though, the evidence says screens and sleep do not mix. As you know (if you read the chapters of this book in order, anyway), sleep is extremely important for kids. Good-quality sleep matters! And a lot of school-age kids do not sleep enough, for various reasons. It seems possible that one of those reasons is television.

To begin with, we have some observational evidence suggesting that more television watching—especially television watching *in bed, near bedtime*—impacts sleep. Kids with TVs in their rooms sleep less.[17] Adolescents who watch more TV have worse sleep in young adulthood, and decreases in TV viewing seem to improve their sleep.[18] Of course, the usual caveats apply, but in this case we have some experimental evidence as well.

One helpful study monitored sleep patterns among adolescents after a single session of extensive TV or video game exposure close to bedtime.[19] The authors followed eleven children in three different settings: no media exposure, an hour of video games from 6 to 7 p.m., or an hour of television from 6 to 7 p.m. Bedtime for the kids was around 8:30 or 9 p.m. The authors found that sleep patterns—continuity, efficacy, and "sleep architecture" (i.e., how much time is spent in each phase of sleep)—were affected by both television and video games. The effects seemed to be a bit different for television versus video games, and clearly more research needs to be done on this before we really understand the mechanisms.

But the fact was, screen exposure close to bedtime made sleep worse. The evidence seems sufficient to provide some caution around allowing television or video games close to bedtime and around letting kids have an in-room TV. Although you may not want to hear it, the same could be said for adults.

WHAT THE DATA SAYS: JOINT MEDIA ENGAGEMENT

In 2016, the American Academy of Pediatrics revised their guidelines on television to, among other things, encourage "joint" media consumption. The basic message is that television or video games or apps are all much more beneficial if you watch or play along with your children, so you can engage and discuss with them.

This isn't based on much evidence, although one can see the logic. If you watch *Frozen II* together, then afterward perhaps there is more scope for discussing why Anna really did have to destroy the bridge, and (perhaps if your kid is older) dissecting whether the implication is that Elsa is going to get involved in a relationship with Honeymaren. (She is, right? I cannot be the only person who picked up on that.)

And when it comes to apps, especially "educational" ones, it seems evident that your child will learn more from them if you're working in the app with them, helping them understand the context.

On the other hand, it's hard for this not to feel like another thing to do. Like, now being a good parent means I have to watch TV with them? Also, kids often like TV that is terrible. Case in point: my children's interest in the Descendants movie trilogy. I once watched 20 minutes with them, and I have to say, I was extremely sorry to have left my phone upstairs. Yes, it was nice to be with them. But honestly, I would not have picked *that* 20 minutes of togetherness.

In the end, this highlights the possible *positive* features of media engagement for kids. Television, video games, apps—they aren't all bad!

They can be a way to connect with your kids, to share interests. Jesse waited for years for the kids to be old enough to share his interest in cartoons, and watching television together on the weekends before dinner is among his favorite times with them.

It's all about balance. Except before bed.

The (Data) Bottom Line

- Time is finite. Watching television takes time that could otherwise be spent doing other things; there is an "opportunity cost" that is worth considering. BUT sometimes it's fine to take a break.
- Kids can absorb content from TV, so it is worth monitoring and curating what they watch.
- The evidence suggesting violent video games lead to violence is based on laboratory studies, and does not seem to be quantitatively important in the real-world context.
- Video game addiction does happen, but it is rare and may well reflect underlying issues.
- **Screens before bed affect sleep and are therefore probably a mistake. For you, too.**

 SOCIAL MEDIA

Your five-year-old can clearly enjoy books and television (even your two-year-old probably likes those). And a kid of seven or eight will often enjoy video games, if they're allowed to play. Interactions on social media, though, aren't likely to come up until kids are a bit older. Most eight-year-olds do not have Instagram accounts, at least not ones that they use for chatting with their friends. And since social media is inherently that—social—if none of the other second graders are doing it, chances are your kid isn't going to be chomping at the bit to do it, either.

But as kids reach middle school, as more of them get phones or more regular computer access, it will be harder to ignore social media. Kids will want to be on Instagram, Snapchat, or whatever the new thing is that kids are actually using that you've never heard of (TikTok?). Many of these sites have minimum ages to sign up—typically thirteen—so these choices are coming up at the tail end of this age range.

It is good to think about social media in advance, though, since the data suggests that teenagers spend a lot of time using it. Even in 2011, surveys suggested that about a quarter of teenagers logged on to social media sites more than ten times a day, and half did it more than once a day.[20] And that was in 2011—the numbers are surely higher a decade later. (Before you freak out, do you check Facebook/Twitter/Instagram more than ten times a day? Yeah, I thought so.)

Before getting into the data, note that this is a place where limits and checks are likely to be key. Social media can be all-consuming, and you may be comfortable with some usage but not comfortable with your child spending all day, every day interacting online. A significant part of the conversation here should focus on what limits will be set, and what checks will be in place. You can get creative here, and perhaps involve the adults also. Maybe one day per week there is no social media use allowed in your household. Maybe it's two days a month. Maybe the use of phones in the house is restricted. Limits like this can help you check in with how social media is making your kids feel. If they seem a lot happier when it's off—or if they seem like they cannot live without it—that's a warning sign.

The general use of social media by adolescents and older teens has sparked a tremendous amount of fear. In 2016, *Time* magazine published a cover story focused on teen anxiety and depression, subtitled "Why the Kids Are Not Alright."[21] The story was wide-ranging but put a focus on social media as at least partially responsible for increased depression and anxiety in teens. The story highlighted the pressure teenagers may feel from constantly being able to know what everyone else is doing (perhaps doing without them). It also pointed to how access to communities around the internet could allow teens who are struggling with, say, eating disorders or suicidal thoughts to find others who would reinforce these tendencies.

As a parent of a not-yet-teenager, this story makes me want to hide my daughter in her room until her early twenties.

Adolescence is a very vulnerable time. In a sense, I see a strong parallel to being a new parent—especially a new mom. You're experiencing body changes, wild hormone fluctuations, an uprooting of your whole life. There's more independence (teens) or less (new moms), new pressures, new schedules, new challenges.

As a new parent, the internet and social connections can be both good and bad. On the one hand, when you're up at 3 a.m. and desperate for suggestions about how to soothe cracked nipples, it's awfully nice to have access to an online community of people at a similar stage, who are also up, who can tell you about lanolin and cabbage leaves. The expansion of community makes it easier to find other parents who share your values, or your challenges.

On the other hand, social media can engender comparisons that aren't healthy. When you're struggling to walk to the shower and wondering why you still look six months pregnant, it's not always helpful to see the "fit blogger" whose six-pack has returned four days after delivery. Scrolling through other people's baby pictures on Instagram doesn't always deliver a dose of reality, and since you are (necessarily) living with your actual reality, it can be easy to make unhappy comparisons.

All this is to say that in the age of new parenting, social media can be a blessing or a curse (or both!) for parents. The same is true for adolescents and teens. Social media can help kids connect to others who share their values and interests, to express themselves, to stay connected with their friends. It can also engender feelings of missing out, of unhappiness, of being lesser. Probably it does both, maybe even in the same moment or day.

I'd challenge you to find many people who look back fondly on middle school. That's not unique to the era of social media. Instagram may be the current venue for this, but adolescent social anxiety predates the iPhone. The phone is not obviously the cause.

The key question for the data, in my mind, is whether social media makes things *worse* for kids, and which kids are especially affected.

WHAT THE DATA SAYS: SOCIAL MEDIA EXPOSURE

In 2014, three authors writing in the journal *Children and Youth Services Review* collated findings from forty-three papers on the impacts of media technology on adolescent well-being. Most of the papers they summarized were narrative—basically, reporting on what kids and their parents said about the benefits and costs of media.[22]

Their bottom-line conclusion: "This systematic narrative review has revealed contradictory evidence while revealing an absence of robust causal research regarding the impact of social media on mental well-being of young people."

To de-jargon that a bit: Social media has both positive and negative impacts in the narrative reports. On the plus side, there is evidence of impacts on self-esteem, and increased ability to experiment with identity and share concerns in a safer space. On the negative side, for some kids, social media seems to increase social isolation and depression, and leaves kids vulnerable to cyber-bullying.

The vast majority of studies, though, showed small, mixed effects or no effects on kids. That is, for most kids, at least those who participated in these studies, social media was neither particularly a blessing nor a curse; it was just neutral.

Note, too, that the "robust causal research" we'd want here is missing. We don't have data that randomly assigns social media and looks at kids' outcomes. For the most part, we don't even have the second best— say, data that tracks kids before and after social media exposure.

A large study currently running out of the National Institutes of Health (NIH) will track kids who were ten at enrollment in the study in 2018 and follow them through adulthood. But that study is focused on screens overall and doesn't have a randomized component, and the results won't be available in time for our parenting. The data does make clear that some share of kids—probably a small share—seems to be at risk of problematic media usage. A 2017 article using data from a nationally representative sample of kids in Hungary showed that about 4.5 percent seemed to have what they term "problematic social media use"—basically, excessive use of social media combined with depressive symptoms and low self-esteem.[23]

A smaller study within the US showed elevated risks of anxiety, depression, and "fear of missing out" (FOMO) symptoms among kids who have a large number of social media accounts.[24] Other work suggests that higher FOMO is associated with more social media accounts, lower self-esteem, and other risk factors.[25]

It's important to be clear on what these results show and what they do not. Specifically, they *do not* show that social media causes FOMO, anxiety, depression, or lower self-esteem. In fact, it seems equally or more likely that the causality goes the other way. Being predisposed to experience FOMO may encourage adoption of social media, and similarly, engagement online may be a response to low self-esteem or depression, not a driving factor of it.

Where does this leave us?

When I'm advising my graduate students on writing their academic papers, I often remind them of something a colleague and mentor once told me: "There is no substitute for thinking." In producing research, it's easy to dive down the data rabbit hole, making a million graphs and tables in the hopes that something will jump out at you.

If you're a person who likes data, this social media area can drive you insane in the same way. There are papers—so many papers!—saying it's bad, or it's good, or it's good for this kind of person or bad for that one. But there is no substitute here (or in parenting generally) for paying attention to what is going on with your kid.

Some kids struggle with social media, some do not. Just as some will struggle with food, or video games, or television. And some will hugely benefit from it, will find an online community that they really connect to and that sustains them through a difficult age. There is no substitute for thinking.

The (Data) Bottom Line

- Some kids report positive benefits from social media interactions.
- Some kids are clearly harmed by social media use.
- Most evidence suggests that there are no effects . . .
- . . . but the evidence isn't very good.
- There is no substitute for thinking.

Application

The Right Age for a Phone

We arrive back at the beginning. You've read this whole book, and now I can finally tell you the right age for a phone.

It's twelve. Happy Parenting!

Oh, you're still here. Well then, let's dig into this a bit more.

The fact is, there is very little systematic data on the phone question. There is certainly no data that can "answer" this question. The choice depends tremendously on your family, and on the individual kid within your family who wants the phone. The question isn't even well posed in terms of the word *phone*. What phone? With what restrictions?

Realizing this can make it feel like you should just pick a time at random—like, when half the other kids their age have a phone (though if everyone did that, no one would ever have a phone, obviously). But a lack of systematic data isn't the same as having no way to approach the problem, and our approach translates well to the phone case.

FRAME THE QUESTION

What are the possible benefits of giving your child a phone? I can see three primary ones: logistical improvements (they can call you for a pickup), safety (you can track where they are, and they can call if there is a problem), and "social benefits" (this is the way their friends interact, they can text their friends, etc.).

And what's the possible cost? One obvious one is money. Phones are expensive. This is a first-line question for many people.

Beyond the money, I see two big concerns. The first is that your child might get so absorbed in the phone (texting, using apps, taking pictures of themselves with a bunny-ears filter) that they neglect other things. And second, possible social friction (online bullying, anxiety, FOMO). Many people worry that their child may *think* a phone will make them popular and happy, but the opposite might be true.

The other piece of structure I'd put on the table here is the question of *what type of phone*. At least in the current technological framework, there is a wide range—from simple "dummy phones" (from which kids can call their parents or emergency services) to advanced iPhones with all kinds of fancy capabilities. Clearly, you want to think about the full range of options.

FACT-FIND

The data is not great. There is no randomized trial that will tell us whether kids who get a phone at eleven are happier and more successful than those who get one at thirteen, so we can scrap the idea of having an answer overall. But there is still fact-finding to do, and some evidence that may help you. There are also some pieces that require reflection, but perhaps not evidence gathering per se.

Logistics

What is the logistical value for your child having a phone? Think through the day. When would they use it? Is there uncertainty around their pickup time from some activity? Are there often times during the day when they'd need to be in touch with you?

If you are finding, for example, that your child is frequently waiting for you in the cold because practice ended early, that could be an argument for a phone. If you are fielding a lot of midday calls from school about forgotten homework, shoes, or jackets, that could argue for a phone (or for a different morning reminder system). Conversely, if you cannot think of a single concrete situation in the last month in which your child would need to call you from a cell phone, this suggests that this particular benefit may be small.

Safety

Do you perceive a safety value in a phone? What would it be? One reason is location tracking. Most phones would let you see where your child is at all times—is there value to this? If your child is walking a long way home from school or between activities, maybe this would make you more comfortable. Some parenting approaches would say this is too much monitoring, too much tracking—kids need to have some freedom of their own. For other parents, the ability to see their child's location opens up the ability to give them more of this freedom.

This is part of a broader conversation around what type of parenting you want to be doing (see more of the "free-range" parenting discussion in early chapters).

The other safety value is, of course, that your child could call you if something bad happens. It's worth saying again that—empirically—kids are safer than ever these days, but bad things do happen, and this should be part of your conversation.

Phone Screen Absorption

I put the issue of phone screen absorption in here because it feels, to me at least, like a question of what limits you want to set. In chapter 11, I talked about the evidence that mostly suggests that the cost of non-social media (television, video games) is a lack of engagement in other activities. Apps on a phone have a similar feel. There is nothing wrong with a little Candy Crush, other than that maybe learning to add fractions is a better use of your time.

So when you think about your family-time management, this is another kind of screen to think about putting limits on. I know families who have written all sorts of rules about this: no screens at the table, no screens upstairs, phones plugged in at the house entryway and not touched, etc.

Depending on your attitude toward within-family fairness, you may need to think about your own habits. In other words, no phone at the table might mean no phone for you, too.

And then there are some pieces of this decision that could rely a bit on data. Think again on the question of whether the social-interaction piece of the phone is likely to make your child happier or less happy. I noted above that this depends a lot on your kid. Think about whether they, in particular, are likely to benefit.

FINAL DECISION

Armed with the data, you're in a better position to make a decision. There's no right answer, but this is about as prepared as you'll be.

Who should come to the decision meeting? You almost certainly want to involve your child in this discussion at some point, but it is possible that you want to come in with an adult-formulated plan. It could be two meetings, or a two-part meeting. At work, I find I am often having the meeting-before-the-meeting. Sometimes it happens at home, too.

Ideally, at this meeting you can talk through the data you've gathered. Are there logistical reasons for your child to have a phone? What kind of limits would you want to set on it if they did have one? How strong are the arguments on the social side, given the overall social environment your child is in, and given their personality?

If you ultimately decide that there are good logistical or safety reasons in favor of a phone, but the social considerations say avoid it, that makes a case for some type of dummy phone.

If the decision is to get a phone, this meeting is a good time to articulate the rules or limits you want to set on its use. There's a case to be made for writing them down. A family phone policy (dare I suggest a Google Doc?).

In addition, the meeting here should end with both a decision and a follow-up plan. If you decide yes on the phone, when will you revisit how it's going? And what are the key points you'll want to consider at that time? If you decide no, when will you reopen this discussion? Six months from now? A year? Agreeing on a timeline for this is an input to harmony. If you just say, "We'll discuss later," a motivated person might take that to mean tomorrow.

FOLLOW-UP

If you decided not to get your child a phone, the follow-up meeting is probably pretty similar to the decision meeting. Has anything changed? Is there a reason to alter the decision? The plus side is that you probably need more limited data gathering this time. You may even have set some milestones or considerations at the decision meeting that you can revisit now.

If the phone has been introduced, now is the time to reflect on how it is going. One question is about responsibility: Has the phone been lost or broken? When I told my daughter about writing this section of the book, her primary suggestion was that the rule should be if you break the phone, you don't get another one until you are much older. This suggestion has the flavor of an eight-year-old (and one who is related to an adult who breaks their phone a lot), but it does have a ring of truth. A phone is a responsibility, and if it's lost three times a week, maybe a break is a good idea.

Beyond that, though, have people been adhering to the rules? Does it seem like phone engagement—either social or not—is becoming a problem? If the value of the phone is logistics, has it actually helped? Maybe you got a dummy phone, it's never been used, it's been lost six times, and everyone's kind of done with it.

The follow-up questions will vary. But no decision of this magnitude should be left without reflection.

Good luck! Like many parenting choices, this isn't an easy one, and it doesn't have a right answer—certainly not ex ante and probably not ex post, either.

(When in doubt, go with twelve.)

Conclusion

Over spring break 2020, our family—Jesse and I, and the kids—were supposed to be visiting Jesse's parents in New York, followed by a drive into Pennsylvania to stay with some close friends for a few days. We had been planning the trip for months.

And then, COVID-19 happened. We didn't go on the trip. Instead, we found ourselves in a rental cottage on a llama farm about an hour from our house in Rhode Island. The kids were on the first floor, absorbed in a DVD of *Spirited Away* that we had been saving for an emergency. Jesse and I were in the small bedroom upstairs. I sat on the bed; he brought in a chair and a tiny desk from the other room. We both had our laptops out.

"Okay," he said. "Let's start by reviewing all the work meetings we both have over the next weeks and seeing which are crucial. We can then move to how to best structure the day with the kids."

"I think I know how I want to do that already," I replied. "Did you see the proposed homeschool schedule in the Google Doc I sent?"

"Yes; broadly it looked good, although I had some questions. But I think we need to work through our work stuff first."

"Fair enough. Let's start with you."

The COVID-19 crisis had spread to the US a few weeks earlier. What started in China with a cold-like illness and some instructions not to shake hands had rapidly morphed into stay-at-home orders and indefinite distance learning.

One day, we were living our busy but highly organized life—school, violin lessons, research, teaching, writing. And then, with almost no warning, we were all at home with no way out. Jesse and I took on altered job and parenting responsibilities—notably, teaching our classes remotely and homeschooling the kids. I, perhaps ill-advisedly, took on new work responsibilities, mainly COVID-19 related. Like everyone on the planet, we were simultaneously deluged with a constant barrage of terrible headlines.

We were very lucky. We have many resources. Our families were safe. At the same time, this experience required a radical reimagining of our lives.

Many of the tools in this book did help. That first weekend conversation was fairly successful. We ended up with a pretty good shared homeschool structure. That I had thought about meal planning before this came in handy when grocery shopping became more difficult and food options more restricted.

On the flip side, the crisis also made clear some of the limits of these tools. I could only do so much to keep us safe. No matter how many Google Forms I used, I could not make more hours in the day. For a few weeks I moved my wake-up time from 5 a.m. to 4 a.m. to get another hour of work in, until Jesse pointedly asked me to think about whether this was unhealthy (yes). As Penelope reminded me often, I "freaked out" a lot.

In the initial weeks of COVID-19, logistics took a front seat (and a back seat, and a middle seat). We were constantly revising our plans to make room for changes to the kids' new homeschool schedule and our own work responsibilities. These decisions all felt very in-the-moment. Can we move the family physical education class by a half hour so Penelope can attend synchronous "morning meeting" with her class? How do we manage the fact that I'm now required to attend a meeting from 5 to 6 p.m. every day during what would have been dinner prep?

As time went on, and things started to slowly reopen, the logistics calmed down. And yet as this happened, we found ourselves facing a million new and unexpected bigger decisions. Decisions without obvious good answers. Should we risk the virus to send our kids to camp? Should we see my parents, knowing my dad was in a high-risk group?

In a sense, this period was a sped-up version of the parenting transition we discussed in the beginning of the book. One minute, you're making a fast choice about moving the schedule by 30 minutes; the next, you are evaluating the trade-off of time with grandparents against serious disease risk.

The tools we used before the virus were there, if slightly modified. A version of the Four Fs helped us make these bigger choices, as hard as they were.

We framed the question. Should we see my parents now or . . . when? We were careful to outline the alternative. You cannot answer the question without asking it. Was the choice to see them now, see them in two weeks, or wait until there was a vaccine? In the case of COVID-19, as in most situations, framing the question was the hardest part.

We did our fact-finding: I spent hours and hours and hours researching COVID-19. Trying to figure out how large the risks really were, and how we could mitigate them. I literally developed an entire website about COVID risks, which may have taken things a bit far.

Was a hike safe? Would it be helpful to have the windows open if we chose to have people at our house? Did it matter if we quarantined for a long time first? Was my dad—on the older side but otherwise healthy—really at high risk?

We made a final decision. We did see my parents, first for a distance hike and then, later, for a longer in-person visit. We tried not to second-guess this in the moment.

And then we followed up. We tried to learn from the decisions we made and will hopefully make better ones in the next opportunity.

It was hard. Among other things, the *uncertainty* in this period was vast. Fact-finding is a challenge when it seems like no one knows anything. We were forced to make many decisions knowing very well that they might be wrong, and accepting that they might turn out to have very extreme consequences.

In the end, the experience of COVID-19 isn't all that different from most parenting. Uncertainty is part of the fear. Facing the unexpected and navigating through it is part of what makes it hard.

But the unexpected also brings adventure. Being home with the kids for months on end was trying, but it wasn't without its joys. We both got to know the kids better. We got a chance to reflect on how fortunate we were to have the options we did during such a complicated time, and a chance to convey this to the kids, especially the older one. We explored every hike in Rhode Island (there are a surprising number).

And most important, perhaps, I learned that while good logistics and decision making helped us navigate this strange and hard moment, they couldn't give me *control*. No matter how well structured your Family Firm is, things will happen that you do not expect—perhaps not a global viral pandemic (I hope), but lesser surprises. At every stage, I am surprised at how parenting forces me to recognize the things I simply cannot command.

What we can hope, though, or at least what I hope, is that by thinking deliberately about our choices, no matter what they may turn out to be, we will know we did our best when we come out the other side.

Acknowledgments

I was very sure I would not write another book after my last one, so the existence of this at all owes the usual tremendous debt to my agent, Suzanne Gluck, and my editor, Ginny Smith. At this point, it really feels like a team effort, and Ginny's careful coaxing of a complete book out of my various pieces feels like her usual magic. The team at Penguin Press also deserves enormous thanks, including Caroline Sydney, Elisabeth Calamari, Danielle Plafsky, Matt Boyd, Ann Godoff, Megan Gerrity, Christopher King, Cassie Garruzzo, and many others.

I'm grateful to a team of amazing students for their research and feedback, including Dora Nathans, Brandon Avendano, and Libby Chamberlin. Kaitlin Bui provided extraordinary overall editing, and Emilia Peters did the graphic design.

It's hard to overstate the value of reader feedback, in sending both ideas for this book and responses to my last. With only two pages for acknowledgments, I cannot thank everyone I hear from. But know that if you write to me—on Twitter, on Instagram, through ParentData— I read it, and somewhere in here you might see yourself or something inspired by what you told me. I feel like the community of parents who are all in this together are, at the core, the fuel, and this book is for all of you.

To all my friends who shared your stories and commented on this, thank you. Especially Jane Risen, Jenna Robins, Tricia Patrick, Hilary

ACKNOWLEDGMENTS

Friedman, Heather Caruso, Katie Kinzler, Kelly Joseph, Nancy Zimmerman, Amy Finkelstein, Ben Olken, and Alix Morse.

This is a book about the school years, and our kids have been so lucky to spend them at Moses Brown. We are tremendously grateful for the partnership of the teachers there, and for the school in general. OJ Marti deserves a special thanks for his leadership, but also for talking through many of the issues in this book with me.

In a sense, all of the people who encouraged me to write *Expecting Better* and *Cribsheet* deserve thanks here, too. This includes, but is by no means limited to, Judy Chevalier, Anna Aizer, David Weil, Matt Notowidigdo, Dave Nussbaum, Nancy Rose, Amy Finkelstein, Andrei Shleifer, the More Dudes, Matt Gentzkow, Heidi Williams, and Laura Wheery.

Finally, my family. The Shapiros: Joyce, Arvin, Emily, Terence, and Leila. The Fairs and Osters: Steve, Rebecca, John, Andrea, James, Emily, Matthew, Connor, Maya, and Marcus. And Mom and Dad. It's hard to overstate how much I owe you both, especially as I navigate this more complicated phase of parenting. I was so lucky to have the foundation that you gave us.

Penelope: Getting to know you as you've grown up is simply a joy. I can't believe I get to be your mom. Thanks for helping me figure out my problems. I love you.

Finn: You're the best minnow. Thanks for helping me see that it's fine to have meatballs for breakfast and for bringing so much joy. I love you.

Jesse: I don't really know what to say. I just feel lucky to get to be your wife. Thanks for supporting all my crazy ideas, for being a great dad, for appreciating my cooking (let's put aside the sausage roll disaster of 2020), and for always being the person I want to talk to at 9 p.m. I love you.

Appendix: Recommended Further Reading and Tools

Readings

ON SCHOOLS, SCHOOL POLICY, AND SCHOOL CHOICE

Ewing, Eve L. *Ghosts in the Schoolyard: Racism and School Closings on Chicago's South Side*. Chicago: University of Chicago Press, 2018.

Garcia, David R. *School Choice*. Cambridge: MIT Press, 2018.

Harris, Douglas N. *Charter School City: What the End of Traditional Public Schools in New Orleans Means for American Education*. Chicago: University of Chicago Press, 2020.

Hannah-Jones, Nikole. "Choosing a School for My Daughter in a Segregated City." *New York Times Magazine* 9, 2016.

ON RACE

Tatum, Beverly Daniel. *Why Are All the Black Kids Sitting Together in the Cafeteria? And Other Conversations About Race*. New York: Basic Books, 2017.

Reynolds, Jason, and Ibram Kendi. *Stamped: Racism, Antiracism, and You: A Remix of the National Book Award–winning Stamped from the Beginning*. Boston: Little, Brown Books for Young Readers, 2020.

PBS Guide to Talking to Kids About Race: https://www.pbs.org/parents/talking -about-racism.

ON INDEPENDENCE

Harris, Malcolm. *Kids These Days: The Making of Millennials*. Boston: Little, Brown and Company, 2017.

APPENDIX

Lieber, Ronr. *The Opposite of Spoiled*. New York: HarperCollins, 2015.

Lukianoff, Greg, and Jonathan Haidt. *The Coddling of the American Mind: How Good Intentions and Bad Ideas Are Setting Up a Generation for Failure*. New York: Penguin Books, 2019.

Phelan, Thomas. *The Manager Mom Epidemic: How Moms Got Stuck Doing Everything for Their Families and What They Can Do About It*. Naperville, IL: Sourcebooks, Inc., 2019.

ON SCREENS

Heitner, Devorah. *Screenwise: Helping Kids Thrive (and Survive) in Their Digital World*. London: Routledge, 2016.

Kamenetz, Anya. *The Art of Screen Time: How Your Family Can Balance Digital Media and Real Life*. London: Hachette UK, 2018.

Turkle, Sherry. *Reclaiming Conversation: The Power of Talk in a Digital Age*. New York: Penguin Books, 2016.

ON SPORTS

Friedman, Hilary Levey. *Playing to Win: Raising Children in a Competitive Culture*. Berkeley: University of California Press, 2013.

O'Sullivan, John. *Changing the Game: The Parent's Guide to Raising Happy, High-Performing Athletes, and Giving Youth Sports Back to Our Kids*. New York: Morgan James Publishing, 2013.

Tools

For Task Management: Asana, Trello

For Meal Planning: Paprika.com

For evaluating the safety of media: Common Sense Media

The Google Suite: Google Docs, Google Sheets, and, do not forget, Google Forms.

Workbook

Creating
THE BIG PICTURE

FAMILY MISSION STATEMENT

What is your main goal for the family?

_____

_____

_____

_____

_____

PRIORITIES FOR KIDS

01. _____

_____

_____

02. _____

_____

_____

03. _____

_____

_____

PRIORITIES FOR ME

01. _____

_____

_____

02. _____

_____

_____

03. _____

_____

_____

Creating
THE BIG PICTURE

WEEKDAY PRIORITIES

01._____

_____

_____

_____

02._____

_____

_____

_____

03._____

_____

_____

_____

WEEKEND PRIORITIES

01._____

_____

_____

_____

02._____

_____

_____

_____

03._____

_____

_____

_____

NEXT STEP: SCHEDULE!

This step involves looking at calendars for the weekdays and weekends, and filling them in. Let's dial into the details—for example, if you've agreed in Step 1 to eat dinner together most nights, you need to figure out how said dinner will be produced (and by whom).

Creating
YOUR SCHEDULE

	(NAME)	(NAME)	(NAME)
6 AM			
7 AM			
8 AM			
9 AM			
10 AM			
11 AM			
12 PM			
1 PM			
2 PM			
3 PM			
4 PM			
5 PM			
6 PM			
7 PM			
8 PM			
9 PM			
10 PM			
11 PM			
12 AM			
1-6 AM			

Creating
FOOD POLICIES

MEAL	TIME	LOCATION	FOOD RULES
MEAL 1			
MEAL 2			
MEAL 3			
MEAL 4			
MEAL 5			
MEAL 6			

"FORBIDDEN" FOODS ——— "SOMETIMES" FOODS

Creating
BEDTIME STRUCTURE

STEPS	(NAME)		(NAME)		(NAME)	
	TIME	DESCRIPTION	TIME	DESCRIPTION	TIME	DESCRIPTION
STEP 1						
STEP 2						
STEP 3						
STEP 4						
STEP 5						
STEP 6						
STEP 7						
STEP 8						
STEP 9						
STEP 10						

Creating
CHILDREN'S RESPONSIBILITIES

	(NAME)	(NAME)	(NAME)
TASK 1			
TASK 2			
TASK 3			
TASK 4			
TASK 5			
TASK 6			
TASK 7			
TASK 8			
TASK 9			
TASK 10			

Allocating
FAMILY ACTIVITIES

TASK	PERSON RESPONSIBLE

Notes

A Sample Case Application: Red Shirt, Green Shirt, School-Entry Age

1. Spira, Greg. "The Boys of Late Summer: Why Do So Many Pro Baseball Players Have August Birthdays?" *Slate*, April 16, 2008.

2. Deming, David, and Susan Dynarski. "The Lengthening of Childhood." *Journal of Economic Perspectives* 22, no. 3 (2008): 71–92.

3. Bassok, Daphna, and Sean F. Reardon. "'Academic Redshirting' in Kindergarten: Prevalence, Patterns, and Implications." *Educational Evaluation and Policy Analysis* 35, no. 3 (2013): 283–97.

4. Angrist, Joshua D., and Alan B. Keueger. "Does Compulsory School Attendance Affect Schooling and Earnings?" *Quarterly Journal of Economics* 106, no. 4 (1991): 979–1014.

5. The particular method they use is instrumental variables—they are "instrumenting" for schooling attainment with quarter of birth because kids who are younger when they start school are forced to finish more of it before they are allowed to drop out at sixteen.

6. Black, Sandra E., Paul J. Devereux, and Kjell G. Salvanes. "Too Young to Leave the Nest? The Effects of School Starting Age." *Review of Economics and Statistics* 93, no. 2 (2011): 455–67.

7. Ibid.

8. Dougan, Kelli, and John Pijanowski. "The Effects of Academic Redshirting and Relative Age on Student Achievement." *International Journal of Educational Leadership Preparation* 6, no. 2 (2011): n2; Elder, Todd E., and Darren H. Lubotsky. "Kindergarten Entrance Age and Children's Achievement: Impacts of State Policies, Family Background, and Peers." *Journal of Human Resources* 44, no. 3 (2009): 641–83; Martin, Roy P., et al. "Season of Birth Is Related to Child Retention Rates, Achievement, and Rate of Diagnosis of Specific LD." *Journal of Learning Disabilities* 37, no. 4 (2004): 307–17.

9. Elder and Lubotsky. "Kindergarten Entrance Age and Children's Achievement: Impacts of State Policies, Family Background, and Peers." 641–83.

10. Ibid.

11. By having different states with different entry-date cutoffs, these authors are also able to separate the impact of age of entry from other month-of-birth effects. If you think kids born in July are different for other reasons than those born in November, this approach fixes that problem. Other papers do not fix this problem, although in practice this doesn't seem to be especially important.

12. Martin et al. "Season of Birth Is Related to Child Retention Rates, Achievement, and Rate of Diagnosis of Specific LD." 307–17.

13. Mühlenweg, Andrea, et al. "Effects of Age at School Entry (ASE) on the Development of Non-cognitive Skills: Evidence from Psychometric Data." *Economics of Education Review* 31, no. 3 (2012): 68–76.

Chapter 4: Sleep

1. Durmer, Jeffrey S., and David F. Dinges. "Neurocognitive Consequences of Sleep Deprivation." *Seminars in Neurology* 25, no. 1.

2. Hirshkowitz, Max, et al. "National Sleep Foundation's Sleep Time Duration Recommendations: Methodology and Results Summary." *Sleep Health* 1, no. 1 (2015): 40–43.

3. Wolfson, Amy R., and Mary A. Carskadon. "Sleep Schedules and Daytime Functioning in Adolescents." *Child Development* 69, no. 4 (1998): 875–87.

4. Dewald, Julia F., et al. "The Influence of Sleep Quality, Sleep Duration and Sleepiness on School Performance in Children and Adolescents: A Meta-analytic Review." *Sleep Medicine Reviews* 14, no. 3 (2010): 179–89.

5. Shin, Chol, et al. "Sleep Habits, Excessive Daytime Sleepiness and School Performance in High School Students." *Psychiatry and Clinical Neurosciences* 57, no. 4 (2003): 451–53.

6. Sadeh, Avi, Reut Gruber, and Amiram Raviv. "Sleep, Neurobehavioral Functioning, and Behavior Problems in School-Age Children." *Child Development* 73, no. 2 (2002): 405–17.

7. Pilcher, June J., and Amy S. Walters. "How Sleep Deprivation Affects Psychological Variables Related to College Students' Cognitive Performance." *Journal of American College Health* 46, no. 3 (1997): 121–26.

8. Vriend, Jennifer L., et al. "Manipulating Sleep Duration Alters Emotional Functioning and Cognitive Performance in Children." *Journal of Pediatric Psychology* 38, no. 10 (2013): 1058–69.

9. This is a bit in the weeds, but doing this kind of design, where everyone is treated both "Long" and "Short," is really helpful for the researchers given their small number of students. This way, they can effectively compare the same child with more and less sleep, which decreases statistical noise a lot, helping them estimate significant effects.

10. Sadeh, Avi, Reut Gruber, and Amiram Raviv. "The Effects of Sleep Restriction and Extension on School-age Children: What a Difference an Hour Makes." *Child Development* 74, no. 2 (2003): 444–55.

11. Gruber, Reut, et al. "School-based Sleep Education Program Improves Sleep and Academic Performance of School-age Children." *Sleep Medicine* 21 (2016): 93–100.

12. Lewin, Daniel S., et al. "Variable School Start Times and Middle School Student's Sleep Health and Academic Performance." *Journal of Adolescent Health* 61, no. 2 (2017): 205–11.

13. Bowers, Jennifer M., and Anne Moyer. "Effects of School Start Time on Students' Sleep Duration, Daytime Sleepiness, and Attendance: A Meta-analysis." *Sleep Health* 3, no. 6 (2017): 423–31.

14. Owens, Judith A., Katherine Belon, and Patricia Moss. "Impact of Delaying School Start Time on Adolescent Sleep, Mood, and Behavior." *Archives of Pediatrics & Adolescent Medicine* 164, no. 7 (2010): 608–14.

15. Ibid.

16. Vorona, Robert Daniel, et al. "Dissimilar Teen Crash Rates in Two Neighboring Southeastern Virginia Cities with Different High School Start Times." *Journal of Clinical Sleep Medicine* 7, no. 2 (2011): 145–51.

17. Lufi, Dubi, Orna Tzischinsky, and Stav Hadar. "Delaying School Starting Time by One Hour: Some Effects on Attention Levels in Adolescents." *Journal of Clinical Sleep Medicine* 15, no. 7 (2011): 183.

18. Hirshkowitz, Max, et al. "National Sleep Foundation's Sleep Time Duration Recommendations: Methodology and Results Summary." *Sleep Health* 1, no. 1 (2015): 40–43.

19. Spruyt, Karen, Dennis L. Molfese, and David Gozal. "Sleep Duration, Sleep Regularity, Body Weight, and Metabolic Homeostasis in School-aged Children." *Pediatrics* 127, no. 2 (2011): e345–52.

20. Matricciani, Lisa, Timothy Olds, and John Petkov. "In Search of Lost Sleep: Secular Trends in the Sleep Time of School-aged Children and Adolescents." *Sleep Medicine Reviews* 16, no. 3 (2012): 203–11.

NOTES

Chapter 5: Childcare and Parental Work

1. An example paper here is Baum, Charles L. "The Long-term Effects of Early and Recent Maternal Employment on a Child's Academic Achievement." *Journal of Family Issues* 25, no. 1 (2004): 29–60.

2. Goldberg, Wendy A., et al. "Maternal Employment and Children's Achievement in Context: A Meta-analysis of Four Decades of Research." *Psychological Bulletin* 134, no. 1 (2008): 77.

3. Note that this is not R0—which you may have heard a lot about during the coronavirus epidemic. It's just little *r* for correlation.

4. Ruhm, Christopher J. "Maternal Employment and Adolescent Development." *Labour Economics* 15, no. 5 (2008): 958–83.

5. Morrissey, Taryn W., Rachel E. Dunifon, and Ariel Kalil. "Maternal Employment, Work Schedules, and Children's Body Mass Index." *Child Development* 82, no. 1 (2011): 66–81; Ruhm. "Maternal Employment and Adolescent Development." 958–83.

6. Ruhm. "Maternal Employment and Adolescent Development." 958–83.

7. Datar, Ashlesha, Nancy Nicosia, and Victoria Shier. "Maternal Work and Children's Diet, Activity, and Obesity." *Social Science & Medicine* 107 (2014): 196–204.

8. Morrissey, Dunifon, and Kalil. "Maternal Employment, Work Schedules, and Children's Body Mass Index." 66–81.

9. Hsin, Amy, and Christina Felfe. "When Does Time Matter? Maternal Employment, Children's Time with Parents, and Child Development." *Demography* 51, no. 5 (2014): 1867–94.

10. Namingit, Sheryll, William Blankenau, and Benjamin Schwab. "Sick and Tell: A Field Experiment Analyzing the Effects of an Illness-related Employment Gap on the Callback Rate." Working Paper (2017).

11. Bertrand, Marianne. "Career, Family, and the Well-being of College-Educated Women." *American Economic Review* 103, no. 3 (2013): 244–50.

Chapter 6: Nutrition

1. Oster, Emily. "Health Recommendations and Selection in Health Behaviors." *American Economic Review: Insights* (2019).

2. Wadhera, Devina, et al. "Perceived Recollection of Frequent Exposure to Foods in Childhood Is Associated with Adulthood Liking." *Appetite* 89 (2015): 22–32.

3. Rose, Chelsea M., Leann L. Birch, and Jennifer S. Savage. "Dietary Patterns in Infancy Are Associated with Child Diet and Weight Outcomes at 6 Years." *International Journal of Obesity* 41, no. 5 (2017): 783–88.

4. Kelder, Steven H., et al. "Longitudinal Tracking of Adolescent Smoking, Physical Activity, and Food Choice Behaviors." *American Journal of Public Health* 84, no. 7 (1994): 1121–26.

5. Rollins, Brandi Y., Eric Loken, and Leann L. Birch. "Stability and Change in Snack Food Likes and Dislikes from 5 to 11 Years." *Appetite* 55, no. 2 (2010): 371–73.

6. Mennella, Julie A., and Jillian C. Trabulsi. "Complementary Foods and Flavor Experiences: Setting the Foundation." *Annals of Nutrition and Metabolism* 60, suppl. 2 (2012): 40–50.

7. Ventura, Alison K., and John Worobey. "Early Influences on the Development of Food Preferences." *Current Biology* 23, no. 9 (2013): R401–8.

8. Atkin, David. "The Caloric Costs of Culture: Evidence from Indian Migrants." *American Economic Review* 106, no. 4 (2016): 1144–81.

9. Bronnenberg, Bart J., Jean-Pierre H. Dubé, and Matthew Gentzkow. "The Evolution of Brand Preferences: Evidence from Consumer Migration." *American Economic Review* 102, no. 6 (2012): 2472–508.

10. Anzman-Frasca, Stephanie, et al. "Repeated Exposure and Associative Conditioning Promote Preschool Children's Liking of Vegetables." *Appetite* 58, no. 2 (2012): 543–53.

11. Wadhera, Devina, Elizabeth D. Capaldi Phillips, and Lynn M. Wilkie. "Teaching Children to Like and Eat Vegetables." *Appetite* 93 (2015): 75–84.

12. Johnston, Craig A., et al. "Increasing Vegetable Intake in Mexican-American Youth: A Randomized Controlled Trial." *Journal of the American Dietetic Association* 111, no. 5 (2011): 716–20.

13. Capaldi-Phillips, Elizabeth D., and Devina Wadhera. "Associative Conditioning Can Increase Liking for and Consumption of Brussels Sprouts in Children Aged 3 to 5 Years." *Journal of the Academy of Nutrition and Dietetics* 114, no. 8 (2014): 1236–41.

14. Savage, Jennifer S., et al. "Serving Smaller Age-appropriate Entree Portions to Children Aged 3–5 y Increases Fruit and Vegetable Intake and Reduces Energy Density and Energy Intake at Lunch." *American Journal of Clinical Nutrition* 95, no. 2 (2012): 335–41.

15. Newman, Joan, and Alan Taylor. "Effect of a Means-end Contingency on Young Children's Food Preferences." *Journal of Experimental Child Psychology* 53, no. 2 (1992): 200–16.

16. Fisher, Jennifer Orlet, and Leann Lipps Birch. "Restricting Access to Palatable Foods Affects Children's Behavioral Response, Food Selection, and Intake." *American Journal of Clinical Nutrition* 69, no. 6 (1999): 1264–72.

17. Fulkerson, Jayne A., et al. "Family Dinner Meal Frequency and Adolescent Development: Relationships with Developmental Assets and High-risk Behaviors." *Journal of Adolescent Health* 39, no. 3 (2006): 337–45.

18. Harrison, Megan E., et al. "Systematic Review of the Effects of Family Meal Frequency on Psychosocial Outcomes in Youth." *Canadian Family Physician* 61, no. 2 (2015): e96–e106; Eisenberg, Marla E., et al. "Correlations Between Family Meals and Psychosocial Well-being Among Adolescents." *Archives of Pediatrics & Adolescent Medicine* 158, no. 8 (2004): 792–96.

19. Fulkerson, Jayne A., et al. "Family Home Food Environment and Nutrition-Related Parent and Child Personal and Behavioral Outcomes of the Healthy Home Offerings via the Mealtime Environment (HOME) Plus Program: A Randomized Controlled Trial." *Journal of the Academy of Nutrition and Dietetics* 118, no. 2 (2018): 240–51.

20. Fulkerson, Jayne A., et al. "Promoting Healthful Family Meals to Prevent Obesity: HOME Plus, A Randomized Controlled Trial." *International Journal of Behavioral Nutrition and Physical Activity* 12, no. 1 (2015): 154; Fulkerson, Jayne A., et al. "Family Home Food Environment and Nutrition-Related Parent and Child Personal and Behavioral Outcomes of the Healthy Home Offerings via the Mealtime Environment (HOME) Plus Program: A Randomized Controlled Trial." *Journal of the Academy of Nutrition and Dietetics* 118, no. 2 (2018): 240–51.

21. The best evidence on kids and food and diets focuses on obesity. But on the other side, many people worry that the messages we send about food—to girls in particular—may influence the development of eating disorders. Unfortunately, the evidence on this is simply very limited. There are papers that study families of girls (it's mostly girls) who have serious eating disorders, but they do not typically draw systematic or robust conclusions.

Chapter 7: Helicopter, Chicken, Tiger, Ostrich

1. Skenazy, Lenore. *Free-Range Kids: Giving Our Children the Freedom We Had Without Going Nuts with Worry.* New York: John Wiley & Sons, 2009.

2. See, for example, Skenazy. *Free-Range Kids*; Lukianoff, Greg, and Jonathan Haidt. *The Coddling of the American Mind: How Good Intentions and Bad Ideas Are Setting Up a Generation for Failure.* New York: Penguin Books, 2019;

Tough, Paul. *How Children Succeed: Grit, Curiosity, and the Hidden Power of Character.* New York: Houghton Mifflin Harcourt, 2012; Lythcott-Haims, Julie. *How to Raise an Adult: Break Free of the Overparenting Trap and Prepare Your Kid for Success.* New York: Henry Holt and Company, 2015.

3. Hewison, Jenny, and Jack Tizard. "Parental Involvement and Reading Attainment." *British Journal of Educational Psychology* 50, no. 3 (1980): 209–15.

4. Sylva, Kathy, et al. "Training Parents to Help Their Children Read: A Randomized Control Trial." *British Journal of Educational Psychology* 78, no. 3 (2008): 435–55.

5. Fehrmann, Paul G., Timothy Z. Keith, and Matthew M. Reimers. "Home Influence on School Learning: Direct and Indirect Effects of Parental Involvement on High School Grades." *Journal of Educational Research* 80, no. 6 (1987): 330–37.

6. Wilder, Sandra. "Effects of Parental Involvement on Academic Achievement: A Meta-synthesis." *Educational Review* 66, no. 3 (2014): 377–97; Hill, Nancy E., and Diana F. Tyson. "Parental Involvement in Middle School: A Meta-analytic Assessment of the Strategies that Promote Achievement." *Developmental Psychology* 45, no. 3 (2009): 740.

7. Stanton, Bonita F., et al. "Parental Underestimates of Adolescent Risk Behavior: A Randomized, Controlled Trial of a Parental Monitoring Intervention." *Journal of Adolescent Health* 26, no. 1 (2000): 18–26.

8. van Ingen, Daniel J., et al. "Helicopter Parenting: The Effect of an Overbearing Caregiving Style on Peer Attachment and Self-efficacy." *Journal of College Counseling* 18, no. 1 (2015): 7–20.

9. LeMoyne, Terri, and Tom Buchanan. "Does 'Hovering' Matter? Helicopter Parenting and Its Effect on Well-being." *Sociological Spectrum* 31, no. 4 (2011): 399–418.

10. Schiffrin, Holly H., et al. "Helping or Hovering? The Effects of Helicopter Parenting on College Students' Well-being." *Journal of Child and Family Studies* 23, no. 3 (2014): 548–57.

11. Nelson, Larry J., Laura M. Padilla-Walker, and Matthew G. Nielson. "Is Hovering Smothering or Loving? An Examination of Parental Warmth as a Moderator of Relations Between Helicopter Parenting and Emerging Adults' Indices of Adjustment." *Emerging Adulthood* 3, no. 4 (2015): 282–85.

12. Lythcott-Haims. *How to Raise an Adult.*

Chapter 8: School: Overview

1. This example and data is drawn from: Angrist, Joshua D., et al. "Inputs and Impacts in Charter Schools: KIPP Lynn." *American Economic Review* 100, no. 2 (2010): 239–43.

2. Chabrier, Julia, Sarah Cohodes, and Philip Oreopoulos. "What Can We Learn from Charter School Lotteries?" *Journal of Economic Perspectives* 30, no. 3 (2016): 57–84.

3. Ibid.

4. Howell, William G., et al. "School Vouchers and Academic Performance: Results from Three Randomized Field Trials." *Journal of Policy Analysis and Management* 21, no. 2 (2002): 191–217.

5. Rouse, Cecilia Elena. "Private School Vouchers and Student Achievement: An Evaluation of the Milwaukee Parental Choice Program." *Quarterly Journal of Economics* 113, no. 2 (1998): 553–602.

6. Abdulkadiroğlu, Atila, Parag A. Pathak, and Christopher R. Walters. "Free to Choose: Can School Choice Reduce Student Achievement?" *American Economic Journal: Applied Economics* 10, no. 1 (2018): 175–206.

7. Chetty, Raj, et al. "How Does Your Kindergarten Classroom Affect Your Earnings? Evidence from Project STAR." NBER Working Paper No. 16381. *National Bureau of Economic Research* (2010).

8. Chetty, Raj, John N. Friedman, and Jonah E. Rockoff. "Measuring the Impacts of Teachers II: Teacher Value-added and Student Outcomes in Adulthood." *American Economic Review* 104, no. 9 (2014): 2633–79.

9. Chetty, Raj, et al. "How Does Your Kindergarten Classroom Affect Your Earnings?"; Krueger, Alan B. "Experimental Estimates of Education Production Functions." *Quarterly Journal of Economics* 114, no. 2 (1999): 497–532; Angrist, Joshua D., and Victor Lavy. "Using Maimonides' Rule to Estimate the Effect of Class Size on Scholastic Achievement." *Quarterly Journal of Economics* 114, no. 2 (1999): 533–75.

10. Dobbie, Will, and Roland G. Fryer Jr. "Getting Beneath the Veil of Effective Schools: Evidence from New York City." *American Economic Journal: Applied Economics* 5, no. 4 (2013): 28–60.

11. Cooper, Harris, Jorgianne Civey Robinson, and Erika A. Patall. "Does Homework Improve Academic Achievement? A Synthesis of Research, 1987–2003." *Review of Educational Research* 76, no. 1 (2006): 1–62.

12. Otterman, Sharon. "At $145 a Session, Tips for the Admissions Test . . . to Kindergarten." *New York Times*, November 20, 2009.

13. Townsend, Andrea. "A Teacher's Defense of Homework." *Atlantic*, September 25, 2013.

14. Kohn, Alfie. *The Homework Myth: Why Our Kids Get Too Much of a Bad Thing.* Cambridge, MA: Perseus Books Group, 2006.

15. Cooper, Civey Robinson, and Patall. "Does Homework Improve Academic Achievement?" 1–62.

16. Foyle, H. *Homework and Cooperative Learning: A Classroom Field Experiment.* Emporia, KS: Emporia State University, Faculty Research and Creativity Committee, 1990. (ERIC Document No. ED350285).

17. Cooper, Civey Robinson, and Patall. "Does Homework Improve Academic Achievement?" 1–62; Trautwein, Ulrich, and Olaf Köller. "The Relationship Between Homework and Achievement—Still Much of a Mystery." *Educational Psychology Review* 15, no. 2 (2003): 115–145.

18. Cooper, Civey Robinson, and Patall. "Does Homework Improve Academic Achievement?" 1–62.

19. Kim, Sunwoong, and Ju-Ho Lee. "Private Tutoring and Demand for Education in South Korea." *Economic Development and Cultural Change* 58, no. 2 (2010): 259–96.

20. Some authors connect the focus on this type of tutoring to Confucian cultural traditions that value effort and learning, and it seems that the focus on these activities has increased since the 1980s. See, for example, Bray, Mark. "Shadow Education: Comparative Perspectives on the Expansion and Implications of Private Supplementary Tutoring." *Procedia-Social and Behavioral Sciences* 77 (2013): 412–20.

21. Ireson, Judith. "Private Tutoring: How Prevalent and Effective Is It?" *London Review of Education* 2, no. 2 (2004): 109–22.

22. Mischo, Christoph, and Ludwig Haag. "Expansion and Effectiveness of Private Tutoring." *European Journal of Psychology of Education* 17, no. 3 (2002): 263–73.

23. See, for example: Begum, Jamila. "Experimental Study to Determine the Effectiveness of Kumon Method in Comparison with Traditional Lecture Method for Teaching of Mathematics to Grade-5." Diss. Islamabad, Pakistan: Foundation University, 2018; Would, Jenna. "The Relationship Between Kumon and Achievement in Mathematics." Diss. Lethbridge, Alberta, Canada: University of Lethbridge, Faculty of Education, 2010; McKenna, Michele A., Patricia L. Hollingsworth, and Laura Barnes. "Developing Latent Mathematics Abilities in Economically Disadvantaged Students." *Roeper Review* 27, no. 4 (2005): 222–27.

24. Lee, Jaekyung. "Two Worlds of Private Tutoring: The Prevalence and Causes of After-school Mathematics Tutoring in Korea and the United States." *Teachers College Record* 109, no. 5 (2007): 1207–34; Kim, Sunwoong, and Ju-Ho Lee. "Private Tutoring and Demand for Education in

South Korea." *Economic Development and Cultural Change* 58, no. 2 (2010): 259–96.

25. Nishio, Masako. "Use of Private Supplementary Instruction (Private Tutoring) by United States High School Students: Its Use and Academic Consequences." Diss. University of Maryland, College Park, 2007.

26. If you're interested in delving more deeply into this, I highly recommend the book *Reading in the Brain*; I will barely scratch the surface here.

27. This section relies on: Dehaene, Stanislas. *Reading in the Brain: The New Science of How We Read*. New York: Penguin Books, 2009.

28. A common early cite for this is Kenneth Goodman in 1967: Goodman, Kenneth S. "Reading: A Psycholinguistic Guessing Game." *Making Sense of Learners Making Sense of Written Language*. London: Routledge, 2014, 115–24.

29. Yoncheva, Yuliya N., Jessica Wise, and Bruce McCandliss. "Hemispheric Specialization for Visual Words Is Shaped by Attention to Sublexical Units During Initial Learning." *Brain and Language* 145 (2015): 23–33.

30. National Reading Panel (US) et al. "Report of the National Reading Panel: Teaching Children to Read: An Evidence-based Assessment of the Scientific Research Literature on Reading and Its Implications for Reading Instruction: Reports of the Subgroups." National Institute of Child Health and Human Development, National Institutes of Health, 2000.

31. Lemann, Nicholas. "The Reading Wars." *Atlantic*, November 1997.

32. Willingham, Daniel T. *Raising Kids Who Read: What Parents and Teachers Can Do*. New York: John Wiley & Sons, 2015.

33. Neuman, Susan B., et al. "Can Babies Learn to Read? A Randomized Trial of Baby Media." *Journal of Educational Psychology* 106, no. 3 (2014): 815.

34. Dehaene. *Reading in the Brain*.

35. The data for this table is drawn directly from their manual (Table 3.7): Tourangeau, Karen, et al. "Early Childhood Longitudinal Study, Kindergarten Class of 1998–99 (ECLS-K): Combined User's Manual for the ECLS-K Eighth-Grade and K-8 Full Sample Data Files and Electronic Codebooks. NCES 2009-004." *National Center for Education Statistics* (2009).

36. Schneider, Wolfgang, Joachim Körkel, and Franz E. Weinert. "Domain-Specific Knowledge and Memory Performance: A Comparison of High- and Low-aptitude Children." *Journal of Educational Psychology* 81, no. 3 (1989): 306.

37. Jones, Troy, and Carol Brown. "Reading Engagement: A Comparison Between E-books and Traditional Print Books in an Elementary Classroom." *International Journal of Instruction* 4, no. 2 (2011).

38. E.g., Buzard, Barbara, et al. "Motivating the Reluctant Reader." (2001); Taylor, Rosemarye. "Creating a System That Gets Results for Older, Reluctant Readers." *Phi Delta Kappan* 84, no. 1 (2002): 85–87.

39. Schmidt, Pauline Skowron. "Carpe Librum: Seize the (YA) Book." *English Journal* 103, no. 3 (2014): 115; Carter, James Bucky. "Transforming English with Graphic Novels: Moving Toward Our 'Optimus Prime.'" *English Journal* 97, no. 2 (2007): 49–53; Snowball, Clare. "Teenage Reluctant Readers and Graphic Novels." *Young Adult Library Services* 3, no. 4 (2005): 43–45.

40. Neumann, Michelle M. "Using Tablets and Apps to Enhance Emergent Literacy Skills in Young Children." *Early Childhood Research Quarterly* 42 (2018): 239–46.

41. Slavin, Robert E., et al. "Effective Programs for Struggling Readers: A Best-Evidence Synthesis." *Educational Research Review* 6, no. 1 (2011): 1–26.

42. Ibid.; Chambers, Bette, et al. "Small-Group, Computer-Assisted Tutoring to Improve Reading Outcomes for Struggling First and Second Graders." *Elementary School Journal* 111, no. 4 (2011): 625–40.

43. During the COVID-19 pandemic, app- and computer-based learning took over many households. We may have to wait a few years, or decades, to learn more about the precise impacts of that. Suffice to say the initial evidence did not suggest remote learning was much of a substitute for in-person.

44. Long, Deanna, and Susan Szabo. "E-readers and the Effects on Students' Reading Motivation, Attitude and Comprehension During Guided Reading." *Cogent Education* 3, no. 1 (2016): 1197818; Jones and Brown. "Reading Engagement"; Reich, Stephanie M., Joanna C. Yau, and Mark Warschauer. "Tablet-Based Ebooks for Young Children: What Does the Research Say?" *Journal of Developmental & Behavioral Pediatrics* 37, no. 7 (2016): 585–91.

45. Jones and Brown. "Reading Engagement."

46. De Boer, Marissa. "The Effects of Teacher Read Audiobooks on Kindergarten Students' Motivation and Desire to Read at Choice Time." Master's Thesis. Orange City, IA: Northwestern College (2018).

47. Noland, Liz. "Why Listening Is Good for All Kids—Especially in the Digital Age." *AudioFile*, 2011, 13–15.

Chapter 9: Extracurriculars: Overview

1. Stieg, Cory. "Chess Grandmasters Can Lose 10 Pounds and Burn 6,000 Calories Just by Sitting." CNBC, September 22, 2019.

2. Hales, Craig M., et al. "Prevalence of Obesity Among Adults and Youth: United States, 2015–2016." *NCHS Data Brief*, no. 288 (2017).

3. "Calories Burned During Soccer Calculator." Captain Calculator, November 16, 2019.

4. Elkins, Whitney L., et al. "After School Activities, Overweight, and Obesity Among Inner-city Youth." *Journal of Adolescence* 27, no. 2 (2004): 181–89.

5. Nelson, Toben F., et al. "Do Youth Sports Prevent Pediatric Obesity? A Systematic Review and Commentary." *Current Sports Medicine Reports* 10, no. 6 (2011): 360.

6. Kriemler, Susi, et al. "Effect of School-based Physical Activity Programme (KISS) on Fitness and Adiposity in Primary Schoolchildren: Cluster Randomised Controlled Trial." *BMJ* 340 (2010): c785.

7. Cawley, John, David Frisvold, and Chad Meyerhoefer. "The Impact of Physical Education on Obesity Among Elementary School Children." *Journal of Health Economics* 32, no. 4 (2013): 743–55.

8. Nelson, et al. "Do Youth Sports Prevent Pediatric Obesity?" 360.

9. Meyer, Ursina, et al. "Long-term Effect of a School-based Physical Activity Program (KISS) on Fitness and Adiposity in Children: A Cluster-Randomized Controlled Trial." *PLOS One* 9, no. 2 (2014).

10. Lee, Jung Eun, Zachary Pope, and Zan Gao. "The Role of Youth Sports in Promoting Children's Physical Activity and Preventing Pediatric Obesity: A Systematic Review." *Behavioral Medicine* 44, no. 1 (2018): 62–76.

11. Kjønniksen, Lise, Nils Anderssen, and Bente Wold. "Organized Youth Sport as a Predictor of Physical Activity in Adulthood." *Scandinavian Journal of Medicine & Science in Sports* 19, no. 5 (2009): 646–54.

12. Ritter, Meredith, and Kathryn Graff Low. "Effects of Dance/Movement Therapy: A Meta-analysis." *The Arts in Psychotherapy* 23, no. 3 (1996): 249–60.

13. Adirim, Terry A., and Tina L. Cheng. "Overview of Injuries in the Young Athlete." *Sports Medicine* 33, no. 1 (2003): 75–81; Merkel, Donna L. "Youth Sport: Positive and Negative Impact on Young Athletes." *Open Access Journal of Sports Medicine* 4 (2013): 151.

14. Scheer, Volker, and Martin D. Hoffman. "Should Children Be Running Ultramarathons?" *Current Sports Medicine Reports* 17, no. 9 (2018): 282–83.

15. Rauscher, Frances H., Gordon L. Shaw, and Catherine N. Ky. "Music and Spatial Task Performance." *Nature* 365, no. 6447 (1993): 611.

16. Chabris, C. "Prelude or Requiem for the 'Mozart Effect'?" *Nature* 400 (1999): 825–27.

17. Demorest, Steven M., and Steven J. Morrison. "Does Music Make You Smarter?" *Music Educators Journal* 87, no. 2 (2000): 33–58.

18. Woodard, Bill. "KU Research Establishes Link Between Music Education, Academic Achievement." University of Kansas (2014).

19. Hodges, Donald A., and Debra S. O'Connell. "The Impact of Music Education on Academic Achievement." University of North Carolina at Greensboro (2005): 2010.

20. Schwenkreis, Peter, et al. "Assessment of Sensorimotor Cortical Representation Asymmetries and Motor Skills in Violin Players." *European Journal of Neuroscience* 26, no. 11 (2007): 3291–302.

21. Schwab, Nicole, and Lili-Naz Hazrati. "Assessing the Limitations and Biases in the Current Understanding of Chronic Traumatic Encephalopathy." *Journal of Alzheimer's Disease* 64, no. 4 (2018): 1067–76.

22. Daneshvar, Daniel H., et al. "Long-term Consequences: Effects on Normal Development Profile After Concussion." *Physical Medicine and Rehabilitation Clinics* 22, no. 4 (2011): 683–700.

23. McAllister, Matthew, and Michael McCrea. "Long-term Cognitive and Neuropsychiatric Consequences of Repetitive Concussion and Head-Impact Exposure." *Journal of Athletic Training* 52, no. 3 (2017): 309–17.

24. McKee, Ann C., et al. "The Spectrum of Disease in Chronic Traumatic Encephalopathy." *Brain* 136, no. 1 (2013): 43–64.

25. Alosco, M. L., et al. "Age of First Exposure to American Football and Long-term Neuropsychiatric and Cognitive Outcomes." *Translational Psychiatry* 7, no. 9 (2017): e1236.

26. Schallmo, Michael S., Joseph A. Weiner, and Wellington K. Hsu. "Sport and Sex-Specific Reporting Trends in the Epidemiology of Concussions Sustained by High School Athletes." *Journal of Bone and Joint Surgery* 99, no. 15 (2017): 1314–20.

27. Fair, Ray C., and Christopher Champa. "Estimated Costs of Contact in College and High School Male Sports." *Journal of Sports Economics* 20, no. 5 (2019): 690–717.

28. Spiotta, Alejandro M., Adam J. Bartsch, and Edward C. Benzel. "Heading in Soccer: Dangerous Play?" *Neurosurgery* 70, no. 1 (2012): 1–11.

29. Mackay, Daniel F., et al. "Neurodegenerative Disease Mortality Among Former Professional Soccer Players." *New England Journal of Medicine* 381 (2019): 1801–8.

30. Tarnutzer, Alexander A., et al. "Persistent Effects of Playing Football and Associated (Subconcussive) Head Trauma on Brain Structure and Function: A Systematic Review of the Literature." *British Journal of Sports Medicine* 51, no. 22 (2017): 1592–604.

31. Baumeister, Roy F., and Mark R. Leary. "The Need to Belong: Desire for Interpersonal Attachments as a Fundamental Human Motivation." *Psychological Bulletin* 117, no. 3 (1995): 497.

32. Eccles, Jacquelynne S., et al. "Extracurricular Activities and Adolescent Development." *Journal of Social Issues* 59, no. 4 (2003): 865–89.

33. Farb, Amy Feldman, and Jennifer L. Matjasko. "Recent Advances in Research on School-based Extracurricular Activities and Adolescent Development." *Developmental Review* 32, no. 1 (2012): 1–48.

34. Mahoney, Joseph L., Angel L. Harris, and Jacquelynne S. Eccles. "Organized Activity Participation, Positive Youth Development, and the Over-Scheduling Hypothesis." *Social Policy Report* 20, no. 4 (2006): 1–32.

35. Metsäpelto, Riitta-Leena, Lea Pulkkinen, and Asko Tolvanen. "A School-based Intervention Program as a Context for Promoting Socioemotional Development in Children." *European Journal of Psychology of Education* 25, no. 3 (2010): 381–98.

36. Dimech, Annemarie Schumacher, and Roland Seiler. "Extra-curricular Sport Participation: A Potential Buffer Against Social Anxiety Symptoms in Primary School Children." *Psychology of Sport and Exercise* 12, no. 4 (2011): 347–54; Farb, Amy Feldman, and Jennifer L. Matjasko. "Recent Advances in Research on School-based Extracurricular Activities and Adolescent Development." *Developmental Review* 32, no. 1 (2012): 1–48.

37. Wang, Jun, et al. "Developmental Trajectories of Youth Character: A Five-Wave Longitudinal Study of Cub Scouts and Non-Scout Boys." *Journal of Youth and Adolescence* 44, no. 12 (2015): 2359–73.

38. Killgore, Leslie. "Merit and Competition in Selective College Admissions." *Review of Higher Education* 32, no. 4 (2009): 469–88.

39. Thurber, Christopher A., et al. "Youth Development Outcomes of the Camp Experience: Evidence for Multidimensional Growth." *Journal of Youth and Adolescence* 36, no. 3 (2007): 241–54.

40. Meltzer, Lisa J., and Mary T. Rourke. "Oncology Summer Camp: Benefits of Social Comparison." *Children's Health Care* 34, no. 4 (2005): 305–14.

41. McCraw, Ronald K., and Luther B. Travis. "Psychological Effects of a Special Summer Camp on Juvenile Diabetics." *Diabetes* 22, no. 4 (1973): 275–78.

42. Goodwin, Donna L., et al. "Connecting Through Summer Camp: Youth with Visual Impairments Find a Sense of Community." *Adapted Physical Activity Quarterly* 28, no. 1 (2011): 40–55.

43. Wong, William W., et al. "An Innovative Summer Camp Program Improves Weight and Self-esteem in Obese Children." *Journal of Pediatric Gastroenterology and Nutrition* 49, no. 4 (2009): 493–97; Huelsing, Jean, et al. "Camp Jump Start: Effects of a Residential Summer Weight-loss Camp for Older Children and Adolescents." *Pediatrics* 125, no. 4 (2010): e884–90.

44. Briery, Brandon G., and Brian Rabian. "Psychosocial Changes Associated with Participation in a Pediatric Summer Camp." *Journal of Pediatric Psychology* 24, no. 2 (1999): 183–90.

45. Cunningham, Lindy G., and Anne N. Rinn. "The Role of Gender and Previous Participation in a Summer Program on Gifted Adolescents' Self-concepts over Time." *Journal for the Education of the Gifted* 30, no. 3 (2007): 326–52.

46. Lattal, K. A. "Contingency Management of Toothbrushing Behavior in a Summer Camp for Children." *Journal of Applied Behavior Analysis* 2, no. 3 (1969): 195–98.

47. Fichman, Laura, Richard Koestner, and David C. Zuroff. "Dependency and Distress at Summer Camp." *Journal of Youth and Adolescence* 26, no. 2 (1997): 217–32.

48. Kerns, Kathryn A., Laura E. Brumariu, and Michelle M. Abraham. "Homesickness at Summer camp: Associations with the Mother-Child Relationship, Social Self-concept, and Peer Relationships in Middle Childhood." *Merrill-Palmer Quarterly* 54 (2008): 473–98.

49. Thurber, Christopher A. "Multimodal Homesickness Prevention in Boys Spending 2 Weeks at a Residential Summer Camp." *Journal of Consulting and Clinical Psychology* 73, no. 3 (2005): 555.

50. Cooper, Harris, et al. "The Effects of Summer Vacation on Achievement Test Scores: A Narrative and Meta-analytic Review." *Review of Educational Research* 66, no. 3 (1996): 227–68.

51. Alexander, Karl L., Doris R. Entwisle, and Linda Steffel Olson. "Lasting Consequences of the Summer Learning Gap." *American Sociological Review* 72, no. 2 (2007): 167–80.

52. Kuhfeld, Megan. "Surprising New Evidence on Summer Learning Loss." *Phi Delta Kappan* 101, no. 1 (2019): 25–29.

53. Cooper, Harris, et al. "Making the Most of Summer School: A Meta-analytic and Narrative Review." *Monographs of the Society for Research in*

Child Development (2000): i–127; Borman, Geoffrey D., Michael E. Goetz, and N. Maritza Dowling. "Halting the Summer Achievement Slide: A Randomized Field Trial of the KindergARTen Summer Camp." *Journal of Education for Students Placed at Risk* 14, no. 2 (2009): 133–47.

Chapter 10: Feelings: Overview

1. Pons, Francisco, Paul L. Harris, and Marc de Rosnay. "Emotion Comprehension Between 3 and 11 Years: Developmental Periods and Hierarchical Organization." *European Journal of Developmental Psychology* 1, no. 2 (2004): 127–52.

2. E.g., Kosse, Fabian, et al. "The Formation of Prosociality: Causal Evidence on the Role of Social Environment." *Journal of Political Economy* 128, no. 2 (2020): 434–67.

3. Ruffman, Ted, Lance Slade, and Elena Crowe. "The Relation Between Children's and Mothers' Mental State Language and Theory-of-Mind Understanding." *Child Development* 73, no. 3 (2002): 734–51.

4. Tenenbaum, Harriet R., et al. "The Effects of Explanatory Conversations on Children's Emotion Understanding." *British Journal of Developmental Psychology* 26, no. 2 (2008): 249–63.

5. Ornaghi, Veronica, Jens Brockmeier, and Ilaria Grazzani. "Enhancing Social Cognition by Training Children in Emotion Understanding: A Primary School Study." *Journal of Experimental Child Psychology* 119 (2014): 26–39.

6. Olweus, D. "Bully/Victim Problems Among Schoolchildren: Basic Facts and Effects of a School Based Intervention Program," *Development and Treatment of Childhood Aggression*, D. J. Pepler and K. H. Rubin, eds. (1991): 411–48.

7. Ttofi, Maria M., and David P. Farrington. "Effectiveness of School-based Programs to Reduce Bullying: A Systematic and Meta-analytic Review." *Journal of Experimental Criminology* 7, no. 1 (2011): 27–56.

8. Kärnä, Antti, et al. "A Large-scale Evaluation of the KiVa Antibullying Program: Grades 4–6." *Child Development* 82, no. 1 (2011): 311–30.

9. Nocentini, Annalaura, and Ersilia Menesini. "KiVa Anti-Bullying Program in Italy: Evidence of Effectiveness in a Randomized Control Trial." *Prevention Science* 17, no. 8 (2016): 1012–23.

10. Frey, Karin S., Miriam K. Hirschstein, and Barbara A. Guzzo. "Second Step: Preventing Aggression by Promoting Social Competence." *Journal of Emotional and Behavioral Disorders* 8, no. 2 (2000): 102–12.

11. Cooke, Michelle Beaulieu, et al. "The Effects of City-wide Implementation of 'Second Step' on Elementary School Students' Prosocial and Aggressive Behaviors." *Journal of Primary Prevention* 28, no. 2 (2007): 93–115.

12. Frey, Karin S., et al. "Effects of a School-based Social–Emotional Competence Program: Linking Children's Goals, Attributions, and Behavior." *Journal of Applied Developmental Psychology* 26, no. 2 (2005): 171–200.

13. Grossman, David C., et al. "Effectiveness of a Violence Prevention Curriculum Among Children in Elementary School: A Randomized Controlled Trial." *Journal of the American Medical Association* 277, no. 20 (1997): 1605–11.

14. Upshur, Carole C., et al. "A Randomized Efficacy Trial of the Second Step Early Learning (SSEL) Curriculum." *Journal of Applied Developmental Psychology* 62 (2019): 145–59.

15. Low, Sabina, et al. "Promoting Social–Emotional Competence: An Evaluation of the Elementary Version of Second Step®." *Journal of School Psychology* 53, no. 6 (2015): 463–77.

16. Baumeister, Roy F., ed. *Self-Esteem: The Puzzle of Low Self-Regard*. New York: Springer Science & Business Media, 2013.

17. Craig, Wendy M. "The Relationship Among Bullying, Victimization, Depression, Anxiety, and Aggression in Elementary School Children." *Personality and Individual Differences* 24, no. 1 (1998): 123–30; Crick, Nicki R., and Gary W. Ladd. "Children's Perceptions of Their Peer Experiences: Attributions, Loneliness, Social Anxiety, and Social Avoidance." *Developmental Psychology* 29, no. 2 (1993): 244.

18. Laursen, Brett, et al. "Friendship Moderates Prospective Associations Between Social Isolation and Adjustment Problems in Young Children." *Child Development* 78, no. 4 (2007): 1395–404.

19. Bowes, Lucy, et al. "Families Promote Emotional and Behavioural Resilience to Bullying: Evidence of an Environmental Effect." *Journal of Child Psychology and Psychiatry* 51, no. 7 (2010): 809–17.

20. They measure this using regression residuals—if you seem to be happy despite what we would predict from the amount of bullying you are experiencing, you're labeled as more resilient. They regress self-esteem on amount of bullying, take the residual, and label it resilience.

21. Ttofi, Maria M., et al. "Protective Factors Interrupting the Continuity from School Bullying to Later Internalizing and Externalizing Problems: A Systematic Review of Prospective Longitudinal Studies." *Journal of School Violence* 13, no. 1 (2014): 5–38; Khamis, Vivian. "Bullying Among School-age Children in the Greater Beirut Area: Risk and Protective Factors." *Child Abuse & Neglect* 39 (2015): 137–46.

22. Heller, Sara B., et al. "Thinking, Fast and Slow? Some Field Experiments to Reduce Crime and Dropout in Chicago." *Quarterly Journal of Economics* 132, no. 1 (2017): 1–54.

23. Cary, Colleen E., and J. Curtis McMillen. "The Data Behind the Dissemination: A Systematic Review of Trauma-Focused Cognitive Behavioral Therapy for Use with Children and Youth." *Children and Youth Services Review* 34, no. 4 (2012): 748–57.

24. Berry, Kathryn, and Caroline J. Hunt. "Evaluation of an Intervention Program for Anxious Adolescent Boys Who Are Bullied at School." *Journal of Adolescent Health* 45, no. 4 (2009): 376–82.

25. Kapçi, Emine Gül, et al. "Cognitive-Behavioral Therapy for Anxiety in Elementary School Students." *Journal of Cognitive-Behavioral Psychotherapy and Research* 1, no. 2 (2012): 121–26.

26. Oar, Ella L., Carly Johnco, and Matthew H. Ollendick. "Cognitive Behavioral Therapy for Anxiety and Depression in Children and Adolescents." *Psychiatric Clinics of North America* (2017).

Chapter 11: Entertainment: Overview

1. Kearney, Melissa S., and Phillip B. Levine. "Early Childhood Education by Television: Lessons from *Sesame Street*." *American Economic Journal: Applied Economics* 11, no. 1 (2019): 318–50.

2. "Kids' Audience Behavior Across Platforms." Nielsen Company Report, 2015.

3. Hernæs, Øystein, Simen Markussen, and Knut Røed. "Television, Cognitive Ability, and High School Completion." *Journal of Human Resources* 54, no. 2 (2019): 371–400.

4. Lieury, Alain, et al. "Video Games vs. Reading and School/Cognitive Performances: A Study on 27,000 Middle School Teenagers." *Educational Psychology* 36, no. 9 (2016): 1560–95.

5. Kearney and Levine. "Early Childhood Education by Television." 318–50.

6. See, for example: Funk, Jeanne B., et al. "Violence Exposure in Real-Life, Video Games, Television, Movies and the Internet: Is There Desensitization?" *Journal of Adolescence* 27, no. 1 (2004): 23–39, and cites therein, as well as Anderson, Craig A., and Brad J. Bushman. "Effects of Violent Video Games on Aggressive Behavior, Aggressive Cognition, Aggressive Affect, Physiological Arousal, and Prosocial Behavior: A Meta-analytic Review of the Scientific Literature." *Psychological Science* 12, no. 5 (2001): 353–59.

7. Anderson, Craig A., and Karen E. Dill. "Video Games and Aggressive Thoughts, Feelings, and Behavior in the Laboratory and in Life." *Journal of Personality and Social Psychology* 78, no. 4 (2000): 772 [see study 2].

8. Anderson and Bushman. "Effects of Violent Video Games on Aggressive Behavior, Aggressive Cognition, Aggressive Affect, Physiological Arousal, and Prosocial Behavior," 353–59.

9. Ferguson, Christopher J., et al. "A Longitudinal Test of Video Game Violence Influences on Dating an Aggression: A 3-year Longitudinal Study of Adolescents." *Journal of Psychiatric Research* 46, no. 2 (2012): 141–46; Dindar, Muhterem. "An Empirical Study on Gender, Video Game Play, Academic Success and Complex Problem Solving Skills." *Computers & Education* 125 (2018): 39–52.

10. DeCamp, Whitney, and Christopher J. Ferguson. "The Impact of Degree of Exposure to Violent Video Games, Family Background, and Other Factors on Youth Violence." *Journal of Youth and Adolescence* 46, no. 2 (2017): 388–400.

11. Beck, Victoria, and Chris Rose. "Is Sexual Objectification and Victimization of Females in Video Games Associated with Victim Blaming or Victim Empathy?" *Journal of Interpersonal Violence* (2018): 0886260518770187; Breuer, Johannes, et al. "Sexist Games=Sexist Gamers? A Longitudinal Study on the Relationship Between Video Game Use and Sexist Attitudes." *Cyberpsychology, Behavior, and Social Networking* 18, no. 4 (2015): 197–202.

12. Masek, Martin, et al. "Improving Mastery of Fractions by Blending Video Games into the Math Classroom." *Journal of Computer Assisted Learning* 33, no. 5 (2017): 486–99.

13. Griffiths, Mark D., Daria J. Kuss, and Daniel L. King. "Video Game Addiction: Past, Present and Future." *Current Psychiatry Reviews* 8, no. 4 (2012): 308–18.

14. Rehbein, Florian, and Dirk Baier. "Family-, Media-, and School-related Risk Factors of Video Game Addiction." *Journal of Media Psychology* (2013); Griffiths, Kuss, and King. "Video Game Addiction." 308–18.

15. E.g., Rehbein and Baier. "Family-, Media-, and School-related Risk Factors of Video Game Addiction."

16. Griffiths, Kuss, and King. "Video Game Addiction." 308–18.

17. Cespedes, Elizabeth M., et al. "Television Viewing, Bedroom Television, and Sleep Duration from Infancy to Mid-Childhood." *Pediatrics* 133, no. 5 (2014): e116371; Owens, Judith, et al. "Television-viewing Habits and Sleep Disturbance in School Children." *Pediatrics* 104, no. 3 (1999): e27.

18. Johnson, Jeffrey G., et al. "Association Between Television Viewing and Sleep Problems During Adolescence and Early Adulthood." *Archives of Pediatrics & Adolescent Medicine* 158, no. 6 (2004): 562–68.

19. Dworak, Markus, et al. "Impact of Singular Excessive Computer Game and Television Exposure on Sleep Patterns and Memory Performance of School-aged Children." *Pediatrics* 120, no. 5 (2007): 978–85.

20. O'Keeffe, Gwenn Schurgin, and Kathleen Clarke-Pearson. "The Impact of Social Media on Children, Adolescents, and Families." *Pediatrics* 127, no. 4 (2011): 800–4.

21. Schrobsdorff, Susanna. "Teen Depression and Anxiety: Why the Kids Are Not Alright." *Time*, October 27, 2016.

22. Best, Paul, Roger Manktelow, and Brian Taylor. "Online Communication, Social Media and Adolescent Wellbeing: A Systematic Narrative Review." *Children and Youth Services Review* 41 (2014): 27–36.

23. Bányai, Fanni, et al. "Problematic Social Media Use: Results from a Large-scale Nationally Representative Adolescent Sample." *PLoS One* 12, no. 1 (2017).

24. Barry, Christopher T., et al. "Adolescent Social Media Use and Mental Health from Adolescent and Parent Perspectives." *Journal of Adolescence* 61 (2017): 1–11.

25. Griffiths, M. D., and D. Kuss. "Adolescent Social Media Addiction (revisited)." *Education and Health* 35, no. 3 (2017): 49–52.

Index

INDEX

INDEX

working mothers. *See* maternal work and
child outcomes
working parents, 12, 17
adding to the Big Picture,
91–93
income and budget considerations,
89–91
logistics and schedules, 81–82,
91–93
stay-at-home parents, 89, 91

working parents and child outcomes,
83–88
data, 83–88
obesity, 86–88
test scores, 83–86

youth sports. *See* sports; *and specific
sports*

Zoo Camp, 3–4